Critical Perspectives on Postcolonial African Children's and Young Adult Literature

Recent Titles in
Contributions in Afro-American and African Studies

Critical Perspectives on Postcolonial African Children's and Young Adult Literature

Edited by
Meena Khorana

Contributions in Afro-American and African Studies,
Number 187

Greenwood Press
Westport, Connecticut • London

Library of Congress Cataloging-in-Publication Data

Critical perspectives on postcolonial African children's and young
    adult literature / edited by Meena Khorana.
        p.   cm.—(Contributions in Afro-American and African
    studies, ISSN 0069-9624 ; no. 187)
    Includes bibliographical references and index.
    ISBN 0-313-29864-5 (alk. paper)
        1. Children's literature, African—History and criticism.
    2. Young adult literature, African—History and criticism.
    I. Khorana, Meena.   II. Series.
    PL8010.C755   1998
    809'.89282'096—dc21   97-48574

British Library Cataloguing in Publication Data is available.

Library of Congress Catalog Card Number: 97-48574
ISBN: 0-313-29864-5
ISSN: 0069-9624

First published in 1998

Greenwood Press, 88 Post Road West, Westport, CT 06881
An imprint of Greenwood Publishing Group, Inc.

Printed in the United States of America

TO MY DAUGHTER, SHOBNA

CONTENTS

PREFACE

We are currently witnessing a growing scholarly interest in African children's literature in the United States. More than twenty years after Nancy J. Schmidt first published her seminal bibliographies, *Children's Books on Africa and Their Authors* (1975), the *Supplement* (1979), and *Children's Fiction about Africa in English* in 1981, there are several more book-length studies on the subject: Yulisa Amadu Maddy and Donnarae MacCann's *African Images in Juvenile Literature: Commentaries on Neocolonialist Fiction* appeared in 1996, Osayimwense Osa's *African Children's and Youth Literature* in 1995, and my *Africa in Literature for Children and Young Adults: An Annotated Bibliography of English-Language Books* in 1994. The number of articles on African children's literature presented at conferences and in scholarly journals also seems to have increased. Publications such as *Research in African Literatures, Reading Teacher, Children's Literature in English, Bookbird: World of Children's Books,* Children's Literature Association's *Quarterly,* and *World Literature Written in English* regularly carry articles on African children's literature. *Journal of African Children's and Youth Literature,* established in 1989 as *Journal of African Children's Literature,* is devoted exclusively to criticism and review of the subject. The January 1997 issue of *ARIEL* had four articles, and the spring 1998 issue of *Bookbird* focuses entirely on African children's literature. Recent publications are moving away from general country surveys or analyses of publishing conditions to articles that analyze the literary structures, themes, and illustrations or that apply Marxist, feminist, or postcolonial theories to interpret the literature.

Research in African children's literature is further encouraged by the African Studies Association. A nonprofit corporation founded in 1957 and open to all persons and institutions interested in African affairs, the association brings together persons with scholarly and professional interest in Africa; provides useful services to schools, businesses, media, and the community at large; and publishes and distributes scholarly materials on Africa. With some 2,800 members, the association is the leading North American learned society promoting African studies and the largest organization of its kind in the world. The African Studies Association also presents the prestigious Children's Book Awards annually to the authors and illustrators of the best children's books on Africa from preschool to grade 12. The awards were established in 1991 to highlight the importance of the production of high-quality children's materials about Africa published in the United States.

The question of an authentic voice in postcolonial African children's literature has emerged as a central concern to those who care about books for African children and young adults. This collection examines the issue from several directions. The essays gathered here either take a postcolonial or revisionist approach to the study of colonial literature, or discuss books published after decolonization. My introductory essay provides a general analysis of some key issues facing the publication of children's books in postcolonial Africa: national identity, language, appropriate genres and relevant themes to inculcate a nationalistic outlook in children and young adults. The individual articles, moving from general to specific, are located within this broad framework. On the one hand, the essays reflect the scholarly interests and expertise of each contributor, and on the other hand they span the entire field of African children's literature, covering North, East, West, and Southern Africa.

The first four essays survey African children's literature from a variety of angles. The issues raised in Asenath Bole Odaga's essay on Kenya are generally representative of the problems faced by authors, illustrators, publishers, and booksellers throughout the continent. Based on her personal experience as a children's author and publisher, she analyzes the social, educational, economic, and infrastructure factors that influence the publication of children's books, especially by small, indigenous publishers: low literacy rates, limited purchasing power, multilingual population, disproportionate demand for textbooks, competition from the more attractive imports, and barriers to marketing and distribution. Nancy J. Schmidt's article on the Noma Award for Publishing in Africa discusses the incentives the award offers to publishing books in Africa, creating original works in indigenous languages, and encouraging research. Focusing on the first 15 years of the award, from 1980 to 1994, the article gives an analytical overview of the honorable mention books and provides a critical study of the two award winners, Meshack Asare of Ghana and Charles Mungoshi of Zimbabwe. The award has led to cooperation among African publishers, and more copublishing and translation projects are under way. Osayimwense Osa's discussion focuses on Nigerian adolescent literature, which includes the richer and more complex novels specifically directed at young adults as well as books marketed for adults but relevant to the lives and experiences of Nigerian youth. These novels portray the disillusionment of youth and their rebellion against governmental corruption, adult hypocrisy, lowered moral standards, and materialism as they come of age in the postindependence era. Mbare Ngom's survey of the young and recently emerging children's literature of Equatorial Guinea points out that the recording of folktales is the first step toward developing a nationalistic literature that defines identity and infuses pride. While the influences of colonization and the dictatorial regime of Francisco Macías Nguema still linger, Ngom's continuing research shows that Guinean Hispanic literature is responding to the challenge of a changing technological world.

The next three essays focus on books written by Western authors for Western readers, projecting values and perspectives that betray a continuing colonial bias or that reflect a "superior" attitude. Claire-Lise Malarte-Feldman and Jack Yeager examine the Babar stories of Jean de Brunhoff in light of the French "mission civilisatrice" to socialize the colonized through the learning modes of the French school system. Jean Perrot's essay, although refuting the "political correctness" of Herbert Kohl's book *Should We Burn Babar? Essays on Children's Literature and the Power of Stories,* offers an interesting counterpoint to the interpretation of Malarte-Feldman and Yeager. He reads the Babar series as an avant-garde work that protests against the slaughter of elephants and offers ideas on the joys of living in a rural community, rather than focusing on the French colonization of Africa. Greta D. Little's study, informed by the "culture shock" theories of Peter Adler and Kalervo Oberg, examines stories written by expatriates who have traveled, lived, or worked in North Africa. Her analysis reveals that colonial models and stereotypes are still being perpetuated in some recent books about North Africa.

The remaining four essays take a thematic or literature-specialist approach. Karen Patricia Smith focuses on Chinua Achebe's sense of responsibility as an author. In his children's stories he is committed to fulfilling the traditional role of elders—or writers—in a community by instructing and educating children. Smith points out that Achebe achieves his aim with aesthetic finesse, so that the moral lessons are not objectionable or overly didactic. Michael Scott Joseph's and Judy Anne White's essays place the structures, symbols, and motifs of selected works in the context of the archetypal and psychoanalytical theories of Northrop Frye, Mircea Eliade, and Carl Jung. Joseph argues that the ritualistic structure of children's journey tales—folktales as well as recent fiction—effaces historical time and connects the reader/protagonist with mythic time, the golden age of the beginning, in order to restore the "primordial unity" that Eliade speaks of in *The Myth of the Eternal Return.* White analyzes the complex archetypal images in Amos Tutuola's *The Brave African Huntress* as the female hero undergoes the psychological process of individuation by engaging in what is traditionally considered a male heroic quest.

Miki Flockemann examines recent developments in South African literature for young adults from the context of the political and social changes that have taken place between Nelson Mandela's release from prison in 1990 and the post-election period in 1995. She states that the emerging "new" genre is taking an interventionist approach in preparation for a nonracial society, because coming to adulthood in the "new" South Africa involves dealing with cross-cultural relationships and crossing boundaries, whether real or imagined, indicating historical shifts in the politics of race and identity.

These essays reveal the depth, complexity, and variety of African children's literature, indicating that serious artistic work is in progress throughout Africa. While not all books are of equally high caliber, there are several excellent authors and works that should be included in the canon of international children's literature. The essays by Joseph and White raise the question of whether or not African books should be analyzed according to Western theories. African children's literature is sophisticated enough to be examined by the highest literary, critical, and theoretical standards for both its inherently indigenous structures and its universal features. As Henry Louis Gates states in his essay, "Talkin' That Talk," in the collection *"Race," Writing, and Difference,* "black" texts do have "white" antecedents and Western literary traditions have relevance for critics of "other" literatures.

I thank all the contributors for helping me realize my vision of this book. Their hard work, excellent research, and cooperation throughout the reviewing, editing, and production stages made working on this book a rewarding experience. Thanks are also due to Dean Burney Hollis, College of Arts and Sciences, and to the English department of Morgan State University for supporting my research in numerous ways, but particularly by granting me one course release per semester. For the final stage of this project, I am indebted to Naomi Greengrass for her conscientious secretarial help, to Susan Clawson for her meticulous copyediting, and to Lesli Lai for her tasteful graphic design and preparation of the camera-ready copy. I am grateful to my husband, Shamsher Khorana, and daughters Shobna and Rohini for their continued support of my work. I am once again pleased to publish through Greenwood Press; its editors, particularly George Butler and Jane Lerner, printers, and marketing staff bring the highest professional standards to the publication of each book.

Critical Perspectives on Postcolonial African Children's and Young Adult Literature

Children's Publishing in Africa: Can the Colonial Past Be Forgotten?

Meena Khorana

Postcolonial African children's literature is best understood by examining what constitutes national identity. My usage of the term *postcolonial* is somewhat ambivalent: while postcolonial implies dismantling the structures of dominance and oppression in literature, politics, and society, it does not emphasize the efforts of the newly independent nations to forge a new identity and to focus on the task of nation building. The alternate term, *postindependence,* while it gives agency to the new nations and its peoples, does not imply "undoing" the effects of colonialism. Both approaches are evident in the literature written and published in Africa for children and young adults. Perhaps it can more appropriately be labeled *nationalistic* literature because it questions the political and cultural definition of "nation" and "national identity" for the emerging countries of the African continent. Is a nation defined by a common territory, race, history, myths, language, beliefs, or lifestyle? Is nation a "pure pedigree," as James Snead puts it (231–38), or is it a new hybrid entity that has emerged from its colonial past and that has to reconcile its westernized urban culture with its ancient traditions?

Postcolonial books are sometimes characterized by their preoccupation with the evils of colonialism, with presenting the precolonial period as mythic and sacred, with emphasizing the dignity and validity of traditional values, and with blaming the postindependence governments for perpetuating colonial policies. Wilfred Cartey writes in *Whispers from a Continent* that "[i]n the course of . . . colonial imposition many native social structures were shattered, family groupings destroyed, and individuals plunged into disillusionment and despair" (45). The reverberations of this breakup, he continues, can be felt in postcolonial literature: "It appears of historical necessity and will continue to be present in many literatures, for its effects on individuals and societies have been deeply wrenching, precipitating 'the falling apart of things'" (45). Chinua Achebe clearly demonstrates in his novels *Things Fall Apart* and *No Longer at Ease* that the precolonial, "old" Africa is in the past. He believes a "new" Africa has to be forged, keeping in mind both the precolonial and colonial past. Likewise, in *A Dance of the Forests* Wole Soyinka forces his characters to confront their personal pasts and the past of the nation in order to hope for a better tomorrow.

How does postcolonial/postindependence African children's literature articulate the idea of nation and nationalism for its young readers? To what extent are children's books used toward nationalistic ends? Are they purely aesthetic? We need to examine children's and young adult books published in Africa to determine what adults believe is important for the younger generation to know, what cherished values the books pass on, how they equip children to lead the nation in the future. A survey of this literature indicates that a new cultural nationalism is being forged to counter the impact of imperialism. However, also evident is a dichotomy between African and European, traditional and modern, rural and urban, neo-colonial and nationalistic. The interplay of this duality is central to an examination of postcolonial/postindependence literature for children and young adults.

LANGUAGE ISSUE

Prior to independence, the books available to African children mainly consisted of biased school texts and leisure books imported from the imperial nations. Written from a colonial perspective, these books advanced the colonial agenda through stereotypical plots, characterization, and themes. To further assimilate Africans, the colonizers imposed European languages, while the indigenous languages were neglected (or forbidden) in schools. What Francesca Blockeel writes about colonial Portuguese children's literature was relevant throughout the continent: "All children—whether living in Portugal, Mozambique, Guinea, or in any other Portuguese colony—had the same schoolbooks, transmitting the same values of God, religion, family, and nation to prepare them to be proud of their history and colonial empire" (12–13). Language became an instrument of subjugation that fostered a sense of inferiority and lack of pride in African languages, culture, and history.

Because of historical factors and practical considerations, European languages continue as the medium of communication and creative expression even after independence. It is not surprising that most of the books discussed in this volume were originally written in English, Spanish, or French. Some of the reasons for the continued use of European languages are that they have become part of the educational, publishing, and governmental infrastructure: they get a wider audience for ideas among the educated elite both within and outside the country; they are necessary to maintain diplomatic, trade, and other international contacts; they provide a uniformity in internal communication amid the cultural and linguistic diversity of African nations; and they make publishing more economically viable because of the multilingual population and lack of sufficient readership in any one language (see Booth 57).

The question of language remains a crucial one. Are African children continuing to be colonized through the literature being written and produced for them?

At the time of independence, neocolonialism was evident in publishing through-out the continent, since the industry was controlled by European multinational firms like Macmillan, Longman, Heinemann, Nouvelles Editions Africaines, Tip. M. Minuesa, and Caminho. As a result of a series of seminars and conferences organized in the 1960s and 1970s by concerned scholars, writers, publishers, and educators, firm directives were outlined to Africanize publishing for children and to take economic, cultural, and ideological control. The foreign publishing houses were nationalized and a number of small, independent publishers emerged in response to the needs of young Africans (see Khorana xxx–xxxii). However, despite these initiatives European languages continue as the medium of commu-nication in instruction, especially in higher education, and the publication of school texts and trade books. The challenge presented by the linguistic diversity of the continent cannot be over-emphasized. Asenath Bole Odaga eloquently points out in this volume that because there are over 41 indigenous languages in Kenya, and because of the high cost of producing good-quality books, it is impossible to meet the reading needs of all children.

Whether children's books are written in English, Spanish, French, German, or Portuguese, another point to consider is that they are addressed to the Western-educated elite of the newly independent nations. Just as the European languages introduced linguistic and cultural homogeneity during the colonial period, so also today they introduce a European-influenced monoculture among the elite. Phanuel Akubueze Egejuru also points out in *Black Writers: White Audience* that the audience for these novels is both European bourgeois and African westernized elite, even if the author is consciously writing only for a native readership. "With his borrowed literary tradition and his borrowed language to express his African experience, the African writer finds himself in the difficult situation in which his audience exerts a great deal of influence on his writing" (16). This awareness, he says, leads to a tendency to insert and explain African customs and experiences, cultural and anthropological terms and material, which eventually influences pre-sentation and choice of subject matter (14–16). These remarks have limited valid-ity for children's literature because children's authors mostly publish through small indigenous presses, and they do not have the dual audience that Egejuru refers to in connection with adult authors.

Are the indigenous languages and cultural groups being marginalized? Ngugi wa Thiong'o forcefully argues in *Decolonising the Mind* that the "elite" segment of the population, which is in power in government, is the extension of paternalism and neocolonialism in Africa today. As education spreads and as the move to write in indigenous languages gains momentum, the center will shift to the non-Western segment of the population. Citing the success of his Gikuyu novel *Caitaani Mũtharabainī* (*Devil on the Cross*), which was reprinted three times in the first seven months of its release and which continues to sell a thousand copies per year, Ngugi maintains that writing in non-African languages denies the poor and illiterate populations access to information and it creates an elite class that is distanced from the mainstream (83–85).

Does using a European language mean that it is not an African voice? Talal Asad and John Dixon wonder how much metaphor and nuances of thought are omitted by using the colonial languages: "what your style cannot easily accommodate, you leave out. Or if you do not leave it out, your style must diminish its significance" (175). In response to a questionnaire, Achebe told Egejuru that "[i]t's really a question of looking around and deciding whether you can tell a story using English words and still keep the meaning of the story. To me it seems you can; you play around and see whether you can do it" (99). Supporters of African writing in European languages assert that these languages have taken root in Africa. According to R. K. Dhawan, P. V. Dhamija, and A. K. Srivastava: "New experiments in form and technique . . . come more readily to the writers from the developing cultures, since they are open to free forms, to new amalgamations of experience and expression. A newness comes from the re-discovery of the old, from the shocks of recognition that reveal the amazing modernity of the residual traditions" (7–8). English words, they continue, carry new meanings and concepts: used in a "new cultural environment, the same English words are referential in a different way" (9). According to Egejuru, the English language, unlike French, is more flexible: it can be Africanized; it is experimental; it can be adapted to African aesthetics (92).

Perhaps a hybrid English, Spanish, French, and Portuguese are evolving in African literature. In English-language books, for instance, an African idiom is distinct in the novels of Chinua Achebe and Amos Tutuola; it can express what they as Nigerians, as Igbos or Yorubas, want to say. To use an Igbo proverb, they have infused into their English "the palm-oil with which words are eaten." Tutuola's prose integrates Yoruba syntax and rhythms of thought; it vigorously narrates Yoruba mythology and folklore by inserting metaphors, proverbs, and cultural references; and it enriches the English language with creative spellings and vocabulary and imaginative descriptions of people and environment. For these stylistic innovations Tutuola suffered the harsh criticism of his countrymen for being "ungrammatical," for giving Western readers the impression that Africans cannot write "correct" English. Western readers were chastized for patronizing and praising Tutuola's "quaint" English, which, critics believe, is a euphemism for "broken" English. Harold R. Collins condemns this attitude as "intellectual snobbery" (111).

It is not within the scope of this introduction to resolve the language controversy; however, the fact remains that European languages impose a cultural homogeneity on children that is often at variance with the diversity of their home cultures and languages. To celebrate the linguistic, cultural, and tribal diversity within the nation, and to develop an overarching national identity, there is a move to publish books in multilingual editions, with the text given in European as well as in the major indigenous languages. We note this trend in Zimbabwe, for instance, with children's books published in Shona, Ndebele, Tonga, and English; in Kenya in English, Gikuyu, and Kiswahili; and in South Africa in English, Afrikaans, Xhosa, and Zulu. As Nancy J. Schmidt points out (in this volume), the Noma Award for Publishing in Africa has encouraged both creative writing and publishing in African languages. Although the winning entries (for children's books) thus far have been in Afrikaans, English, French, and Gikuyu, the award has stimulated the translation and publication of these outstanding books in several African and non-African languages. This development indicates that a multicultural ideology is at work in African children's publishing, an ideology that values differences.

LITERARY GENRES

Because imported books were irrelevant, and because they were directed at a Western audience, after independence African authors were deeply concerned about providing children with books written especially for them, reflecting their experiences, sociocultural environment, and worldview. Some of this fiction—school stories, Enid Blyton-style adventures and mysteries, and stories of social progress—can be criticized as poor imitations of colonial models because of their predictable plots, lack of in-depth character development, and stilted language. To counter the impact of imported European books, it was vital to inculcate in children pride in their culture and heritage.

One can detect an indigenous tradition developing in the two most popular genres for children in the postindependence period: retellings of folktales and narrative fiction. In each region of Africa, there has been a tremendous effort to record and publish collections of prose narratives, folktales, genealogies, songs, myths, legends, heroic sagas, children's rhymes, and proverbs and riddles. This activity not only preserves an oral tradition that is in danger of being lost as a result of rapid industrialization, modern media, and telecommunications, but it also forges a national and cultural identity. Instead of drawing creative inspiration from the culture and literary heritage of Spain, Portugal, Britain, Germany, or France, authors and students can turn to indigenous models. Mbare Ngom notes (in this volume) that the recording of folktales was the first step in the development of a children's literature canon in Equatorial Guinea. Perhaps this recovery of the history, folklore, and culture of various ethnic groups is an extension of the négritude movement. Despite the criticism that the movement was reductive, that its proponents universalized African culture, it cannot be denied that in celebrating their cultural roots they infused an African consciousness in literature.

Collections of folktales range from bare plot summaries to detailed narrations that provide descriptions of setting, circumstances of storytelling, and local customs. There are many outstanding collections that incorporate oral techniques in the written form. D. T. Niane recorded the extraordinary story of the birth, exile, and triumphant return of Sundiata, a thirteenth-century ruler of Mali, from the *griot* Mamadou Kouyate of the village of Djeliba Koro. Niane also emphasizes the role of *griot* as a counselor of kings, a recorder of history and laws, and repository of customs, traditions, and wisdom. Kariuki Gakuo's *Nyumba Ya Mumbi* is an evocative account of the origin of the Gikuyu cultural group of Kenya and the formation of its nine clans. In Zimbabwe, Norman Atkinson records 16 fables from the Shona, Ndebele, and Venda cultures in *The Broken Promise,* while Tim Matthews in *Tales of the Secret Valley* preserves the creation myths, legends, and animal stories of the Leya, Inde, and Dimba clans before the valley was submerged under water because of the dam built on the Zambezi River. In *Naa Kcnga: A Collection of Dagaaba Folktales,* Dannabang Kuwabong places 11 stories of daily life in their social and cultural context. Village youth narrate these stories night after night while shelling groundnuts: the playful banter and teasing of villagers, interruptions in the storytelling and task of shelling, and details of activities and comments between stories are carefully reproduced. The written version also reflects the influence of storytelling techniques: rich cultural background, songs interspersed in the narrative, insertion of key Dagaaba words and ideas, and passing on of cherished values and rules of conduct.

Scholars have also researched theories of indigenous verbal arts by emphasizing the qualities of a good storyteller, the communal function of storytelling, and the influence of traditional art forms on the written version. Osayimwense Osa writes in *African Children's and Youth Literature* that literature is not just for aesthetic pleasure, but serves as a link with the past: "it is the repository of cultural life of the people and is a major source of education for the young" (136). In Malawi, Steve Chimombo has examined *Ulimbaso,* which is an integrated theory for the creation and appreciation of indigenous Chichewa art. Wanjiku Mukabi Kabira and Karenga Mutahi in *Gikuyu Oral Literature* analyze tale types and outline the skills and techniques essential to a good performance. Odaga's *Yesterday's Today: The Study of Oral Literature* and *Thu Tinda!,* both pioneering works that record and translate Luo and other tales, provide methodology for collecting tales from storytellers, analysis of tale types, and role of tales in society. Benedict Onyango-Ogutu and Adrian Roscoe's *Keep My Words,* a collection of 36 Luo tales, also discusses the essential elements of a true storytelling performance and points out how Luo traditions are being incorporated in modern verse and short stories.

In the area of fiction a hybrid form is evolving, which combines Western novelistic techniques with the art of storytelling and African aesthetics. Cyprian Ekwensi, Achebe, and Tutuola intersperse the traditional stylistic devices of *orature*—songs, proverbs, idioms, dialogue, direct address to reader—in their prose. Jack Berry writes that spoken art has had a tremendous impact on literature in West Africa: "The political quest for the African personality is reflected . . . in a growing preoccupation with African modes of expression, and some stimulus has undoubtedly been provided by the critical acclaim accorded in Europe to recent literary efforts by West Africans that have drawn deeply on the traditional repertory of their cultures" (xxii). For instance, Odaga's *The Storm* is a fictional story that provides an ideal framework for introducing children to the myths, folklore, and historical legends associated with the Yimbo region of Kenya. Tutuola turns to the abundant folklore and mythology on which he was raised to create quest novels that display rich and varied descriptions of environment, fantastical happenings, exciting, suspense-filled adventures, and memorable characters who are both magical and human. Meshack Asare's *Chipo and the Bird on the Hill* is enriched by details from historical accounts and archaeological findings at Great Zimbabwe, while his Asante heritage—crafting goldweights, art motifs, fishing lore, and rituals of canoe-making—are intrinsic elements in the text and illustrations of *The Brassman's Secret* and *Taiwa Goes to Sea.*

However, this emerging African genre has led to controversy among African scholars. While some trace the development of the African novel to oral traditions and storytelling, others like Eustace Palmer argue that the novel is not an indigenous African genre but is based on Western fictional models (5). Hence she believes that the African novel should be judged by the same standards as Western novels for technique and artistry, and not just for subject matter (9). Collins suggests that perhaps Nigerians' embarrassment at some of Tutuola's mythological source material—old superstitions, witchcraft, tribal rituals, monstrous creatures—is based on their fear that it will feed the prejudices of Westerners who think of African customs as primitive and barbaric (89–90).

While Eurocentric critics focus on the novel's bourgeois nature—that it is a written form with a fixed European structure, such as a tightly knit plot and in-depth character delineation—Chinweizu, Onwuchekwa Jemie, and Ihechukwu Madubuike respond by saying that these critics "fail to give due weight to influences from Africa's oral antecedents to the African novel" (25). Citing both oral and written narratives from pre-European times, they point out that "[t]hese novels have made thematic, technical and formal contributions to the African novel. Among the formal are contributions in the area of length, structural complexity, and textural complexity. In their themes and techniques, African novelists have utilized material from African tales, fables, epigrams, proverbs, etc." (27). They state that for a genuine African literary genre to evolve, "a deliberate and calculated process of syncretism" must be pursued; there should be experimentation and "vitalizing contributions from other cultures," but only within the parameters of African tradition, so that "valuable continuities with our precolonial culture" may be maintained (239). The emerging African novel, whether based on oral tradition or on social realism, appears to be such a hybrid genre.

Biographies and autobiographies have also been instrumental in providing continuity with the past. They symbolize the forming of new nations by tracing how individuals and families have negotiated various geographical, cultural, historical, and social changes in their lives. For instance, in *My Father's Daughter* Mabel Segun describes her life as the daughter of a Christian pastor; Camara Laye in *L'Enfant Noir* (*The Dark Child*) provides a frank and intimate portrait of life under French rule and emphasizes that despite his French education and training, traditional beliefs continued to be essential to his family; and Nafissatou Diallo in *De Tilène au Plateau: Une Enfance dakaroise* (*A Dakar Childhood*) subtly reflects on the many changes that crept into her Muslim family with the social and political turmoil that marked the end of colonialism. Biographies and autobiographies almost function as traditional epics or heroic sagas because they provide role models, encourage self-pride, and forge national cohesiveness.

DOMINANT THEMES

Literature for children attempts to fill the void created by the "rootlessness" or "nonbelonging" that is a legacy of colonialism. Some of the more sophisticated works develop complex themes of protest, alienation, corruption, and the harsh realities of urban life. An examination of the dominant themes in children's and young adult literature indicates that there is a binary tension between modernity and tradition: westernization versus Africanization, rural versus urban, community versus individual.

The modern outlook in children's books is characterized by an emphasis on the themes of social, educational, medical, and scientific progress, because postcolonial societies faced overwhelming problems at the time of independence. Louis James believes that while the négritude movement was a necessary phase in shaking off the colonial yoke, today it has extended its influence to protest against social and political wrongs within Africa (116).

Prominent among the novels of progress are school stories, which are intended to inspire children to participate in the task of nation building. Marjorie Oludhe-MacGoye's *Growing Up at Lina School*, Anezi Okoro's *One Week, One Trouble*, and Ekwensi's *Trouble in Form Six* capture the atmosphere of the British boarding school, with the protagonists getting in trouble with the teachers and prefects for playing pranks and breaking rules. Importance is placed on sports competitions and athletics to build team spirit and to develop a moral character. Similarly, *The Race* and Mabel Segun's *Youth Day Parade* inculcate leadership qualities and school spirit. In contrast, F. K. Anane's *Kofi Mensah*, Chukwuemeka Ike's *The Potter's Wheel*, Ifeoma Okoye's *Village Boy!*, and Martina Nwakoby's *A Lucky Chance* inspire rural youth with the dream of success through education and hard work. The agenda of these stories is to convince village youth to work hard to get a Western-style education and become productive members of society. Bernard Chahilu's *The Herdsman's Daughter* and Henry R. ole Kulet's *To Become a Man* raise important questions of the value of formal education and the fast-disappearing traditional lifestyles. Both worlds have their strengths and weaknesses, but the resulting confusion often leads to alienation and a rejection of traditions.

Novels of progress also demand the uplifting of women, their right to education, employment, and equal opportunities. Teresa Meniru's *Unoma*, Onuora Nzekwu and Michael Crowder's *Eze Goes to School*, and Odaga's *Jande's Ambition* and *The Angry Flames* champion the rights of women. Each novel has a strong female character who works hard to fulfill her ambition to study, become financially independent, and exert her personal autonomy. Feminist authors want to provide young girls with positive role models and to empower them through their reading.

The social realism novels of Ekwensi, Meja Mwangi, and Ben Okri describe the harsh realities of urban life with brutal honesty. They depict the city as attractive, tempting, corrupting; urban life leads to governmental corruption, social inequities, and moral decay. The tone displays both the disillusionment and idealism, the apathy and involvement, of youth. Ekwensi's *The Motherless Baby* is about teenage pregnancy and the clash between traditional values and the influence of Western culture on youth; Mwangi's *Kill Me Quick* portrays the frustration of two village youth who come to the city for better opportunities, only to find a life of poverty, crime, and imprisonment; and Okri's *Flowers and Shadows* is a revealing portrait of power politics, corruption, disorder, and the hedonistic culture of the westernized elite of Lagos.

Bonnie Barthold suggests in *Black Time* that with the growing dominance of industrialization and technology, emphasis is placed on linear time, on progress and advancement here and now. This attitude has led to political and personal upheaval because an African worldview, which sees time as spiritual and cyclical, is ignored in the desire to forge a new society (14–27). Michael Scott Joseph's essay (in this volume) on children's journey tales identifies the mythological sources and symbolic rituals that efface profane historical time and invoke the sacred time that Mircea Eliade refers to (Eliade 78). In a sense, writers want to re-create for young readers the precolonial period that symbolizes the beginning, the mythic golden age. As Joseph's analysis reveals, the golden age is eventually lost, resulting in suffering and destruction.

While recognizing the importance of progress, writers also want to inculcate in young readers a respect for tradition: sense of community, time-honored beliefs and customs, kinship with nature and the land. Folktales, didactic stories, and legends emphasize varying relationships with the soil: it is the site of the spiritual connection with the gods, the dwelling of ancestors, and source of their livelihood. Soyinka's play, *A Dance of the Forests*, which is read by young adults, employs the trope of the gathering of the tribes to represent redemption and regeneration. In the scene where the spirits of nature—River, Palm, Precious Stone, Sun—are summoned to dance, the destinies of the natural world, society, Yoruba rituals and beliefs, and individuals are linked with the past and present. In traditional African societies, spiritual and political concerns were one; the community's strength lay in this unified vision, a vision that was disrupted during the colonial period. Postcolonial literature attempts to integrate these disparate elements in new fiction as well as in traditional tales. The fate of animals displaced by the creation of Lake Kariba is the subject of the Zimbabwean novel *Tsoko: The Story of a Vervet Monkey*. Richard Rayner evokes compassion for the feelings of Tsoko, who was separated from his mother because of a poacher's trap, and reflects on the spiritual affinity between humans and animals. Similarly, in Musa Nagenda's *Dogs of Fear* the protagonist learns that book knowledge and the practical lessons of his traditional upbringing can be reconciled. Esther Bali's *Taroh Folktales,* a collection of 15 tales from the Langtang region of Nigeria, reflects this farming community's belief that harmony among supernatural beings, animals, and humans is essential for happiness, and that family solidarity can be achieved through the peaceful coexistence of wives, stepmothers, and marital partners.

Historical books on the *Chimurenga* (independence) war in Zimbabwe and the Mau Mau movement in Kenya glorify the nationalism, sacrifice, and heroism of freedom fighters and the common folk who helped them. Mwangi's ironic stance in *Little White Man* presents the Mau Mau movement from the perspective of young Kariuki's friendship with a British boy: both Kenyans and whites are kind and loving in their personal lives, but the colonial situation introduces violence in their interpersonal relationships; hope and transformation rest with the children. The revolutionary Njamba Nene stories by Ngugi combine history, heroic myth, and fantasy to emphasize the bravery of the Mau Mau guerillas and to condemn colonialism and the unpatriotic behavior of those who support it.

According to feminist and Marxist critics, the status of women in children's books symbolizes the emerging nations of Africa: their subjugation and oppression, fight for independence from all forms of colonization, and demand to be treated as equals. Barthold writes that "[i]n traditional Africa, women were the biological embodiment of the mythic cycle, by virtue of procreation and childbirth. But they were often spiritual leaders, priestesses, as well, charged along with their male counterparts with nurturing the mythic cycle through appropriate rituals and sacrifice" (100). Buchi Emecheta's *Rape of Shavi* is an allegory about the impact of Western civilization on Africa. The rape of their future queen and the exploitation of their resources shatter the dignity of Shavians and their harmonious and economically self-sufficient country. Dreams of power, war, and technological might mesmerize the crown prince, till the wisdom of the Queen Mother makes him realize that Shavi was a highly cultured and civilized kingdom before the arrival of Europeans. In *The Moonlight Bride,* Emecheta sensitively portrays the feelings of co-wives and their daughters, and their differing treatment depending on the mother's status in the patriarchal household. Phebean Itayemi and Mabel Dove-Danquah's *The Torn Veil and Other Stories* is a bitter, and at times unfair, invective against the social norms and customs surrounding the marriage issue: in each short story, the victimized female is victorious over lechery, forced marriage, fickleness, and sexual abuse. In her Jungian analysis of Tutuola's *The Brave African Huntress,* Judy Anne White argues (in this volume) that the personal quest of the female hero follows the same archetypal pattern of individuation and self-knowledge as do male heroes. Although the heroine, Adebisi, has to constantly reassert her identity as a woman and hero, she is successful only because she "looks to herself as both source and beneficiary of her own inner strength."

Children's literature is going through a rite of passage similar to Tutuola's heroine, a quest for an identity that includes the many voices of postcolonial Africa. The journey involves seeking two divergent paths: developing an overarching national identity that embraces all segments of the population and celebrating the cultural uniqueness of the individual regions. Children's literature is assuming an African identity through multilingual and indigenous publications, recording traditional tales, and exploring themes that represent an African worldview and interpretation of history.

These divergent trends are most evident in South Africa and Namibia, two countries that have recently become democratic. The move is to publish books that will appeal to all children, regardless of culture, language, race, or class in order to bridge the "dreadful chasm" created by apartheid (Hepker 52). As Andree-Jeanne Tötemeyer writes of the emergent Namibian children's literature, "It is becoming a literature that does not primarily put people into racial or ethnic categories, but rather emphasizes a common Namibian culture that transcends ethnicity and apartheid" (50). At the same time folktales and stories about Southern Africa's numerous cultural and ethnic groups are also being written to preserve the identity of each community.

Above all, children's books published in Africa are dedicated to entertaining as well as giving children a sense of values. Writers bring to children's literature the spirit of communal responsibility for instructing the younger generation. Chinua Achebe sees the writer in the role of a teacher: "I would be quite satisfied if my novels (especially the ones I set in the past) did no more than teach my readers that their past—with all its imperfections—was not one long night of savagery from which the first Europeans acting on God's behalf delivered them. Perhaps what I write is applied art as distinct from pure. But who cares? Art is important, but so is education of the kind I have in mind" ("The Novelist as Teacher" 72).

WORKS CITED

Achebe, Chinua. *No Longer at Ease.* 1960. Rpt. London: Heinemann, 1987.

———. "The Novelist as Teacher." *Morning Yet on Creation Day.* Garden City, N.Y.: Anchor-Doubleday, 1975. 67–73.

———. *Things Fall Apart.* 1958. Rpt. London: Heinemann, 1986.

Anane, F. K. *Kofi Mensah.* Accra: Ghana Publishing House, 1968.

Asad, Talal, and John Dixon. "Translating Europe's Others." *Europe and Its Others.* Ed. Francis Baker et al. Vol. 1. Colchester, U.K.: University of Essex, 1985. 170–77.

Asare, Meshack. *The Brassman's Secret.* Accra: Educational Press and Manufacturers, 1981.

———. *Chipo and the Bird on the Hill.* Harare: Zimbabwe Publishing House, 1984.

———. *Taiwa Goes to Sea.* Accra: Ghana Publishing Corporation, 1970.

Atkinson, Norman. *The Broken Promise and Other Traditional Fables from Zimbabwe.* Harare: Academic, 1989.

Bali, Esther. *Taroh Folktales.* Ibadan: Spectrum, 1990.

Barthold, Bonnie J. *Black Time: Fiction of Africa, the Caribbean and the United States.* New Haven, Conn. and London: Yale University Press, 1980.

Berry, Jack. "Spoken Art in West Africa." *West African Folktales.* Collect. and trans. Jack Berry. Introd. and ed. Richard A. Spears. Evanston, Ill.: Northwestern University Press, 1991. vii–xxvi.

Blockeel, Francesca. "Colonial and Postcolonial Portuguese Children's Literature." *Bookbird* 34.4 (Winter 1996): 12–17.

Booth, James. *Writers and Politics in Nigeria.* New York: Africana, 1981.

Cartey, Wilfred. *Whispers from a Continent: The Literature of Contemporary Black Africa.* New York: Random House, 1969.

Chahilu, Bernard P. *The Herdsman's Daughter.* Nairobi: East African Publishing House, 1974.

Chimombo, Steve. *Malawian Oral Literature: The Aesthetics of Indigenous Arts.* Zomba: Centre for Social Research and University of Malawi, 1988.

Chinweizu, Onwuchekwa Jemie, and Ihechukwu Madubuike. *Toward the Decolonization of African Literature.* Vol. 1: *African Fiction and Poetry and Their Critics.* Washington, D.C.: Howard University Press, 1983.

Collins, Harold R. *Amos Tutuola.* New York: Twayne, 1969.

Dhawan, R. K., P. V. Dhamija, and A. K. Srivastava. "Commonwealth Literatures." *Recent Commonwealth Literature.* Ed. R. K. Dhawan, P. V. Dhamija, and A. K. Srivastava. New Delhi: Prestige Books, 1989. 1: 5–10.

Diallo, Nafissatou. *De Tilène au Plateau: Une Enfance dakaroise (A Dakar Childhood;* trans.

Dorothy S. Blair). Harlow, Essex: Longman, 1982.

Egejuru, Phanuel Akubueze. *Black Writers: White Audience. A Critical Approach to African Literature.* Hicksville, N.Y.: Exposition, 1978.

Ekwensi, Cyprian. *The Motherless Baby.* Nairobi: Heinemann, 1990.

———. *Trouble in Form Six.* Cambridge: Cambridge University Press, 1966.

Eliade, Mircea. *The Myth of the Eternal Return.* Trans. Willard R. Trask. 1949. Princeton, N.J.: Princeton University Press, 1971.

Emecheta, Buchi. *The Moonlight Bride.* 1980. Rpt. New York: Braziller, 1983.

———. *The Rape of Shavi.* London: Flamingo/Fontana, 1985.

Gakuo, Kariuki. *Nyumba Ya Mumbi: The Gikuyu Creation Myth.* Nairobi: Jacaranda, 1992.

Hepker, Sue. "Little Voices, Big Stories: The Role of Children in Creating The Little Library." *Bookbird* 34.3 (Fall 1996): 52–56.

Ike, Chukwuemeka. *The Potter's Wheel.* London: Fontana/Collins, 1974.

Itayemi, Phebean, and Mabel Dove-Danquah. *The Torn Veil and Other Stories.* London: Evans, 1975.

James, Louis. "The Protest Tradition: *Black Orpheus* and *Transition.*" *Protest and Conflict in African Literature.* Ed. Cosmo Pieterse and Donald Munro. New York: Africana Publishing, 1969. 109–24.

Kabira, Wanjiku Mukabi, and Karenga Mutahi. *Gikuyu Oral Literature.* Nairobi: Heinemann, 1988.

Khorana, Meena. *Africa in Literature for Children and Young Adults: An Annotated Bibliography of English-Language Books.* Westport, Conn. and London: Greenwood, 1994.

Kulet, Henry R. *To Become a Man.* Nairobi: Longman, 1972.

Kuwabong, Dannabang. *Naa Kcnga: A Collection of Dagaaba Folktales.* Accra: Woeli, 1992.

Laye, Camara. *L'Enfant Noir* (*The Dark Child;* trans. James Kirkup). London: Collins, 1959.

Matthews, Tim. *Tales of the Secret Valley.* Harare: Baobab, 1988.

Meniru, Teresa E. *Unoma.* Lagos and Ibadan: Macmillan, 1982.

Mwangi, Meja. *Kill Me Quick.* London: Heinemann, 1973.

———. *Little White Man.* Nairobi: Longman, 1990.

Nagenda, Musa, pseud. *Dogs of Fear.* London, Nairobi, Ibadan, Lusaka: Heinemann, 1971.

Ngugi wa Thiong'o. *Caitaani Mūtharabainī.* Nairobi: Heinemann, 1980.

———. *Decolonising the Mind: The Politics of Language in African Literature.* London: Currey; Nairobi: Heinemann Kenya; Portsmouth, N.H.: Heinemann, 1986.

———. *Njamba Nene and the Flying Bus.* Trans. from the Gikuyu by Wangui wa Goro. Nairobi: Heinemann, 1986.

———. *Njamba Nene's Pistol.* Trans. from the Gikuyu by Wangui wa Goro. Nairobi: Heinemann, 1986.

Niane, Djibril Tamsi. *Sundiata: An Epic of Old Mali.* Trans. from the French *Soundjata, ou l'Épopée Mandingue* by G. D. Pickett. Harlow, Essex: Longman, 1965.

Nwakoby, Martina. *A Lucky Chance.* Ibadan: Macmillan, 1980.

Nzekwu, Onuora, and Michael Crowder. *Eze Goes to School.* Ibadan: African Universities Press, 1963.

Odaga, Asenath Bole. *The Angry Flames.* Kisumu: Lake Publishers & Enterprises, 1968.

———. *Jande's Ambition.* Kisumu: Lake Publishers & Enterprises, 1966.

———. *The Storm.* Kisumu: Lake Publishers & Enterprises, 1985.

———. *Thu Tinda!* Nairobi: Uzima, 1980.

———. *Yesterday's Today: The Study of Oral Literature.* Kisumu: Lake Publishers & Enterprises, 1984.

Okoro, Anezi. *One Week, One Trouble*. Ibadan: African Universities Press, 1972.

Okoye, Ifeoma. *Village Boy!* Ibadan: Macmillan, 1980.

Okri, Ben. *Flowers and Shadows*. Harlow, Essex: Longman, 1980.

Oludhe-MacGoye, Marjorie. *Growing Up at Lina School*. Nairobi: Heinemann, 1971.

Onyango-Ogutu, Benedict, and Adrian A. Roscoe. *Keep My Words*. Nairobi: Heinemann, 1974.

Osa, Osayimwense. *African Children's and Youth Literature*. New York: Twayne, 1995.

Palmer, Eustace. *Growth of the African Novel*. London: Heinemann, 1979.

The Race. London: Collins, 1980.

Rayner, Richard. *Tsoko: The Story of a Vervet Monkey*. Harare: Baobab, 1990.

Segun, Mabel D. *My Father's Daughter*. Nairobi: East African Publishing House, 1965.

———. *Youth Day Parade*. Ibadan, Nairobi, Kampala, and Accra: DUCA,1984.

Snead, James. "European Pedigrees/African Contagions: Nationality, Narrative, and Communality in Tutuola, Achebe, and Reed." *Nation and Narration*. Ed. Homi K. Bhabha. London and New York: Routledge, 1990. 231–49.

Soyinka, Wole. *A Dance of the Forests*. Oxford: Oxford University Press, 1963.

Tötemeyer, Andree-Jeanne. "Country Survey: Namibia." *Bookbird* 35.2 (Summer 1997): 46–50.

Tutuola, Amos. *The Brave African Huntress*. New York: Grove, 1958.

2

The Excitement and Challenges of Publishing for Kenyan Children: A Writer's Perspective

Asenath Bole Odaga

Writing and publishing for children is a very complicated business, and I went into it well prepared. Initially, I had no problems, although there were some male chauvinists who felt I, a woman, was too daring; they even suggested I would be better off with a restaurant! But I ventured into writing for children with high expectations, seeking inspiration from my love of storytelling, which dates back to my childhood and school days. To date, I have written more than thirty books for children. Although I have received very little financial gain, I have derived much personal satisfaction from writing for children.

I grew up in a large family and a home full of laughter, where we enjoyed story-telling by moonlight, accompanied by singing, handclapping, and dancing in a happy, carefree atmosphere. As a young woman, after I trained as a teacher and started to teach, I was concerned that the beautiful stories I had enjoyed as a child were no longer available to most Kenyan children. It was then that I decided to collect oral narratives and to write some fiction for young children and teenagers. This was not for monetary gain, because I was well aware of the enormous problems facing a children's author in postcolonial Kenya.

I wanted Kenyan children to read books written especially for them and to encourage Kenyans to write for children. Literature is very much a part of a people's culture, and over the years I have come to realize that no outsider can develop or preserve our culture. We have to do it ourselves, as a nation and as patriotic citizens.

BACKGROUND

At the advent of colonialism in Africa, only Egypt and a few other countries had some form of writing or recording their thoughts. Most African countries, such as Kenya, had not invented any methods of writing at the beginning of the nineteenth century. Thus literature for children and adults in Kenya was oral in form; however, it was well developed and occupied a central place in the community, playing a significant role in the daily lives of the people. Most communities had some sort of "classroom" arrangement through which children were, at an early age, introduced to the various genres of oral literature.

Oral literature provided a unique forum for education, entertainment, and interaction among children and between children and adults. Because it played an important role in the process of socialization of children, it acted as a carrier and transmitter of cultural and aesthetic values, modes of behaviors, and moral standards that society expected them to project as adults. A people's philosophies, attitude toward life, beliefs, social ethics, and skills and knowledge were subtly conveyed to the younger generation through beautiful proverbs, songs, and folktales.

Today it is no longer possible for these communities to rely solely on verbal transmission of literature because of social, economic, and political changes and modernization. For instance, some children no longer speak the indigenous languages used to transmit oral literature, because their families have been urbanized or have moved from their ancestral homes to find employment in cities and on large plantations. In addition, political upheavals in certain countries of Africa have disturbed the traditional social set up. As a result, traditional modes of transmission are no longer effective or practical.

Kenyans now feel compelled to research, collect, write, and publish oral literature from various ethnic groups. This material helps to build Kenyan literature and is available to all children wherever they may be. However, publishing narratives and other oral literature alone does not solve the problem of the scarcity of good, interesting children's literature. Kenyans must also write and produce more creative works, using events and settings that are familiar to children.

While the number of young and upcoming children's writers is steadily increasing, there is still an apparent lack of seriousness and full commitment to writing for children. Children's writers are viewed as having a lower status than writers for adults. A number of Kenyans still write only casually for children. They may produce a collection or two of oral stories or they may write just one children's novel and then stop. Because readership and sales of children's books is low and one cannot earn enough to live on, few Kenyans take writing for children seriously enough to fully develop their talents to write quality children's books that can compete in the world market. Book sales in Africa are so low that no writer, not even a Chinua Achebe or a Ngugi wa Thiong'o, can live on his or her royalties.

Factors that contribute to low readership in Kenya are illiteracy, poverty, and a poor infrastructure that makes books inaccessible. Children who drop out of school at the primary level have no suitable books to read, hence a percentage of such youth often regress into illiteracy. The buying capacity of most Kenyans has gone down tremendously. The situation is worse when it comes to buying non-textbooks, especially for rural parents who are often forced by poverty to remove their young daughters from school. The young girl may be married off or sent away to work in town to support the family. Hence the dropout rate is higher for girls, resulting in more illiterate women than men in Kenya. Poverty is an obstacle to the development of Kenyan literature for both children and adults. Since independence, Kenya has experienced rapid population growth. This development, together with other economic factors, has put a great strain on resources, slowing the development of nonessential services such as libraries.

THE LANGUAGE ISSUE

A major problem a children's writer faces is the lack of a unifying language. There are more than 41 indigenous languages spoken in Kenya, and obviously one cannot produce books in all languages to meet the reading needs of all children. As with literature for adults, children's books are written in either English, Kiswahili, or the languages of the major ethnic groups. More often than not, children's writers are forced to use the language of the ex-colonial masters, English, because it is the language in which formal education is conducted.

However, the scenario is different in the vast rural areas, where more than 80 percent of Kenyan children live. For the first three years of school, children speak and learn in various mother tongues. In high-cost schools for middle- and upper-class children, located mostly in urban areas, English is taught from day one. In some town schools, however, children learn in Kiswahili for the first three years, while English is just one of the subjects in the curriculum. In both rural and urban schools, the switch to English is made in the fourth year, when English becomes the medium of instruction.

It is not possible for a children's writer in Kenya to create a story for the six-to-nine-year-old age group, regardless of the language in which it is written, that will be read by children all over the country. To translate books for younger children into the numerous mother tongues is expensive. Hence literature for younger children is fragmented. Some ethnic groups have books for beginners written in their mother tongues and Kiswahili, while others have none.

We may try to dismiss the language problem as unimportant, but it is quite serious, particularly because it has adverse effects on the reading abilities of rural children and those who come from homes and communities where no other languages except the local ones are spoken. As books are mostly written in English and Kiswahili,[1] and rarely in the local languages, these children are confronted at an early age with the problem of not being able to correlate their home environment with their education and reading. Hence they are unable to comprehend and formulate clear ideas on anything. As S. J. Smith, an American specialist on children's literature, writes, "A child's intellectual and emotional well-being depends on his developing the full possession of his native language—the effect of the amplified view is more marked so far in primary school than elsewhere" (120). He further states that "[a] student brings to his reading a moral and religious code and social philosophy assimilated primarily from his family and community background" (120). Language is a carrier of values, and it is these values that have to be passed on to children through their literature. The oral story was popular as children's literature because its creators made use of children's culture, background, experiences, and, above all, a language which all the children could speak and understand.

INDIGENOUS PUBLISHING

Even after Kenya had attained political independence, its book market continued to be dominated by multinational publishers with parent companies in the United Kingdom. However, the last ten years or so have been characterized by positive changes due to the emergence of a number of local publishing firms—the indigenous publishers—in major urban centers, who have ventured into publishing trade books for both adults and children, as well as textbooks and other relevant materials. Some, such as my Lake Publishers & Enterprises Limited (LPE), have focused on children's publishing. Indigenous publishers are harder hit by the problems of publishing for children than are the well-established multinational firms. As a result of the increased competition in the children's book market in recent years, indigenous publishers are unable to compete with multinational publishers for good authors. Neither can they afford the high rates for advertising their publications in newspapers, magazines, and other information media. As a result, most of them go out of business within a few years. Indigenous publishers of children's fiction are especially disadvantaged when it comes to actual sales, because they do not publish textbooks, which are in higher demand.

Many indigenous publishers are afraid of expanding through bank facilities because of the high interest rates and the low economic activities brought about by Structural Adjustments Programmes (SAPs) commonly known as cost sharing. According to this plan, parents are responsible for purchasing textbooks, contributing money or materials for the construction of school buildings, and providing other facilities, while the government only pays teachers' salaries. Government subsidies for education have been curtailed, as have medical and other benefits. The introduction of SAPs came abruptly, and because of their low earning capacity, parents can barely afford textbooks for their children.

The Kenyan government owns two publishing firms, the Jomo Kenyatta Foundation and the Kenya Literature Bureau, which was created in place of the defunct East African Literature Bureau. The Jomo Kenyatta Foundation publishes mainly educational materials that have been researched, field-tested, and developed by the Kenya Institute of Education for use in preprimary, primary, and secondary schools. In contrast, the Kenya Literature Bureau is a parastatal body charged with the responsibility of publishing both educational and noneducational materials. In fact, it is not meant to compete with other publishing houses or to make a profit. Both firms also publish children's literature, which is a positive move.

The colonial mentality that judges children's books written and produced in Kenya to be inferior to Western children's books still dominates our thinking. This attitude stems from our colonial background, when Africans were subjected to subordination and their background and culture were despised as inferior. This negativity has been counterproductive and has made Africans regard their culture and even their language as less valuable and lower in status than those of foreigners. Most Kenyans, and indeed Africans as a whole, tend to disparage each other's works as not being of high quality when compared to books by non-Africans. Until recently, many bookshops in urban centers would not display Kenyan books on the same shelves with the more colorful Western children's books. Of course, Western books are of better quality and well produced compared with those published in Kenya, which appear dull and unattractive by comparison. In our situation, however, it is the content and its relevance to children that matters and not the appearance.

Indigenous publishers cannot produce books in full color because of the prohibitive cost of materials and color separations. If books were to be published in full color, and on good-quality paper suitable for children, the sale price would be exorbitant, making even a small book unaffordable for the majority. Similarly, indigenous books are not well illustrated or designed because the number of Kenyan illustrators is still miserably small. The reason for this is historical: publishers have mainly been British, so that illustrators, even of books written by Kenyans, have been commissioned from abroad by the publisher.

In recent years, however, the new generation of local artists has begun to take courses on illustrating at the diploma and postgraduate levels, while others train at polytechnical institutes or at one of the few art schools that exist in the country. In addition, art education has been given emphasis in school curricula. Kenyans have also established well-organized firms that specialize in graphic design and book illustration. The only major limitation facing young artists is the lack of employment opportunities, which compels many to turn to freelancing. The situation is worsened because most publishing houses do not engage illustrators on a permanent basis but prefer to utilize their services as required. With more and more indigenous publishing houses being set up, one hopes that local artists will have greater opportunities to produce better-quality illustrations for books published in Kenya.

MARKETING AND DISTRIBUTION

As is the case with publishers, bookstores and distributors of children's books also concentrate mainly in cities and large towns. Since there are very few independent book distributors and book agents in Kenya, publishers act as distributors of their books as well. They sell books to agents, who in turn sell them to the public, making books expensive for bookstores and buyers alike. Again, this is a monopoly that does not augur well for indigenous publishers, who lack the funds to compete with the powerful multinational publishing giants.

The concentration of book activities in urban centers has also thwarted the growth of the book industry in rural areas. Because of the poor infrastructure—long distances on rough roads and few railway lines—not many books are available to rural children. Schools, which could serve as a means of disseminating literature for children, often lack the funds to buy supplementary books or library books. While parents are required to buy schoolbooks, they seldom buy trade books, which are generally unknown outside urban centers. Sales of books that are not prescribed as school texts are so low that most bookstores do not even display them.

A positive development in postcolonial times, which aims at decentralizing book industry services, is the move to establish bookshops in rural shopping centers. Publishers supply these bookshops with children's and other books, and although sales are weak, rural children are at least exposed to the books, which they can buy when the need arises.

Library facilities are inadequate throughout the country. Public libraries and school libraries, which could make children's literature available to young readers, are also concentrated in urban centers. Rural areas lack such facilities, leaving the majority of the country's population with few or no libraries and reading rooms. Even in urban areas, there are only a handful of well-stocked libraries in Kenya. Most are run by the partly government-owned Kenya National Library Services. While these libraries are manned by well-qualified and trained Kenyans, the children's sections are poorly stocked. The heavy usage to which the books are subjected leads to rapid wear and tear. According to Muthoni Kibandi, more than 50 percent of their volumes in the children's section of the country's libraries are foreign books that have been donated. Libraries cannot afford to replenish their holdings or purchase books published in Kenya. There are also a few private libraries in some Kenyan towns, including Nairobi. The British Council has three well-stocked and efficiently run libraries in Nairobi, Mombasa, and Kisumu. Membership is open to any Kenyan over 18. Some urban schools also provide libraries for their students and teachers, but most of them are poorly stocked and managed because of lack of funds. Book clubs and reading houses, which could assist in the dissemination of the literature, are almost unheard of in Kenya. The lack of reading opportunities that would create a reading culture is a situation that a publisher or writer can do very little to remedy.[2]

Children may not prefer books produced in Kenya to well-produced Western ones, but they have no option but to buy and read them, because imported books are very expensive and not readily available. Usually imported books are sold only in larger urban centers such as Nairobi, while those produced locally are sold everywhere, even in the small bookshops in rural shopping centers and open-air markets.

COOPERATION WITH OTHER AFRICAN COUNTRIES

Some of the problems experienced by Kenyan publishers, which in turn affect writers, could be solved through closer cooperation between Kenya and its neighbors. Copublishing and translation of good children's books into the common languages used in various regions of Africa could assist in the dissemination of Kenyan children's literature throughout the continent.

The three East African countries of Tanzania, Uganda, and Kenya are geographically close and hence have much in common. Because Tanzania decided to use

Kiswahili as its official language, while Kenya and Uganda chose English, everyone speaks, reads, writes, and studies all subjects in Kiswahili from primary school to university. Tanzania thus has a higher literacy rate because Kiswahili is spoken by everybody. However, years of internal strife have slowed the growth of its publishing industry, which is not as developed as Kenya's. Uganda, in contrast, has the most limited facilities. Only in the last five years has Uganda tried to catch up with the production of children's books. Ugandan writers sometimes are able to publish their books in Kenya. LPE has published *The African Children's Stories,* a collection of five Ugandan narratives, by Evangeline Barongo and Ruth Mwayi, which has been very well received throughout East Africa. *The Shadow and the Substance,* a fictional book by the Ugandan writer V. R. Barungi, is scheduled to be released shortly. Since I visited Tanzania in 1993 and 1994 to teach children's writing, the country has produced some excellent and well-illustrated books in Kiswahili. Tanzania is also getting assistance with its children's book project from a Canadian nongovernmental organization (NGO-CODE), which has enabled Tanzanians to publish many children's books. Occasionally, Kenyan children's books are translated and sold in schools in Tanzania and Uganda; however, because of their weak currencies the average Ugandans and Tanzanians cannot afford to buy books from Kenya.

The opening of South Africa after the dismantling of apartheid has also exposed Kenyan children's books to a wider market. This is posing a stiff but healthy competition for Kenyan publishers. Some are already copublishing children's books with South African publishers. Book dealers in Southern Africa are beginning to work with Kenyan dealers and are participating in seminars and workshops. This is a welcome development that can only benefit children's literature. APNET, the African Publishing Network, a Zimbabwe-based organization, which was created in 1992 to coordinate publishing in Africa, is doing much to foster closer cooperation among African publishers. In recent years, seminars on children's literature have been held in Kenya and other African countries such as Zimbabwe during their annual book fair. Publishers and book dealers from several countries such as India have become regular visitors to both the Nairobi and Harare book fairs.

We also look forward to the development of closer cooperation with publishers in developed countries to herald the emergence of a worldwide book market.

CHILDREN'S LITERATURE RESEARCH

Children's literature is as much a product of its time as adult literature and must be subjected to rigorous appraisal and criticism, which is presently lacking in Kenya and indeed in Africa as a whole, with the exception of South Africa. As I stated in my study of Kenyan children's literature: "Children's literature is very much an integral part of the general creative scene. It grows out of, and is shaped by the same forces that give rise and influence to adult literature. It therefore deserves greater critical attention than it has hitherto been accorded, especially in the criticism of African literature. It is in fact very important that we see children's literature as . . . play[ing] a significant role in the image-forming process of individuals" (xxiii).

Although its funding is limited, the Kenyan section of the International Board on Books for Young People (KeBBY) would like to carry out research in children's literature starting with the compilation of a bibliography of locally written children's publications. KeBBY would also like to initiate the publication of critical works on children's literature, magazines, and journals. However, KeBBY has been successful in creating awareness through seminars organized for both illustrators and writers to promote writing for children. This has provided grand opportunities for artists to discuss relevant aspects of the subject and to identify common areas of cooperation. Three of our local universities—Nairobi, Kenyatta, and Egerton—are currently offering courses on children's literature at the graduate level.

Book critics, especially of children's literature, are scarce, and more often than not a new book can take a year or so to be reviewed. Furthermore, newspapers devote very little space to book reviews. Music, musicians, soccer, and other sporting activities often get better publicity and coverage than writers and their books. Part of the problem is the lack of active professional associations or organizations of writers, librarians, and illustrators.

ROLE OF A CHILDREN'S AUTHOR IN POSTCOLONIAL KENYA

The children's book industry has changed a great deal from the time I began to write nearly thirty years ago. Writing and publishing for the Kenyan child is an exciting undertaking. Since writing for children is a relatively new development, there is abundant traditional material from which an author can draw. The precolonial era offers a rich reservoir of oral literature made up of myths, legends, and folktales. The colonial era, which introduced Western children's literature in Kenya, also has plenty of material from which great works of literature are still being created. In addition, the 34 years of Kenya's political independence have been packed with activities and events from which a children's writer may create interesting, relevant works on economic, religious, political, or social issues.

A Kenyan writer has many faces and many missions. She is an explorer, a philosopher, and a historian; she entertains, teaches, and informs. Besides, she is a social commentator and a missionary. Because of her artistic qualities and abilities, she is sensitive to both negative and positive developments in her society. One of her major tasks is to decolonize the thinking of her young readers, to make them proud of being Kenyans with a dignity and identity of their own: "a writer, whether she produces works for youth or for adults, is part and parcel of her society, which she must observe with interest in order to write realistically about it. The writer uses her society and background to produce authentic literature that distinguishes itself as an African (Kenyan) literature by evoking experiences which are peculiarly African (Kenyan) in nature" (Odaga, *Literature for Children* 39). The objective of the Kenyan author is to offer an essential service to the country. Knowing that the average Kenyan child can at least afford to buy and read locally produced books, even though they are in black and white, is a fact that encourages her to work with greater determination.

Children's writers can also be instrumental in shaping attitudes and values and removing stereotypes. While society's methods of socializing its members cannot be changed in a day, editors and writers can be sensitized to the harmful effects of perpetuating gender disparity in children's literature. The image of girls and women in locally published books is gradually changing, although negative beliefs and attitudes survive in oral tales and fiction. LPE has countered such images by publishing stories such as *Jande's Ambition* that depict boys and girls, men and women, as equals. According to a major survey conducted by a Kenyan researcher, Dr. Anne Obura, there are some improvements in the portrayal of girls and women in Kenyan textbooks. The research acted as an eye-opener for teachers, editors, and publishers when it revealed that girls and women are discriminated against and marginalized in textbooks and storybooks alike. They are featured as diminutive characters: a weak, helpless, and unintelligent lot that must always be protected by male relatives. They are considered fit only for production and service jobs, or for their reproductive functions and tiresome domestic chores. In the majority of oral narratives, and indeed in some creative works for adults and children as well, women are identified with evil and inhuman acts; yet, at the same time, they are revered as mothers, providers, and nurturers of life.

The conflict between modernity and traditional ways has not been a great problem in my writing. A good writer in a developing country realizes the country is going through a transitional period and always tries to harmonize useful traditions with new ideas to benefit children and the country as a whole. Being objective and balancing the issues between the old and the young, the traditional and the modern, is difficult, but it can be and has been done with marked success.

A Kenyan children's writer, like writers elsewhere in the world, is first and foremost an artist who creates literary works from experiences and activities central to her community. She is, therefore, a keen observer of all that goes on around her. Such works, at one level, may seem to be local and peculiar to Kenyan society only; at another level, the works may raise issues that transcend national boundaries and touch on universal issues pertaining to the developing world and to human societies.

FUTURE OF CHILDREN'S LITERATURE IN KENYA

Since the country gained political independence in 1963, the Kenyan child has had a variety of books to choose from. While the multinational publishers and large booksellers continue to import Western children's books, such books are proving to be too expensive for the average Kenyan. Sales are low due to their high cost; in some cases, one imported book may sell for the price of two or three local ones. Only affluent parents can afford to purchase such expensive books for their children. In this respect, high prices have worked for the benefit of books written, illustrated, and produced by Kenyans.

The majority of Kenyan children find imported books to be irrelevant because the content, setting, and cultural values are from a totally different background. For these reasons the majority of Kenyan children have begun to prefer locally produced books, because they depict experiences and characters with whom they can identify. Kibandi writes that it is crucial to provide children with books that reflect their surroundings and culture during their formative years, because "[a]lienation at this stage leaves no room for accepting one's culture" (4).

Much progress has been made in developing children's literature written and illustrated by Kenyans. Both fictional works and recorded folk narratives offer a rich variety of reading material for Kenya's culturally and racially diverse population. Another positive development is that not all locally produced books are in English. In response to a demand for suitable reading material, the new generation of Kenyan writers is encouraged to write in Kiswahili and the regional languages. The move to publish books in the mother tongues of young children in rural areas is gradually becoming popular.

Because 60 percent of Kenya's population is under the age of twenty, children's literature has great potential and a bright future. The market has also grown as a result of the rapid growth in population. In the last five years, there has been a marked improvement in readership of children's fiction in primary and lower secondary schools. Those who first read my books in the late 1960s are now educated young parents, holding professional jobs, who know the value of reading and are willing to spend money on buying books for their children.

The printing industry, which is a vital component of book publishing, is also well established in Kenya, and the quality of work has improved considerably in the last ten years. The new trend in Kenya is to publish better-quality and cheaper children's books in order to promote literature and culture. The most recently produced children's books have large, clear illustrations in black and white, while covers are made bright and attractive. Computers are also being used to typeset children's books in bolder and larger typefaces. The market for these books is encouraging, especially since the inauguration of the former Children's Literature Association of Kenya in 1988 and the formation of KeBBY in 1996, which sensitized the public and publishers to the importance of children's literature. Even the multinational publishers, who in the past concentrated only on publishing school texts, have now initiated programs to publish children's books by Kenyans in addition to importing Western books from their parent firms.

Writing for Kenyan children is still in its infancy, and we are all hopeful it will grow. I believe that the problems and obstacles—such as lack of committed writers for children's books, lack of training for book industry personnel, inadequate school library facilities, and economic constraints—that hinder the rapid growth of an indigenous children's literature will be overcome in time. We look forward to a bright future in development and growth of the book industry in Kenya that will enhance production of high-quality children's literature.

NOTES

1. According to a survey conducted by the Council for the Promotion of Children's Scientific Publications in Africa, only 1.69 percent of the books published in Kenya are in Kiswahili and the mother tongues (cited in Kibandi).

2. See Lily Msae Nyariki, "Reading Opportunities for the Young in Kenya," *Bookbird* 34.4 (Winter 1996): 31–32.

WORKS CITED

Barongo, Evangeline L., and Ruth M. Mwayi. *The African Children's Stories.* Kisumu: Lake Publishers & Enterprises, 1994.

Barungi, V. R. *The Shadow and the Substance.* Kisumu: Lake Publishers & Enterprises, forthcoming.

Kibandi, Muthoni. "A Study of the Availability and Relevance of Children's Recreational Literature in Selected Libraries in Kenya." Paper presented at the seminar on Publishing and Promotion of Reading among Children, Nairobi, 1992.

Obura, Anne. *Changing Images: Portrayal of Girls and Women in Kenyan Textbooks.* Nairobi: African Centre for Technology Studies, 1991.

Odaga, Asenath Bole. *Jande's Ambition.* Kisumu: Lake Publishers & Enterprises, 1986.

———. *Literature for Children and Young People in Kenya.* Nairobi: Kenya Literature Bureau, 1985.

Smith, S. J. *A Critical Approach to Children's Literature.* London: McGraw, 1967.

3

AWARD-WINNING CHILDREN'S BOOKS: THE NOMA SELECTIONS 1980–1994

Nancy J. Schmidt

The Noma Award for Publishing in Africa was established in 1980 by Shoichi Noma, then president of Kodansha Limited, the largest publishing house in Japan.[1] The influence of the award was immediately evident for award winners in the early years, since the books were translated into many languages and widely distributed. In 1982 UNESCO acknowledged the success of the 1980 and 1981 awards (Noma Award Archive, Committee minutes 2 February 1982). Within four years of its foundation, the Noma Award had become the major book award in Africa (Irele 104), because it is not just another literature award, but an award by Africans for African publishing within African contexts. By the time the award was ten years old its impact on African publishing was evident in the improved quality of many of the books submitted for the award in addition to the winning and honorable mention books, which suggested a bright future for African publishing (Jones 111–12). The Noma Award has succeeded in drawing attention to the scope and vitality of African publishing despite declining economic conditions in many African countries.

Shoichi Noma firmly believed in the influence of books as a powerful force for social change, for economic, social, and cultural development, and for enlightening people in general. Before establishing the Noma Award for Publishing in Africa, Mr. Noma was active in promoting publishing in Asia. He founded the Tokyo Centre for Book Development in Asia and served as president of the Japanese Publishers' Association for Cultural Exchange. In 1974 he received the International Book Award for his sponsorship of UNESCO assistance programs for book publishing in Asia. When he established the Noma Award for Publishing in Africa, he also started a Noma Fund for the Promotion of Readership to support activities of the International Reading Association in the developing world, and provided funds to improve the quality of children's book publishing in Asia, Africa, and the Arab states by holding contests for illustrators (Lottman, "Kodansha" 31).

The Noma Award has three aims:

[F]irstly, to encourage the research work of African scholars, the writing and illustrating of children's books—especially picture-story books for younger children—and to aid new creative writing by African writers, particularly aspiring new authors. Second, the Award will seek to encourage the publication of the work of African writers and scholars in Africa, rather than in Britain, France, or the United States as is often the case at present. Thirdly, the prize will have the effect of giving a boost to the growing number of indigenous African publishers, and will thus contribute not only to the advancement of knowledge, literary output, and authorship, but also to the promotion of book development and publishing in Africa. ("Noma Award" 229)

The Noma Award has been given annually since 1980 for books in any of three categories: scholarly or academic work, children's books, and literature and creative writing, including criticism of African literature. Books are submitted for the award by African publishers located in Africa to the Noma Award Secretariat in Oxford, England. The Noma Award Managing Committee, composed of distinguished African scholars and book experts, serves as the jury. The Managing Committee examines all books submitted for the award, recommends books to be submitted to expert reviewers, and selects the winning entries. Because books may be submitted in any African language in which materials are published as well as on a wide variety of subjects, the services of some three hundred reviewers have been used in the first 15 years that the award has been given. In order to promote African publishing, each year five or more honorable mention books are selected in addition to the award winner, or award co-winners in a few cases. The winning author receives a monetary award, and the winning author and publisher both receive a plaque. Each year all the books submitted for the award are donated to a library in Africa; a nonprofit organization pays for the transportation.

The Noma Award trust was initially established with $100,000, and the prize money was $3,000. In 1986 the trust was augmented by $50,000, and in 1989 the award was increased to $5,000. Shoichi Noma took a keen interest in the award until his death in 1984, and members of his family have been equally supportive since then.

Since one of the aims of the Noma Award is to encourage children's book publishing and one of the three categories for submissions is children's books, it is appropriate to focus on children's books that have received Noma awards and honorable mentions. It is beyond the scope of a short essay to provide a detailed analysis of all children's books submitted for the award or to discuss all the prizewinning and honorable mention books in the contexts in which they were written and published. This essay will provide general information on the children's books submitted for the Noma Award, a brief account of the honorable mention books, and detailed discussion of books written by two award-winning authors, Meshack Asare of Ghana and Charles Mungoshi of Zimbabwe.

All the children's books submitted for the Noma Award have been published in the postcolonial period. Between 1980 and 1994, 185 children's books were submitted for the award. Table 1 charts the submissions over the years for children's

Table 1
Books Submitted for Noma Award

Year	Children's Books	Total
1980	9[a]	120+[b]
1981	2	60
1982	13	97
1983	11	87
1984	14	94
1985	10[c]	60
1986	9	102
1987	14	98
1988	8[d]	73
1989	17	101
1990	14	73
1991	7	90
1992	20	106
1993	27	145[e]
1994	10	146

Source: Data on this table were compiled from reports and entry forms in the Noma Award Archive. It is possible that children's books may be undercounted for some years because of insufficient information on books in African languages.

a. One title included 3 volumes, another included 10 volumes of stories.
b. Entries for the first award were from 1977–1979.
c. One title included 17 volumes, another included 2 volumes of stories.
d. One title included 2 volumes of stories.
e. The increase in entries is related to all "new" South African publishers being eligible, rather than only "oppositional" publishers as in previous years.

books and total submissions. Children's books, like submissions in general, are written in African languages as well as in English, French, and other European languages. Most of the children's books submitted have been retellings of oral literature and fiction. Few works of nonfiction for children have been submitted for the award in contrast to general submissions, which are frequently nonfiction. Since most children's books are published in series of supplementary school readers or to encourage reading by school children, this contrast is not surprising.

Two Noma Awards have been given for children's books written in English and twelve other children's books written in Afrikaans, English, French, and Gikuyu have received honorable mention (Table 2). The award-winning and honorable mention books include fiction and retellings of oral traditions. Five were published in South Africa, three each in Ghana and Zimbabwe, and one each in Côte d'Ivoire, Kenya, and Nigeria. The countries in which the award-winning books were published are not those with the largest production of children's books. Nigeria is the leader in the publication of children's books, following South Africa. However, until 1992 only "oppositional" publishers in South Africa were invited

Table 2
Noma Awards for Children's Books

1980	Mercy Owusu-Nimoh. *The Walking Calabash and Other Stories*
1982*	Meshack Asare. *The Brassman's Secret*
1983	Ngugi wa Thiong'o. *Njamba Nene Na Mbaathi i Mathagu*
1985	Meshack Asare. *Chipo and the Bird on the Hill*
1987	*Two Dogs and Freedom: Children of the Townships Speak Out*
1989	Fatima Pam. *Amina the Milkmaid* Jenny Seed. *Ntombi's Song*
1990	Charles Mungoshi. *Stories from a Shona Childhood*
1991	Gcina Mhlophe. *Queen of the Tortoises*
1992*	Charles Mungoshi. *One Day Long Ago: More Stories from a Shona Childhood*
1993	Don Mattera. *The Five Pebbles and Other Stories* Alexander H. T. Yankah. *I Am River Densu*
1994	Corlia Fourie. *Die Wit Vlinder* Véronique Tadjo. *Mamy Wata et le monstre*

*Asterisked titles are award books. All others are honorable mention books.

to submit books for the Noma Award, which meant that most South African children's books were not eligible for the award.[2]

The honorable mention children's books are diverse in theme and format. Véronique Tadjo's *Mamy Wata et le monstre* (Mamy Wata and the monster) is a picture storybook for younger readers that retells one story about Mamy Wata with brightly colored illustrations by the author based on Ivorian art motifs, while Gcina Mhlophe's *Queen of the Tortoises* is an original animal story for younger children complemented by bright color drawings by Hargreaves Ntukwana. While Tadjo's story is grounded in West African oral traditions about Mamy Wata, Mhlophe's original story has the ring of a universal animal tale. *Mamy Wata et le monstre* is a small book measuring 6 3/4 by 9 3/4 inches, while *Queen of the Tortoises* is significantly larger, measuring 8 1/4 by 11 3/4 inches, the general size range of most of the other books.

Two Dogs and Freedom is the only book written and illustrated by children. In children's own unedited words, handwriting, and drawings, it depicts some of the harsh realities of living in a South African township in the 1980s. A totally different South African "reality" is incorporated in Jenny Seed's fictional *Ntombi's Song,* about a young girl who gains confidence and self-esteem by going to the store alone for the first time, passing through a forest inhabited by a monster, and entertaining tourists with her own song and dance. Anno Berry's color drawings of a lively girl in a rural setting add a visual dimension to the story.[3]

Alexander H. T. Yankah's *I Am River Densu* is a didactic story told in the first person by the river about its course from source to mouth and the good and bad experiences encountered en route. Realistic three-color drawings by Kwabena Ofori-Panin depict an animated river traveling through rural and urban landscapes. A map shows the Densu River's real course. Realistic color drawings by K. Ofori-Pani[4] are the focus of Fatima Pam's *Amina the Milkmaid*, a picture storybook for younger children with minimal text, which appeared in a supplementary school reader series. It is the story of a ten-year-old girl who is kidnapped while earning money to support her family, but eventually marries a prince and lives happily ever after.[5]

Mercy Owusu-Nimoh's *The Walking Calabash and Other Stories* and Don Mattera's *The Five Pebbles and Other Stories* are collections of stories that incorporate oral traditions of the past and present. The two collections are markedly different not only because they are based on Ghanaian and Southern and East African oral traditions, but also because Owusu-Nimoh is primarily a children's writer whose stories are for younger children, while Mattera is a well-known poet and writer for adults whose stories are for older children, but also are appropriate for adults.

Ngugi wa Thiong'o, the well-known creative writer for adults, received honorable mention for *Njamba Nene Na Mbaathi i Mathagu*,[6] first in a series of adventure stories written in Gikuyu about Njamba Nene, a small boy with a firm identity as a Kenyan. In this story, which takes place in the colonial period, the hero's knowledge of Kenya saves his classmates but results in his expulsion from school. The strong populist message in Ngugi's adult fiction is just as evident in this series written for children. Corlia Fourie's novel for young adults, *Die Wit Vlinder* (The Rain Maker), written in Afrikaans, is a collection of three original stories told with characteristics of the oral tradition that are also appropriate for adults at a deeper symbolic level.

All of these children's books were published in paperback editions, which is typical of African publishing in general. There is far greater variation in production quality among the 12 Noma Award and honorable mention books than there would be among a dozen books submitted for an American award, such as the Caldecott or Newbery, because of the differences in publishing infrastructure in the countries of publication. Even in the 1990s not all African countries have equipment for producing full-color illustrations like those in *Mamy Wata et le monstre* and *Queen of the Tortoises*. Nor do all countries have access to the high-quality paper stock used in these two books. All Noma Award books are evaluated both for the quality of their content relative to other books published in Africa and in relation to the publishing infrastructure in the country at the time of publication. Thus considerable variation in the production quality of award-winning and honorable mention books is evident over time, as well as among books produced in different countries.

As chance would have it, the two prizewinning authors come from countries with very different postcolonial histories: Ghana was one of the first countries to gain independence in 1957, while Zimbabwe was one of the last countries to gain independence in 1980. All of Asare's writing has been in the postcolonial period, whereas Mungoshi has written in both the colonial and postcolonial periods.

Asare's winning title, *The Brassman's Secret,* is an original story based on Ghanaian oral and cultural traditions in which his full-page illustrations are an integral part of the story. In contrast, Mungoshi's *One Day Long Ago: More Stories from a Shona Childhood* is a collection of oral traditions retold by a master storyteller, part of a trilogy in which the illustrations by Luke Toronga enhance the stories but are not integral to telling them. Since both Asare and Mungoshi are prolific writers, it will not be possible to comment on their complete oeuvre in this essay, although an attempt will be made to indicate its range.

MESHACK ASARE

Ghana became independent in 1957 and was at the forefront of the wave of independence from colonial control that swept across the continent in the 1960s and following decades. From the British colony of Gold Coast, Ghana inherited at independence the basis for the development of the postcolonial publishing industry in the form of newspaper, mission, government, and commercial publishing. Despite colonial control, Ghanaian oral traditions and culture remained strong, and materials were published in Ghanaian languages as well as in English in both the colonial and postcolonial periods.

The Ghana Publishing Corporation, which was responsible to the Ministry of Information in the early years, was founded in 1965 to produce textbooks appropriate for Ghanaian schools and encourage the development of a national literature. Although it had support from the British publisher Macmillan until 1970, and its first manager was British, it has been controlled by Ghanaians for most of its history (Lottman, "Ghana" 35). Like other publishers in Ghana, it has experienced some basic problems from its foundation to the present, including receiving more acceptable manuscripts than could be published because of the lack of capital to purchase and maintain equipment, import paper, and effectively distribute its books inside and outside the country. For most of its history its printing equipment could produce materials in a maximum of four colors. Nevertheless, Ghana Publishing Corporation has been a major publisher of children's books, including Asare's *Taiwa Goes to Sea, I Am Kofi, Mansa Helps at Home, Seeing the Wind,* and *Akousa in Brazil,* which he illustrated but which was written by Alero Olympio and Cecile McHardy. Asare's first children's books were published there in 1970 in the Children's Library series, which included fiction by Africans and others familiar with Africa that was considered appropriate for school children in Ghana.

Meshack Asare was born in Nyankumasi in southern Ghana near Cape Coast on September 18, 1945. As a child he was interested in his Asante heritage, which he learned about through stories told by his grandparents, from an uncle who was a chief, and from participation in community life. Before he attended the University of Science and Technology in Kumasi, where he studied fine arts, he worked at the Department of Art and Culture in Accra as an assistant to the organizer of arts and crafts. He also received training in journalism at the University of Wisconsin, Madison, and the School of Journalism and Television in Berkshire,

England. He had ample opportunity to learn about children's interests in books during the 12 years that he taught in Ghanaian schools. In addition to writing and illustrating children's books, Asare is a practicing artist who makes glasswork, murals, and fountain sculpture. For more than two decades he has attended writers' conferences and led workshops for book illustrators in Ghana and other African countries from Sierra Leone to Zimbabwe.

Although Asare began his writing career with a book on Ghanaian arts for the American employees of the Volta Aluminum Company (Perry 1073), the focus of his writing career has been on picture storybooks for children in which his art is an integral part of the story. Asare articulated his goals in writing for children in "The African Writer in the Child's World," a paper he presented at the Seminar on Creative Writing and Publishing for Children in Africa Today, held in Freetown, Sierra Leone, in January 1983. He pointed to the importance of the heritage of the African children's writer and defended the "soundness" of the oral tradition. He identified social conditioning, knowledge, and creativity as three "progressive factors" to which African children's writers should give attention. In particular, he emphasized a child-centered approach.

[T]he first thing the Children's Writer can do in the African society is to stress the importance of the child as an individual. Our work must recognize and treat the child as a person with a mind of his own, with feelings and ideas to express and the driving desire to succeed. . . . all of my work have [sic] been consistently based on this concept of the child as an individual. . . . after making the child an individual, the next thing the Writer must do is to strengthen and reinforce his character. This may be done by helping him to build a balanced and rational image of himself and the world. . . . Lastly, the Writer must help the child to project himself into the world. The written word must inspire the child to explore with his mind and create with his hands. (17–18)

In his paper Asare also described his standards for children's books and problems getting his work published in Ghana. Although he had prepared 12 projects, after the publication of his first book he did not get another book published for ten years because of the economic situation in the country and his insistence on high production standards: "although I wrote and illustrated my stories, I could simply not accept the poor production that obtained as a result of inadequate supplies. I also believe that children's books must be as beautiful as possible" (19). Despite these production problems Asare has continued to publish in Ghana, as well as in Zimbabwe and Namibia in Africa, Europe, and America.

The Brassman's Secret, for which Asare received the Noma Award in 1982, was published by Educational Press and Manufacturers Ltd., which is located in Kumasi although it has editorial offices in Accra. This press was founded in 1974 to produce materials for the Ghanaian educational system and continues to do so today. By 1981, when Asare's book was published, Educational Press and Manufacturers Ltd. had published seven children's books. Asare had worked there since 1979 as an illustrator and art director.

The Brassman's Secret is a picture storybook with Asare's black drawings on pink paper[7] dominating every page as they flesh out the details of Asante material culture related to the story. As the story opens Kwajo, the hero, is helping his father make goldweights, while other boys are weaving kente cloth and stamping adinkra patterns on cloth. Kwajo is shown kneeling as he works the bellows and in all stages of lost wax casting, until the goldweights are finished. More than a dozen different goldweights are depicted, and details of looms and adinkra patterns are shown as other boys work.

In the evening young people sing and dance while the elders sit and talk. Kwajo is preoccupied with a goldweight whose secret he wants to know. He closes his eyes and travels to the past with the goldweight, where he sees gold dust being measured; goes to the royal court, which is depicted in detail; and learns that the royal treasurer has stolen some gold dust. The goldweight promises to show Kwajo where the dust is hidden, and he becomes excited in anticipation of being the richest boy in Asante. The hidden treasure is in the shrine room, and Kwajo has to identify all the goldweight symbols to get there, which involves reciting the appropriate proverb for each goldweight. At the door of the shrine room a bird appears, but Kwajo cannot identify it. When Kwajo tries to pass through the door, the bird crows and alerts the whole palace. The goldweight reminds him that it is the Sankofa bird, but Kwajo has to flee as he hears drumming. Kwajo awakes to find children surrounding him and the brass drummer goldweight in his hand.

In addition to being illustrated in great cultural detail, the story is told well with extensive dialogue. *The Brassman's Secret* won the Noma Award because the jury members were "impressed by an exciting and unusual children's story, beautifully and imaginatively illustrated, to bring out important aspects of Asante culture, particularly the crafting of the famous goldweights, and traditional Asante architecture.... the jury was also impressed by the production quality of the book. The book industries in Ghana are labouring under extremely difficult conditions at the present time, and the jury thought it remarkable that a book of such high quality could be produced in these circumstances" (Zell 6).

Of the child-centered picture storybooks that Asare wrote and published through Ghana Publishing Corporation in the early 1970s, *Taiwa Goes to Sea* is more like *The Brassman's Secret* than *I Am Kofi* and *Mansa Helps at Home*, which have color illustrations and reflect the influence of colonial models of British multinational publishers despite some specific African content. The brown and white illustrations in Asare's distinctive style on every page of *Taiwa Goes to Sea* help tell the story and depict details in it. Taiwa, like Kwajo, is a hardworking, imaginative boy. He lives in a fishing village near Accra where he helps the fishermen when he is not at school, although he is considered too young to go to sea. By building his own small canoe and filling it with twig men, Taiwa has a boating adventure that attracts the attention of others at the seashore and earns him a ride in a real boat. The story is infused with the warmth of Taiwa's enthusiasm when his toy canoe sails out to sea and with the concern of adults who think that he is in trouble and then show their approval of his accomplishment.

Feelings of warmth and pride also are conveyed in *The Canoe's Story,* which was published a dozen years after *Taiwa Goes to Sea* but clearly is related to it. The main character is a giant wawa tree from the inland forest who tells how humans came and removed many of his friends, and finally cut him down, with libations and due respect, and skillfully made him into a canoe. He then describes how he was taken to the sea and welcomed by other canoes that had come from the Asante forest. He is proud of his new Ga name, Ka she me, which means never leave me, and his numerous accomplishments as he became a seasoned seafarer. Men offer him food and drink as rewards for his many successes, and children pat him gently and call his name with fondness. The story teaches lessons about respect for the environment and appropriate behavior without overt didacticism. The illustrations, in a style similar to those in *Taiwa Goes to Sea,* depict many details of the stately old tree in the forest and the transformations and adventures it experiences. Again Asare demonstrates that color illustrations are not essential for beautiful and appealing children's storybooks.

The Noma Award has been important in helping Asare achieve his goals as a creator of illustrated storybooks for children. Not only was *The Brassman's Secret* reprinted and widely distributed in Ghana as well as overseas, it also has been translated into other languages including Dutch, French, German, and Japanese, providing Asare with an international audience. Asare also was commissioned to write books for Zimbabwean and Namibian publishing houses that admired his skill in creating illustrated storybooks based on cultural traditions.

Chipo and the Bird on the Hill, a Noma honorable mention book in 1985, was commissioned by Zimbabwe Publishing House (ZPH), which was founded in 1981, the year after Zimbabwe's independence, to offer an alternative form of publishing to that which was dominant in colonial Rhodesia. At independence educational publishing was dominated by two British multinational publishers, Longman and Oxford. With approval from the Ministry of Education, ZPH has published educational materials for school children. One of ZPH's innovations was to form literature advisory committees to assist in making publishing decisions. The children's advisory committee in the early 1980s had ten members aged 7 to 14 (Martin 183). The ZPH logo is the Zimbabwe Bird and the enclosure wall from Great Zimbabwe, the same bird that is featured in Asare's picture storybook.

ZPH invited Asare to visit Great Zimbabwe, the remains of a precolonial city-state, and to write an original children's story about it. Asare did research on precolonial Zimbabwean history and used information from Peter Garlake's *Life at Great Zimbabwe* as a source for his illustrations of Great Zimbabwe. The story focuses on children several centuries ago at the time of Great Zimbabwe and court life as it might have been then. The sepia drawings on light tan paper depict children in their adventures, the structure of Great Zimbabwe, storytelling, beer brewing, iron smelting, a ritual sacrifice, and other aspects of domestic and ritual life related to the story. Chipo is a princess whose curiosity to see the great carved bird on the hill is stimulated by old Sekuru's stories. Dambudzo, a weaver's son, helps her enter the forbidden palace and see the bird. In the process, Chipo falls from the hill. The story conveys the warmth of Dambudzo's and Chipo's friendship and the greater concern of the king and his courtiers for the children's safety than for the completion of their rituals. Asare successfully familiarized himself with another culture and produced an outstanding picture storybook that enables

Zimbabwean children to take pride in their history and also appeals to children in other African countries.

Asare's second work commissioned by an African country came in 1990, the year of Namibia's independence, from the Namibia Project, a group of teachers interested in creating educational materials appropriate for all of Namibia's children. Asare was selected to write a story on the Omumborombonga tree, the focus of many traditions in Namibia, because he is an outstanding writer, artist, and illustrator whose work focuses on universal values and particular cultural details. Nangolo Mbumba, a member of the Namibia Project, recounts: "We contacted Meshack Asare, the renowned author and illustrator of children's books, and provided him with the basic outline of the story. In a lively interchange of ideas with us he wrote the story anew and painted the illustrations" (Mbumba n.pg.). The result was *The Children of the Omumborombonga Tree,* which was published in Namibia but printed in Germany. Asare states that the text is based on legend and fact, deriving from Namibian folklore, historical accounts, and archaeological findings, while the illustrations "reflect the character of the Namibian people and the awesome beauty of their country" (Asare, *Children* n.pg.).

The Children of the Omumborombonga Tree is an origin myth about a man and woman who emerge from the large old tree with special powers into a beautiful world of plains, rocks, a large river, and animals, where people of the fire and people of the rock already live. The couple works hard hunting and gathering and have a daughter who marries a prince of the people of the rock. They, in turn, have two daughters who marry men from the people of the fields and people of the fire and become mothers of smiths, stock raisers, farmers, and hunters, all of whom are ultimately children of the tree. Each of the characters has a personal name with a special meaning, which is explained at the end of the book. As in Asare's other children's books, the realistic illustrations depict details of the Namibian landscape and culture and help to tell the story. These illustrations are in full color, in contrast to those in most of his other children's books published in Africa, although various shades of brown are dominant in them.

Asare is a diverse creator of children's picture storybooks who began his career by writing books that embodied Ghanaian culture. His talent and the recognition received from the Noma Award have enabled him to become an African writer in the broader sense of the term and to use different artistic techniques in his illustrations by publishing in several countries that have printing equipment that enables him to achieve the high standard he has set for his work.

CHARLES MUNGOSHI

Zimbabwe became independent under majority rule in 1980, following a period of white settler rule as Rhodesia after the country unilaterally declared independence from Britain in 1965. Previously it had been the British colony of Southern Rhodesia. As a result of the late date of independence, 23 years after Ghana's, and the large white settler population, Zimbabwe had a well-established publishing industry as well as local production of 18,000 tons of newsprint a year (Martin 184), although this did not fill all of the country's needs and some paper had to be imported. A dozen commercial publishers were well established at the time of independence, producing academic, educational, religious, and general materials. One of the larger noncommercial publishers was the Ministry of Education's Literature Bureau, which was founded in 1954 as the Southern Rhodesian African Literature Bureau to encourage reading and writing in Shona and Ndebele. It encouraged writing by holding annual literary competitions. Zimbabwe also had a more extensive book distribution system than Ghana at independence (see Bolze 229–233). However, despite the relatively strong publishing infrastructure, Zimbabwean writers had less access to it than Ghanaian writers had to theirs at independence, because of racial discrimination that prevailed throughout the colonial period in Rhodesia.

Charles Mungoshi was born on December 2, 1947, on a farm near Chivhu in southern Rhodesia, the oldest of eight children. As a child he herded cattle and helped in the fields of maize, beans, groundnuts, and monkey nuts. Mungoshi's grandmother was a "wonderful story-teller" (Veit-Wild 270). He also frequently listened to a teenage cousin tell stories. Mungoshi started attending primary school in 1955 and left secondary school in 1966 to look for a job. In interviews he explains that he performed poorly in school, although he was very interested in writing poems and stories. "Looking at my schoolmates, I saw that no-one was satisfied with conventional reading which did not really relate to our immediate experience" (Seroke 18). In 1965 his involvement in writing led to the publication of two stories when he was in the third year of secondary school, in a local magazine called *[African] Parade,* which is still being published, followed by another two in 1966. In an interview with Carol Sicherman, he stated: "English came easy for me at that time because when I went into secondary school our teachers stopped teaching us Shona—Shona being my mother tongue. They felt it didn't have a future, so I had four years of French, English, and Latin. After 1966 I left school to look for a job. My examination results weren't that good; I didn't qualify to go further, for A-level. The main reason was I'd become very much involved in writing stories" (112).

While in secondary school Mungoshi was encouraged to write by his English teacher, Father Keble Prosser, who also encouraged him to act in school plays (Veit-Wild 272–73). Mungoshi took this encouragement seriously and has become a prize-winning author in both Shona and English. Most of Mungoshi's employment has been related to publishing, including being an invoice clerk for Textbook Sales in Salisbury, now Harare, and an editor for the Literature Bureau from 1975 to 1981 and for Zimbabwe Publishing House from 1981 to 1988. Mungoshi obtained his editorial positions because of his success as a writer of social realist fiction and drama in Shona and English. Since 1988 he has devoted his attention full-time to writing, although few authors anywhere in Africa have been able to earn their living from writing.

When Mungoshi began to write books in the colonial period, it was easier to publish in Rhodesia in Shona than in English. The first novel in Shona was published in Rhodesia in 1956, while the first novel in English was published in 1966. Between 1956 and 1984, 112 novels in Shona were published in the country, but only 22 were published in English (Kahari, *Rise of the Shona Novel* 3). It has been said that Zimbabwean creative writing in English was born in exile (Kahari, "New Literatures" 21).

Mungoshi's first novel in Shona, *Makunun'unu Maodzamwoyo* (means heartbreak; not translatable [Sicherman 112]), won a Literature Bureau award and was published in 1970. It focuses on conflict caused by the custom of parents' pledging their daughter in marriage to a man of their choice. It is still in print, and like many of Mungoshi's other books has been adopted as a text in Zimbabwean schools. Mungoshi's first collection of stories in English, *Coming of the Dry Season,* was published in Nairobi, Kenya, in 1972 in a series of new fiction from Africa. Banned in Rhodesia in 1974 because the Censorship Board felt that one of the stories was subversive of race relations, it was finally published in the country in 1981 by Zimbabwe Publishing House.

Mungoshi explains the circumstances that led to the publication of his prizewinning Shona novel *Ndiko Kupindana Kwamazuva* (How time passes):

At the end of 1974, after I'd completed *Ndiko Kupindana Kwamazuva,* I sent it to the Literature Bureau, which was then the only institution where you could have books published in the local languages, Ndebele and Shona. It was a government institution under the Ministry of Education, and they didn't publish in English. The government then felt that the African didn't know enough English to write anything worth looking at. So most of what we wrote was in our languages, and their Literature Bureau acted as a kind of literary agent for most of us. They would scout for manuscripts, look at them, give recommendations. They didn't have their own publishing house. They would recommend a book to an established publishing house with a promise that if the book wasn't sold out in three years, they would buy the remainder. So the publishers didn't feel they were risking anything. Otherwise we couldn't publish anything in Rhodesia. (Sicherman 113)

Mungoshi set a record by winning two PEN International awards in 1976, one for *Ndiko Kupindana Kwamazuva* in Shona and the other for *Waiting for the Rain* in English, which was published in the Heinemann African Writers Series in London, and within the country by Zimbabwe Publishing House in 1981. This established his reputation as the preeminent writer in Zimbabwe. He has continued to be a prolific author in both languages and to win more awards. In addition to novels and short stories, he has written plays, including *Inongova Njakenjake* (Each person does his own thing) in Shona, which was a Noma honorable mention book in 1981, poetry, and a Shona translation of Ngugi wa Thiongo's *A Grain of Wheat.*[8]

Mungoshi started to write for children only recently, even though his adult short stories in English are about children. *Stories from a Shona Childhood,* his first book for young readers, is a collection of traditional tales generally told to children. According to Mungoshi: "In these books I found a new fascination with [folktales]. They are not only for children but for all age groups. If one takes a closer look you will find that the stories talk about human cruelty, human failures in understanding, how people look down at the disadvantaged or disabled who are sometimes viewed with disapproval. Therefore, the wisdom in the books is also for adults. The human failures in understanding are a universal issue" (quoted in Choto 45).

Mungoshi's three stories for older children and adults—*Stories from a Shona Childhood, One Day Long Ago: More Stories from a Shona Childhood,* and *Long, Long Ago: Stories from a Shona Childhood,* all illustrated by Luke Toronga—are published by Baobab Books, which was founded in 1988 to publish Zimbabwean literature, including children's literature. By 1995 twelve books published by Baobab, including two by Mungoshi, had won awards.

In 1990 *Stories from a Shona Childhood* was a Noma honorable mention book. The jury commended the stories as "well written in clear and concise language" and having "well-developed plots and characterization. Their morals are clear without being explicitly stated." The jury considered some of the color illustrations "brilliant" ("Study" 230). In addition, Emmanuel Ngara, a Zimbabwean literature scholar, observed in a review: "Mungoshi has used the English language in a manner which effectively captures the narrative technique of Shona story telling. The language is simple; where necessary the author has retained key Shona words so as not to lose the meaning of the original; and, as in traditional folklore, the narrative is interspersed with song or a suitable rhyme. As in traditional folklore, animals are given human attributes which enables the reader to identify with them as if they were human characters. The result of all this is enchanting and artistically satisfying. The stories have a compelling power which transports the reader to the world of myths so that he temporarily lives in the world of fantasy as in traditional Shona story telling" (163).

The setting for *Stories from a Shona Childhood* is created by the cover drawing of an old man telling a story to a child by a fire at sunset. The stories include extensive dialogue and songs. In the two stories about animals, the songs include ideophones for animal sounds and drum beats. Although the stories deal with universal human problems of greed, two focus on animal characters and two on human characters. "The Hare and the Animals of the Jungle" is about Hare's cleverness in getting water during a time of drought and in saving himself from death, Lion's bullying of other animals, and Frog's finding water for the animals and catching Hare, even though the animals discriminate against Frog because of his small size. The general plot of the story is familiar in stories about animal cooperation to obtain water during a drought, Hare's laziness and trickery, and the animals' suspicion of the motives of Chief Lion. The original twists in the story come from Frog's success in finding water and in capturing Hare when larger animals are humiliated by their failure to do so, and from Hare's invoking his ancestor spirits to kill him on an ashheap, which provides for his escape from a death sentence for greed and trickery. In "The Pumpkin That Talked" Hare is a hardworking farmer who relies for protection on Elephant, who is lazy. During a period of drought, Hare plants pumpkins, but Elephant plants nothing. Elephant takes advantage of Hare's dependence on him for protection and eats Hare's largest pumpkins, but Hare gets his revenge by hiding in a pumpkin that Elephant eats, speaking to Elephant from his stomach, and driving him to distraction and eventually death from exhaustion in searching for the source of the voice. After Hare crawls out of Elephant's stomach, he makes a drum from Elephant's skin. Thereafter Hare has a reputation for power and cleverness.

The two stories that focus on human characters also take place in a time of drought. "The Slave Who Became Chief" is about Kabore, the slave of Chief Chisvo, who must live alone and is harshly treated by other young men until he demonstrates his power to bring rain by playing his *mbira* and singing. Chief Chisvo shows his wisdom in protecting Kabore from harm, finding a peaceful way to get Kabore to demonstrate his rainmaking power, selecting Kabore as the new chief, and giving him one of his own daughters in marriage. Kabore's unusual power is demonstrated not only in his rainmaking but also in his ability to get others to work without coercion and in the peacefulness of his reign. "The Spirit of the Ashpit" is about Kuruta, a hunter who finds honey during a drought and decides to keep it for himself rather than share it with his wife, Madiro, and their two children. Kuruta buries the honey in a jar by the ashpit in the family's compound and concocts a story about his ancestor spirits wanting people to stay away from the ashpit. He refuses food from Madiro, but stays well fed by praying daily at the ashpit and sipping honey through a straw, while she and the children become weak and thin. Madiro becomes suspicious and discovers Kuruta's secret by braving the wrath of the ancestor spirits and praying at the ashpit. She teaches Kuruta a lesson by digging up the honey, feeding it to her children, and replacing it with a pot of water and ashes. The next time Kuruta prays at the ashpit, he chokes and is shamed into collecting more honey and sharing it with his family.

In 1992 *One Day Long Ago: More Stories from a Shona Childhood* was a co-winner of the Noma Award with Souad Khodja's *A comme Algérienne* (Like an Algerian). The Noma Award jury cited Mungoshi's book as "four stories from the Shona oral tradition, beautifully told and vividly illustrated, with an imaginative use of language, an element of mystery and magic, the occasional sting in the tail, and a gentle, controlled sense of humour. Charles Mungoshi is at the height of his powers as a story-teller and has added significantly to the canon of African legends" ("Two Books" 93).

"Hare's Medicine Bag," the first story in the collection, exemplifies Mungoshi's talent as a master storyteller. Baboon asks Hare if his son can accompany him on a journey to visit his relatives. Hare agrees. As they travel, Baboon prevents the young Hare from eating, drinking, and resting by telling him a series of lies. Once they arrive, Baboon prevents Hare from sharing the feast prepared for them by sending Hare to get leaves to soothe his burns and blisters. When Hare and Baboon finally return home, the Hare tells his father what happened, even though Baboon has threatened to skin him alive. The next time Baboon asks for Hare's son as his traveling companion, Hare accompanies Baboon and gets his revenge. Hare leads Baboon on a circuitous route that makes him extremely hungry, thirsty, and tired. He offers Baboon some medicine from his medicine bag on the condition that Baboon not eat or drink anything for the rest of the day. Baboon takes more medicine than he should, and then Hare further punishes him by preventing him from eating anything, including the feast his relatives had prepared for him. Hare also convinces Baboon's relatives to tie him up for three days so he can recover from the ill-effects of the medicine. The cunning of Hare and Baboon is skillfully developed, primarily through dialogue, as they travel through the "jungle," tricking each other into not eating or drinking. The innocence of the young Hare who accompanies Baboon on the first journey and the graciousness of Baboon's relatives are appropriately portrayed. Baboon's humiliation at the end is thorough and well deserved.

The other three stories in this collection depend more on plot than characterization for their success. Two of the stories are based on widespread themes in African folklore, with their own unique details. "The Prince and the Leper" is about a poor girl who is chosen by a prince to be his wife in preference to more beautiful, talented, and wealthy girls. In this version both the girl and the prince are lepers, but they are cured after the girl passes the test of humility and courtesy. "The Lazy Young Man and His Dog" is about a stranger who wins the hand of the chief's daughter by performing a feat that no one else can. In this version the daughter is mute and the young man quite unintentionally makes her laugh when his dog strips him of his coat, made from the dog's skin, and leaves him naked in the chief's court. Dialogue and songs in both of these stories make them appropriate for reading aloud, as does the extensive dialogue in "Hare's Medicine Bag." The fourth story, "The Blind Man and the Lion," tells how an old blind man becomes chief of the Women's Village and his nephew finds a wife when the old man fearlessly confronts the lion and tricks him, so that he can shoot him. Although the lion had killed all the men in the village, when confronted by the old man's wisdom and courage, he appears to be a "paper tiger."

Mungoshi's talent as a master storyteller had been recognized by numerous awards before he began to write for children. He is the only author to have three books recognized by the Noma Award jury for an award or honorable mention. Like Asare, Mungoshi has faced challenges in getting his work published, although the challenges were related primarily to discrimination in colonial Rhodesia, rather than to economic constraints as in postcolonial Ghana. Mungoshi obtained all of his formal education in Rhodesia and, despite his fame as a writer, has remained in his country to work and has focused almost exclusively on Rhodesian/Zimbabwean themes. Asare, in contrast, obtained his formal education in Ghana and abroad, has published in Ghana and abroad, and has written about cultural traditions of other African countries in addition to those of Ghana. Whereas Mungoshi writes in both Shona and English, Asare has chosen to write only in English. Although Asare is a skillful storyteller, he is primarily an artist who integrates words and images in storybooks for younger children. Mungoshi's children's books bring the telling of oral traditions to the printed page far more skillfully than do those by most authors who retell oral traditions.

The contrast between the lives and work of these two authors who have received Noma Awards for children's books provides only a brief glimpse at the diversity of African children's literature. A detailed analysis of all of the children's books found meritorious by the Noma Award jury in relation to the author's career and publishing industry in the author's country would contribute to a better understanding of the history of postcolonial African children's literature as well as the influence of the Noma Award on the publication of books for children in Africa.

NOTES

1. Background material on the Noma Award has been obtained from published sources listed in the works cited and from the Noma Award Archive, which is housed at Lilly Library, Indiana University, Bloomington, Indiana. The archive is the official repository of material related to the founding and history of the Noma Award for Publishing in Africa.

2. South African books have been problematical in terms of the purpose of the Noma Award because the publishing infrastructure in South Africa is well developed and not in need of encouragement and support as in the rest of the continent. The limitation to submissions from "oppositional" or anti-apartheid publishers was an attempt to keep within the spirit of indigenous publishing for Africans. However, the momentous political changes of the 1990s, which have led to publishers redefining themselves in relation to the "new" South Africa and the opening of the award to all publishers that define themselves as "new," has resulted in a flood of South African submissions, representing approximately 30 percent of the total submissions in the last few years.

3. This book was first published in 1966 as *Tombi's Song* by Hamish Hamilton in London, with illustrations by Dugald MacDougall. The text has been slightly reduced in length in the Ravan Press edition, the heroine's name changed, and her identity changed from Zulu to South African, even though some Zulu words and phrases have been added.

4. This appears to be the same illustrator despite the different spellings of the name.

5. Although the illustrations are the core of the book, the illustrator's name appears only on the verso of the title page.

6. Translated by Wangui wa Goro as *Njamba Nene and The Flying Bus* (Nairobi: Heinemann Kenya, 1986).

7. The 1985 edition is printed on white paper.

8. Space precludes providing more information about Mungoshi's writing for adults. Brief summaries in English of his works written in Shona appear on the covers of the books. More information about his work, criticism of it, and other literature awards he won can be found in Brown and McLoughlin (1996).

WORKS CITED

Asare, Meshack. "The African Writer in the Child's World." *Proceedings of the Seminar on Creative Writing and Publishing for Children in Africa Today, Freetown 12–14 January, 1983*. Freetown: Sierra Leone Library Board, 1983. 13–19.

———. *The Brassman's Secret*. Accra: Educational Press and Manufacturers, 1981.

———. *The Canoe's Story*. Accra: Miracle, 1982.

———. *The Children of the Omumborombonga Tree*. Bremen: Centre for African Studies/ Windhoek: Namibia Project, 1990.

———. *Chipo and the Bird on the Hill*. Harare: Zimbabwe Publishing House, 1984.

———. *I Am Kofi*. Accra: Ghana Publishing Corporation, 1971.

———. *Mansa Helps at Home*. Accra: Ghana Publishing Corporation, 1971.

———. *Seeing the Wind*. Tema: Ghana Publishing Corporation, 1989.

————. *Taiwa Goes to Sea*. Accra: Ghana Publishing Corporation, 1970.

Bolze, Louis W. "The Book Publishing Scene in Zimbabwe." *African Book Publishing Record* 6.3–4 (1980): 229–36.

Brown, G. R., and T. O. McLoughlin. "Charles Mungoshi." *Twentieth-Century Caribbean and Black African Writers*. 3rd Ser. Ed. Bernth Lindfors and Reinhard Sander. Detroit: Gale Research, 1996. 209–17.

Choto, Roy. "What It Takes to Be a Winning Writer." *Horizon* [Harare] Jan. 1993: 45.

Fourie, Corlia. *Die Wit Vlinder*. Cape Town: Tafelberg, 1993.

Garlake, Peter. *Life at Great Zimbabwe*. Gweru: Mambo, 1982.

Irele, Abiola. "The Noma Award and African Publishing." *African Book Publishing Record* 9.2–3 (1983): 103–4.

Jones, Eldred. "The Noma Award for Publishing—Ten Years On." *Scholarly Publishing* 21.2 (1990): 108–16.

Kahari, George P. "New Literatures in Zimbabwe." *Imagination and the Creative Impulse in the New Literatures in English*. Ed. M.-T. Bindella and G. V. Davis. Amsterdam: Rodopi, 1993. 13–23.

————. *The Rise of the Shona Novel*. Gweru: Mambo, 1990.

Khodja, Souad. *A comme Algérienne*. Algiers: Entreprise Nationale du Livre, 1991.

Lottman, Herbert R. "Ghana Enters the Publishing Age." *Publisher's Weekly* 6 Mar. 1972: 34–36.

————. "Kodansha to Celebrate 70 Years of Publishing." *Publisher's Weekly* 9 Apr. 1979: 31.

Martin, David. "Zimbabwe Publishing House—The First Two Years." *African Book Publishing Record* 9.4 (1983): 181–84.

Mattera, Don. *The Five Magic Pebbles and Other Stories*. Braamfontein: Skotaville, 1992.

Mbumba, Nangolo. "How the Picture Book Came About." In Asare, *The Children of the Omumborombonga Tree*. N.pg.

Mhlophe, Gcina. *Queen of the Tortoises*. Braamfontein: Skotaville, 1991.

Mungoshi, Charles. *Coming of the Dry Season*. Nairobi: Oxford, 1972.

————. *Inongova Njakenjake*. Salisbury: Longman, 1980.

————. *Long, Long Ago: Stories from a Shona Childhood*. Harare: Baobab, forthcoming.

————. *Makunun'unu Maodzamuwoyo*. Salisbury: College, 1970.

————. *Ndiko Kupindana Kwamazuva*. Gwelo: Mambo, 1975.

————. *One Day Long Ago: More Stories from a Shona Childhood*. Harare: Baobab, 1991.

————. *Stories from a Shona Childhood*. Harare: Baobab, 1989.

————. *Waiting for the Rain*. London: Heinemann, 1975.

Ngara, Emmanuel. Review of *Stories from a Shona Childhood* by Charles Mungoshi. *African Book Publishing Record* 16.3 (1990): 162–63.

Ngugi wa Thiong'o. *Njamba Nene Na Mbaathi i Mathagu*. Nairobi: Heinemann, 1982.

Noma Award Archive. Lilly Library. Indiana University. Bloomington, Ind.

"Noma Award for Publishing in Africa." *African Book Publishing Record* 4.4 (1978): 229.

Olympio, Alero, and Cecile McHardy. *Akousa in Brazil*. Accra: Ghana Publishing Corporation, 1970.

Owusu-Nimoh, Mercy. *The Walking Calabash and Other Stories*. Tema: Ghana Publishing Corporation, 1977.

Pam, Fatima. *Amina the Milkmaid*. Ikeja: Longman Nigeria, 1988.

Perry, Alison. "Portrait of an Artist." *West Africa* 2 May 1983: 1073–4.

Seed, Jenny. *Ntombi's Song*. Johannesburg: Ravan, 1988.

Seroke, Jaki. "We Were Brought Up in a Literary Desert." *Staffrider* 3.4 (1980–81): 18–19.

Sicherman, Carol. "We Have Still to Shed a Few of Lucifer's Feathers . . . An Interview with

Charles Mungoshi." *Matatu* 7 (1990): 111–25.

"Study of South African Poverty Wins 1990 Noma Award." *African Book Publishing Record* 16.4 (1990): 229–30.

Tadjo, Véronique. *Mamy Wata et le monstre.* Abidjan: Nouvelles Editions Ivoiriennes, 1993.

"Two Books Share 1992 Noma Award." *African Book Publishing Record* 18.2 (1992): 93.

Two Dogs and Freedom: Children of the Townships Speak Out. Johannesburg: Ravan, 1986.

Veit-Wild, Flora. *Teachers, Preachers, Non-Believers.* London: Zell, 1992.

Yankah, Alexander H. T. *I Am River Densu.* Accra: Afram, 1992.

Zell, Hans M. "The 1982 Noma Award for Publishing in Africa." *African Book Publishing Record* 8.1 (1982): 6–7.

4

"To Build a Nation Where Peace and Justice Reign": Postcolonial Nigerian Young Adult Literature

Osayimwense Osa

Nigeria's political independence from Britain in 1960 was perceived as the beginning of an era of freedom, peace, progress, and potential for the new nation. Contained in Nigeria's first national anthem, which we were taught in school and which we committed to memory, was a recognition of Nigeria's diversity and a need for genuine unity, pride, and patriotism. Relevant lines in this anthem read:

> Nigeria we hail thee
> Our own dear native land
> Though tribes and tongues may differ
> In brotherhood we stand
> Nigerians all are proud to serve
> Our sovereign motherland.

Acknowledged in this anthem is the multicultural and multilingual nature of the country, a situation where the use of the English language has proven invaluable. In spite of the loftiness of the above lines, Nigeria was engulfed in a three-year civil war only six years after political independence, and its existence as a united nation was threatened. Put together without regard to tribal domains, Nigeria, like many African countries, is still developing the spirit of togetherness and nationhood. The place of youth and their potential to build a united nation is also evident in the new national anthem, adopted in 1977 to replace the one composed by the British:

> Help our Youth the truth to know
> In love and honesty to grow
> And living just and true
> Great lofty heights attain,
> To build a nation where peace and justice reign.

The spirit in these anthems, both composed in English, is the same: the country needs a disciplined young population to build the new nation. Fiction produced for Nigerian adolescents during that period had a touch of the didactic, and youth were charged with emulating positive values in life. Chinua Achebe realized that this new generation needed the nurturing of an equally disciplined adult population: "[O]ur responsibility as Nigerians of this generation is to strive to realize the potential good and avoid the ill. Clearly, children are central in all this, for it is their legacy and patrimony that we are talking about. If Nigeria is to become a united and humane society in the future, her children must now be brought up on a common vocabulary for the heroic and the cowardly, the just and the unjust. Which means preserving and refurbishing the landscape of the imagination and the domain of stories, and not—as our leaders seem to think—a verbal bombardment of patriotic exhortation and daily recitations of the National pledge and anthem"("Chinua Achebe: At the Crossroads" 192). What is striking in Achebe's statement is that literature is seen as an instrument for uniting the country and affirming its nationhood. Postcolonial literature for young adults has contributed to the realization of the lofty aims of the national anthem.

A discussion of representative works suggests the scope, vitality, and relevance of contemporary young adult fiction against a panoramic sociocultural, economic, and political backdrop. While books published in the 1960s and early 1970s focused on socializing Nigerian youth, from the late 1970s onward they reflect a disillusionment with adult society and the rebellion of youth.

The emergence of a promising, politically independent nation in 1960 prompted enthusiasm to publish relevant and meaningful works for its young population. Before independence, books for children and young adults had been imported from Britain. They were paraphrased and abridged versions of the classics: *Gulliver's Travels, King Solomon's Mines, Treasure Island, The Thirty-Nine Steps, Oliver Twist,* and the like. Besides being simplified versions of the originals, some were "quite clearly inappropriate to the Nigerian context and, in some cases, harmful to the psychology of our young population" (Irele 150). Relevant works were scarce. It is against this background that the African Universities Press (AUP) prides itself as the first indigenous publishing house in independent Africa. It was established in Lagos to address the problem of irrelevance and scarcity, and it energetically responded to the vision of producing meaningful and exciting literature. Although educational books for Nigerian schools and colleges made up the greater part of AUP's output, with the inception of the African Reader's Library Series, the press launched what promised to be a glowing future for literature written by Nigerian authors for young people in Nigeria and in other African countries. Within a few years thirty titles were published in this series, which has for more than three decades offered exciting reading for youth.

DIDACTIC FICTION: SOCIALIZING YOUNG ADULTS

The first work in the African Reader's Library of AUP, Cyprian Ekwensi's *An African Night's Entertainment*, significantly established for Nigerian children and young adults that a literature rooted in their familiar sociocultural milieu can be available to them. Although written in English, it rendered in print a traditional storytelling session intended for the entertainment or relaxation of an entire community. Based on a story Ekwensi states he had heard from an aged Hausa *mallam*, the setting for *An African Night's Entertainment* is provided in the eager audience of "young men, old men, children, women" surrounding the old story-teller, who patiently waits for his listeners to be comfortably seated. With this cross section of Africans eager to listen to him, the old storyteller expresses his thoughts on love, disappointment, and the unquenchable desire for vengeance.

The storyteller's attitude toward revenge, as reflected in his closing admonition that one should not take it upon oneself to wreak vengeance, implies a belief that the survival of the human community depends primarily on mutual respect, reason, and sometimes on a large heart to forgive when one has been wronged. While this moral is meant for listeners of all ages, it is particularly relevant to young adults, who out of pride or inexperience are more likely to seek revenge. Young adults who decide to emulate the wronged lover Abu Bakir by passionately protecting their egos and self-esteem may expect a fate similar to his. To warn the young against calamity is partly why the old man tells the story of *An African Night's Entertainment*, which he describes at the beginning of his narrative as "A long tale of vengeance."

After the publication of *An African Night's Entertainment*, Nigerian adolescent literature reflected a society's desire to have an honest, hardworking, conscientious, and dedicated young population. Three milestones in the early development of fiction for young adults are Ekwensi's *The Drummer Boy*, Achebe's *Chike and the River*, and Mabel Segun's *Youth Day Parade*. All three writers were educated at British-style schools, and their early exposure to written literature was that of England. They chose to write in English rather than in their respective indigenous African languages. While their works reflect some Western forms, they are African in content.

The publication of *The Drummer Boy*, intended primarily for the 9-12-year-old age group coincided with Nigeria's attainment of political independence in 1960. Not surprisingly, it shows a bias toward such glowing moral themes as social and personal reform (see Roscoe 137). This short novel is about a young blind boy, Akin, who has been rejected by his parents because of his handicap. Akin learns to transcend his physical handicap by capitalizing on his drumming talent. At first he refuses to depend on any charitable organization, but later goes to a school for the blind where he continues to spread happiness through his drumming. Nothing has a greater, longer-lasting impression upon another person than the awareness that someone has transcended suffering and is embodying a value that inspires, ennobles, and uplifts (see Covey).

In reminiscing on his childhood reading in "Named for Victoria, Queen of England," Achebe clearly has a serious argument with the literary legacy English writers bequeathed to his society (120–21). Hence he directs part of his creativity to children's and adolescent literature, and we can expect his literature for young people to reflect many of the broad moral and political concerns which characterize his adult novels and nonfiction (Miller 10). In his novella, *Chike and the River*, young Chike leaves his family and the traditional life of his village of

Umuofia for the attractions of the city of Onitsha. Chike's adventures in Onitsha teach him self-reliance, honor, love of country, courage, hard work, diligence, and honesty—all qualities demanded of youth in the new Nigeria. Achebe does not evoke the past but concentrates on the future, on the positive attributes needed to sustain a growing, disciplined youth population. He complicates the message by introducing into the story a highly religious man as a robber, hence illustrating the hypocrisy of some churchgoers.

The African school story, which was quite popular in the 1960s in Nigeria, depicts the introduction of Western education during colonial times, the Africans' early suspicion and distrust of Western education, and their later acceptance of its virtues. *Eze Goes to School, Akin Goes to School,* and *Sani Goes to School,* which Michael Crowder co-authored with Onuora Nzekwu, Christie Ajayi, and Umaru Ladan respectively, address this phenomenon. The literary quality of these works is very thin indeed, and as Abiola Odejide rightly observes: "Their plots are formulaic, the characters often stereotypical, and the point of view adult. The basic story line is that a young boy determines to acquire western education, meets considerable opposition, reverses and finally achieves his aim. His success comes through a combination of his own resourcefulness, help from some progressive adults, and good luck" (80). Mabel Segun's *Youth Day Parade* continues the genre of the school story but focuses on character building and leadership qualities. It is the story of a group of school children who put on an impressive parade for Youth Day. Tunde, organizer of the parade, after some initial fear of the onerous task, draws on his organizational resources, makes do with what is available locally, and infuses enthusiasm in his schoolmates. This short story demonstrates that unity, patriotism, and determination are indispensable in any worthwhile achievement. The selection of the young characters Tunde (Yoruba), Audu (Hausa), Ekpo (Efik), and Chike Wachukwu (Igbo) reflects the ethnic plurality of Nigeria and subtly indicates that overcoming ethnic differences in a multiethnic country like Nigeria will always produce positive results. Likewise in Segun's *Olu and the Broken Statue,* Olu, Aigbe, and Ikem are friends from three ethnic groups: Yoruba, Edo, and Igbo. The major didactic thrust of this short story is patriotism. At a time when Nigeria's ancient artifacts were being sold to foreigners for exorbitant amounts of money, Olu and his friends' decision to send their rare find to the museum is unique and worthy of emulation. Their interest is not to profit from the sale of the broken statue but to preserve the cultural heritage of their nation.

THE PUBLISHING SCENE

The grand publishing dream of the 1960s to provide young adults with inspirational stories has not become a reality in the Nigeria of today. After the short-lived oil boom of the 1970s, whose effect was felt in many spheres of Nigerian life, economic recession slowly crept in, bringing with it a depressing climate that affected publishing and other areas of Nigerian life. The once dynamic and aggressive African Universities Press fell victim to the economic slump in Nigeria and is almost nonexistent today.

This bleak publishing scene has curbed the vigorous development of young adult literature in Nigeria. Outlets for African writers, especially for the new ones, are very limited. Besides the economic problem of African Universities Press, it was even rumored that "Heinemann of Great Britain were going to close down their vaunted African Writers Series, which was a major outlet for African writers especially those from Anglophone areas. The series has survived, but in a newer and much costlier format, and seems more concerned with reprinting older best sellers than vigorously seeking out, as it once did, new works and younger writers" (Hughes 379). In addition to local publishers like Onibonoje and Fourth Dimension that have limited distribution and few international outlets if any, the African literature series of multinationals like Longman and Nelson—Pan Africa Library and Collier's African/American library, respectively—are now almost inactive except, like Heinemann, for old reprintings.[1] School texts or educational books, however, have survived the economic stress because they are required and publishers know there are ready markets for them. Even then the sales may be seasonal, limited to the academic year. The trend to concentrate on educational or textbook publishing is likely to continue for some time until the country's pool of educated citizens can support general publishing (Olanlokun 84).

To produce novels, especially new ones by new writers, in very large quantities is a risk to publishers because a solid reading culture does not presently exist in Nigeria. Furthermore, the buying power of many Nigerians is now very weak. They are not likely to spend on novels when there are more pressing financial matters to contend with. Having established a picture of the publishing scene, both past and present, let me focus on some specific works for Nigerian young adults.

THE NEW REALISM: A MIRROR OF SOCIETY

The emergence of a substantive corpus of Nigerian young adult novels in English, especially in the late 1970s, is an interesting development. Macmillan Publishing House established the Macmillan Pacesetters series, which accelerated publication for young people in Nigeria and in other parts of Africa. Agbo Areo, formerly the deputy publishing manager of Macmillan Nigeria Publishers Limited, now of Paperback Publishers Nigeria, was instrumental in beginning the series. To a certain extent, the series was a reaction against the romances of Hadley Chase, Denis Robins, Mills and Boon, and the like, which many young Nigerians were reading. The policy of the series, which is stated in the preface of every Pacesetter novel, is as follows: "All the novels in the Macmillan Pacesetters series deal with contemporary issues and problems in a way that is particularly designed to interest young adults, although the stories are such that they appeal to all ages." While some of the novels in the series are formulaic, dealing with adventure, romance, and mystery, quite a number of them like *Naira Power, Director!, A Kind of Marriage, For Mbatha and Rabeka,* and a host of others deal with young Africans and realistic social issues they can identify with. These are the ones that merit attention; hence "[y]oung people interested primarily in raw sex would have to seek their literary thrills elsewhere" (Lindfors 91). The series made its debut with Agbo Areo's *Director!,* Mohammed Sule's *The Undesirable Element,* and Sam Adewoye's *The Betrayer,* novels that are quite popular among young people. Today the number in the series is quite staggering. Of the more than eighty novels, most are from Nigeria, although there are some from other African countries as well. While the central characters in several of these novels are young adults—high school and young college students—in some they are clearly adults.

The novels deal realistically with contemporary events in Nigeria. The 1970s was the oil boom era in Nigeria, the decade when this country was one of the world's wealthiest nations. While there was prosperity in various spheres of Nigerian life, the abundance was not carefully managed. The novels of this period depict the ills of society: greed, corruption, materialism, and the lowering of moral standards. Contemporary young adult novels are quite serious in tone, probing and sometimes focusing on the dingy side of Nigerian society. Some find it difficult to classify them as young adult novels even though their central characters are Nigerian youth. This exploration of some fundamentally serious issues—the problem of the individual and society, nonconformism, momentous choices in love and marriage—does not mean that they are completely outside the realm of young adult literature. The boundaries between the young adult novel and the adult novel are sometimes blurred.

A condemnation of the hedonistic lifestyle is implicit in contemporary young adult fiction. The Nigerian currency, the naira, assumed the dimension of a god whom many "worshiped." Buchi Emecheta's *Naira Power* successfully depicts this period in Nigerian history and the social problems that ensued. Emecheta employs an oral mode of transmitting stories by presenting two women telling stories about contemporary Nigerian society and its negative influence on its young population, reminding one of Ekwensi's *An African Night's Entertainment.* This return to an oral narrative form "is not merely a fleeting fancy but a continuation and purposeful revival of an art solidly grounded in African [and Nigerian] culture" (Osa 139). The characters Amina and Bintu indict their society in this interchange:

"How can one walk in a place like this? There are too many cars, motorcycles, cycles, open gutters, and wandering people. No, walking in this part of the country is out of the question. You'll get killed."

She sighed. "But only ten years ago, we could walk the streets of Lagos."

"Now you are beginning to sound like me. Ten, fifteen years ago, were years before the oil boom, before Nigeria became rich. Now she is rich, we are all condemned to choke in our wealth." *(Naira Power* 11)

This excerpt reflects the abundance without real control or direction that oil wealth brings. In the story, the race to acquire money and property destroys relationships and families, promotes charlatans, and produces a young criminal and murderer who is burned alive by an angry crowd when he is mistaken for a thief at a football match. The burning of this youth serves as a warning to young adults to shun the ignoble race for money. *Naira Power* subtly indicts the adults for emphasizing material wealth as a measure of success without realizing that they are promoting in young adults unwholesome thoughts of rushing into wealth.

This period is also characterized by governmental instability and violence in Nigeria, when military coups d'etat and takeovers are common. Since 1960, the country has been ruled by the Nigerian military more frequently than by the civilian government. In Chuma Nwokolo's *The Extortionist,* phenomenal promotion in the military is resented, especially by those who have been passed over in the process. It is sometimes the cause of a military coup d'etat. General Kamazolu Gwarzo's rival, Colonel Kwazu, plans a takeover of power with the assistance of the chief of police, but it fails, and the novel ends on a very cynical note. According to Virginia Coulon: "The cynicism in this novel is not characteristic of Nigerian Pacesetters in general. What is significant, however, is that the place-name of the country in which the novel is set is not Nigeria but Songhai, a code name for Nigeria that has already been used by V. C. Ike in *The Naked Gods.* By masking the place-name, the author gives himself free rein to explore imaginatively his perceptions of Nigeria while refusing either to commit himself or to conclude. His vision is one of political disorder in which all the alternatives are equally bad" (313). Such disorder is also contained in Chukwuemeka Ike's recent novel, *Our Children Are Coming.* This novel is important primarily for its illustration of the generation-gap war between African young adults and their parents, who set standards they themselves sometimes find difficult to meet. The blurb on the jacket describes this 341-page novel as "a great work of fiction which serves as a mirror of society" and stresses that "every parent, teacher and child needs to own this mirror for a better perception of his role." Truly, one's understanding of his or her position in society as well as the attendant duties is very important in Nigeria. In general, age is respected: the young are expected to give due respect to their parents and seniors; they are also expected to honor traditional rulers, government functionaries, and their bosses in the workplace.

In *Our Children Are Coming,* when those in authority consistently fail to perform their legitimate duties, young adults feel justified in questioning the status quo by talking back or rebelling. However, adults consider such behavior insubordination and a lack of discipline. A desire to probe the underlying causes of such lack of discipline in youth below the age of 21 prompts the Nigerian civilian administration to set up a commission of inquiry, called the Presidential Commission on Juveniles. It attempts to be national in its composition: there is representation not just from one ethnic group or geographical region but from several. Justice Okpetun, the head of the commission, had risen through sycophancy in the previous military administration: "he knew how much he had gained, psychologically and materially, from his loyal service as chairman of a couple of tribunals of enquiry" (102–3). With the return of the civilian regime made up of democratically elected officials, Justice Okpetun frantically makes an effort to be known and recognized by the new administration. He sees his appointment as head of the commission as a means of gaining access to those in power.

Justice Okpetun resolves to do his master's bidding to the letter, with the hope that his performance will secure him another appointment from the president. His ultimate ambition is to have a seat on the nation's supreme court before the expiration of the first four-year term of the president. Evidently, Okpetun's steady rise to power and fame are characterized by a calm and scheming disposition. The young students actively demand representation on the commission which is supposed to investigate matters affecting youth. As chairman, Okpetun states that the students have nothing worthwhile to offer because of their youth and inexperience, and he blames the university vice chancellors for incompetence:"What business has a student whose parents sent him to university to acquire a degree to do with service on a presidential commission? Sometimes I wonder whether the vice-chancellors keep those students sufficiently busy or how else would they have time to jump around like this, poking their noses everywhere!"(74). The students retaliate by setting up their own commission of inquiry to examine the role of parents in the upbringing of their children, particularly their role as pacesetters for their children. The students' commission succeeds in exposing the fraud, extravagance, and hypocrisy of the adult world. Their slogan is "Youth must save the nation." While youth activism is visible in the novel, the true voice of African youth does not emerge because the chairman of their own commission is a popular attorney and not of their age group, although he does support and sympathize with the students.

Unlike *Our Children Are Coming*, Victor Ulojiofor's *Sweet Revenge* and Agbo Areo's *Director!* and *A Paradise for the Masses* are written mainly from the point of view of African young adults. The purpose of the demonstration by the City Comprehensive High School students in *Director!* is to demand more amenities and better accommodations from the school authorities. But their approach is marred by youthful exuberance and the reckless need for fun. They assault the principal and his secretary, the teaching staff, and the house mistress, and cause damage to school property. By smearing cooked mashed beans on the principal and his staff, the students make those in authority appear ridiculous: "The principal cut the picture of a fat village pig which had revelled in a muddy pond and come out with rags sticking on its muddy body . . . they saw his bleeding secretary also hardly recognizable as a human being. . . . When the policeman peeped through the window of the Staff Room and saw what the helpless vice-principal and other teachers looked like, they could not restrain their spontaneous laughter. The students must have had a good sense of humor!" (50). Even in the hospital the nurses cannot help laughing from time to time as they clean up the principal and his staff members. With the exception of a few boys, the vast majority of the students do not have any prior knowledge of the demonstration and its purpose. According to the author, "the whole thing had been a spontaneous, exciting and welcome comic interlude" (48).

It is this same sense of fun that prompts the students' noble gesture to clean up the city in *A Paradise for the Masses*. Unfortunately, their effort degenerates into hooliganism: they empty loads of stinking debris at the health minister's house and burn government vehicles, as well as two vehicles given to them by well-meaning citizens. As in *Director!*, the majority of the students are not aware of the master action plan of cleaning the city; they just want some fun. To change any system for the better is a serious matter. This novel illustrates how a radical student movement for justice can collapse under pressure from the government and society, and as a result of the weaknesses of the students themselves. *A Paradise for the Masses* is relevant reading for any community that is at odds with itself and is in need of direction.

Whenever a student movement indulges in fun, it is bound to end in failure, as is also the case with Ulojiofor's *Sweet Revenge*. When a dormitory built by a construction firm, JOMBCO, collapses after 33 days, killing two students, the students blame the disaster on the firm's incompetence and corruption—a malaise they believe plagues many contractors in their country. This tragic incident draws out their deep-seated revulsion against the ills of their society:

Many of those in important positions are doing nothing but getting rich quick without regard for the common people. I have read about the cement deal, the fertilizer deal, even the stockfish deal, involving millions of naira going into a few people's pockets. Last week my mother told us that the stockfish which she bought cost six naira. . . . My father did not believe her. But it was because the importation of stockfish had been banned. They did not stop there. They also banned laces, thereby running away from "Made in Nigeria" goods which we are told to patronize. Our eyes are further blinded by someone going low profile and riding officially in 504 cars [Peugeot] but at the same time owning Mercedes for jolly rides and visits to their numerous girlfriends. (30)

The immorality and hypocrisy of the adult world as described above seriously disturb Chukwudi and his friends. Makaranta notices the poor housing in their community: even in high-rent areas there are no toilet systems, no water, and no electricity. To him, "It is absurd that we are inhabitants of a country with all the oil, rich and strong, yet with all our wealth, we are still living in squalor and poverty" (31). How they intend to put things right is intriguing: by harassing those in power, by kidnapping landlords who charge exorbitant rents, by hijacking an airplane. They naively believe that acts of mischief and vengeance can wipe out the disorder in their country and transform it into a paradise for the masses. But this does not mean that these high school students are irresponsible. They need nurturing and direction to channel their cleverness and youthful energy toward positive goals.

In fact, the five high school students demonstrate a strong sense of unity. As a result of the death of Ovie's girlfriend in the collapse of the dorm, Ovie and his four friends devise a bold plan to get even with the building contractors. With the toy rifles they successfully seize one of JOMBCO's vans loaded with boxes of money. They tie up the security guard and bury the stolen money and their toy rifles in a specific spot in a training ground. The whole operation lasts only eight minutes. All newspapers make it their top story. The radio station interrupts its regular program for a "Special News Flash" to give its version of the prank and to appeal to the public for assistance in arresting the "robbers." A handsome reward is offered for any information leading to the recovery of the money. Bayo, one of the students, discloses the whole operation because he wants the promised reward of 50,000 naira. This betrayal leads to their arrest; however, they receive only a reprimand because they had no criminal intention and no criminal record. But the betrayal by a fellow student is cause for alarm: at a relatively young age Bayo already manifests a treacherous bent by disclosing the secrets of his friends. This is an indication that complete solidarity is impossible.

The importance of *Sweet Revenge* lies primarily in the fact that young high school students are sensitive to the social ills of their country and that they are articulate about it. They justify their action in a press release entitled, "THE JOM-BCO AFFAIR":

WE OBSERVED THAT OUR SOCIETY IS ROTTEN. BUSINESSMEN CHASE WEALTH BY FOUL MEANS. THAT WAS WHY JOMBCO COLLECTED ALL THE MONEY BUT FAILED TO DELIVER THE GOODS. INSTEAD THEY BROUGHT SORROW . . . WE THEREFORE DECIDED TO POINT OUT THESE EVIL PRACTICES TO THE PUB-LIC. (116)

By making high school students the spokespersons for justice, dedication, and fair play in Nigeria, the authors of young adult novels emphasize that the next genera-tion is unlikely to condone corruption. These novels attempt to be national by using young people from different ethnic groups as central characters.

Traditionally, Nigerian culture expects conformity from its young population on the question of marriage, and most traditional stories favor this approach. But in Emecheta's *The Bride Price,* the teenage heroine, Aku-nna, does not conform to the tradition of her Ibuza community. She decisively chooses Chike, an *osu* ("out-cast" in Ibuza), as her sweetheart and elopes with him. Emecheta employs the experiences of Aku-nna to subtly indict the Ibuza customs of bride price, polygamy, and prejudice against *osus.* In contrast, Aku-nna and Chike demonstrate a true love that is based not on money but on mutual appreciation. Although Aku-nna dies in childbirth at the end of the novel, her brief marriage was more pleas-ant and fulfilling than all the arranged marriages and polygamous marriages in the story. It is the intriguing blend of content and form that makes *The Bride Price* a successful novel of genuine relationships among young adults.

Like *The Bride Price,* Jide Oguntoye's *Too Cold for Comfort* illustrates that spiri-tual incompatibility can seriously weaken and even destroy a marriage. It stresses that compromise is at the root of a successful marriage. The sometimes vulgar lan-guage of the novel is not an end in itself but is intended to emphasize some major lessons for young adults. For instance, Hannah's mother plans to tell her daughter that "sex is the bolt to wedlock. When a lock has no bolt in it, it is no lock at all" (14). Other works, such as Areo's *The Hopeful Lovers,* Chukwuemeka Ike's *Toads for Supper,* and Mohammed Sule's *The Undesirable Element,* provide a good counter-point to *The Bride Price* and *Too Cold for Comfort.* They are transparently didactic. The three novels reflect the shortcomings of philandering by giving a subtle warn-ing to youths to shun such a lifestyle.[2]

Three and a half decades have wrought some notable changes in Nigerian young adult literature. While there are still some didactic works, the new realism deals with once taboo topics: profane language and sex as seen in *Too Cold for Comfort;* nonconformism or rebellion as seen in *The Bride Price;* and a subtle call to the adult population to reexamine its role as parents, guardians, and responsible adults as in *Sweet Revenge, A Paradise for the Masses, Our Children Are Coming,* and *The Bride Price.* Nigerian young adult literature is moving away from pure didacticism aimed at youth to the adult population's examination of itself. Adults are seen as poor role models. In measuring success by material wealth, they ultimately destroy the young by subliminally implanting in their minds that the frenzied rush to make money fast and by any means necessary is important. Besides, the revolutionary attempt by youth in *Sweet Revenge, Director!,* and *A Paradise for the Masses* to challenge the prevalent corruption in their society is refreshingly new.

NOTES

1. See Hughes for an account of the economic and publishing problems in Africa.

2. See my essay, "Touchstones in Nigerian Youth Literature," *The ALAN Review* 15. 3 (Spring 1988), where I discuss three accomplished Nigerian youth novels: *The Bride Price, Too Cold for Comfort,* and *Director!*

WORKS CITED

Achebe, Chinua. *Chike and the River.* Cambridge: Cambridge University Press, 1966.

———. "Chinua Achebe: At the Crossroads." *Piper at the Gates of Dawn—The Wisdom of Children's Literature.* Ed. Jonathan Scott. New York: Random House, 1981. 159–92.

———. "Named for Victoria, Queen of England." *Morning Yet on Creation Day.* Garden City, N.Y.: Anchor-Doubleday, 1975. 115–24.

Adewoye, Sam. *The Betrayer.* London: Macmillan, 1979.

Ajayi, Christie, and Michael Crowder. *Akin Goes to School.* Ibadan: African Universities Press, 1978.

Areo, Agbo. *Director!* London: Macmillan, 1977.

———. *The Hopeful Lovers.* London: Macmillan, 1979.

———. *A Paradise for the Masses.* Lagos: Paperback, 1985.

Coulon, Virginia. "Nigerian Writing in Pacesetter Series." *Research in African Literatures* 18.2 (1987): 304–19.

Covey, Stephen R. *The Seven Habits of Highly Effective People.* New York: Fireside/Simon, 1989.

Ekwensi, Cyprian. *An African Night's Entertainment.* Ibadan: African Universities Press, 1962.

———. *The Drummer Boy.* Cambridge: Cambridge University Press, 1960.

Emecheta, Buchi. *The Bride Price.* New York: Braziller, 1976.

———. *Naira Power.* London: Macmillan, 1982.

Hughes, Shaun F. D. Preface. Postcolonial African Fiction. *Modern Fiction Studies* 37.3 (1991): 377–83.

Ike, Chukwuemeka. *Our Children Are Coming.* Ibadan: Spectrum, 1990.

———. *Toads for Supper.* London: Fontana/Collins, 1965.

Irele, Abiola. "The Ethiope Experience." *Publishing in Africa in the Seventies.* Ed. Edwina Oluwasanmi, Eva McLean, and Hans Zell. Ile-Ife: University of Ife Press, 1975. 143–65.

Ladan, Umaru. *Sani Goes to School.* Ibadan: African Universities Press, 1978.

Lindfors, Bernth. *Popular Literatures in Africa.* Trenton, N.J.: Africa World, 1991.

Maillu, David. *For Mbatha and Rabeka.* London: Macmillan, 1980.

Miller, James. "The Novelist as Teacher: Chinua Achebe's Literature for Children." *Children's Literature* 9 (1981): 7–18.

Nwokolo, Chuma. *The Extortionist.* London: Macmillan, 1983.

Nzekwu, Onuora, and Michael Crowder. *Eze Goes to School.* Ibadan: African Universities Press, 1963.

Odejide, Abiola. "Education as Quest: The Nigerian School Story." *Children's Literature in Education* 18.2 (1987): 77–87.

Oguntoye, Jide. *Too Cold for Comfort.* London: Macmillan, 1980.

Olanlokun, S. O. "Textbook Publishing in Nigeria." *International Library Review* 14 (1982): 83–90.

Osa, Osayimwense. *African Children's and Youth Literature.* New York: Twayne, 1995.

Roscoe, Adrian A. *Mother Is Gold: A Study in West African Literature.* Cambridge: Cambridge University Press, 1971.

Segun, Mabel. *Olu and the Broken Statue.* Ibadan: New Horn, 1985.

———. *Youth Day Parade.* Ibadan: Daystar, 1984.

Sule, Mohammed. *The Undesirable Element.* London: Macmillan, 1977.

Ulojiofor, Victor. *Sweet Revenge.* London: Macmillan, 1982.

5

POSTCOLONIAL HISPANIC AFRICAN CHILDREN'S LITERATURE

Mbare Ngom

Even a cursory examination of African literature written in Spanish reveals that children's and adolescent[1] literature has received very little attention, if any, compared with that focused on adult literature. It is only in the past few years, more than 20 years after Equatorial Guinea gained its independence from Spain, that Hispanic African literature for children and adolescents has begun to receive some critical and theoretical attention.

Formerly "Territorios Españoles del Golfo de Guinea," and later renamed "Guinea Española," the republic of Equatorial Guinea gained its independence from Spain on October 12, 1968. Located in the Gulf of Guinea or Biafra, as the case may be, the country consists of two main parts: Río Muni, an enclave on the African mainland, and the Island of Bioko (formerly Fernando Póo), where the capital, Malabo, is located. Also as part of Guinea are the small islands of Annobón, Elobey Grande and Elobey Chico, Mbanié, and Cocotiers. Although France has attempted to become a major player in Guinea, and although Guinea has joined the Zone Franc and adopted the Franc CFA as its national currency, the French language has never been a threat to Spanish. Guineans are committed to "Hispanidad," and Spanish is the official language used in schools and in the government.

As a consequence of the neglect of children's literature, a crucial group in Equato-Guinean society—children and adolescents—remains marginalized in the area of literature and publishing.[2] This paper explores the genesis and evolution of Hispanic African children's literature in Equatorial Guinea, the only former Spanish colony in Sub-Saharan Africa. Raquel Ilonbe's *Leyendas guineanas* (Guinean legends), the first children's book to be published by a native writer in Equatorial Guinea, serves as a central text in this examination.

LITERATURE OF THE COLONIAL ERA

The colonial era and the emergence of African literature in the Spanish language changed the function, focus, and priorities of literary discourse in Equatorial Guinea. The historical and political reality of the colonial situation, coupled with the birth of a written Guinean literature in Spanish in the mid-1940s, transformed literary creation from a communal oral literature into a restricted and individual activity produced by a minority group, the Guinean literary elite. The audience also changed from a traditional rural audience to a metropolitan, reading audience, limited to Spanish speakers. By the late colonial period, Spanish Guinea had one of the highest ratios of schools to population in Sub-Saharan Africa: in 1966, there were 147 elementary schools, with 21,421 pupils; 32 upper-level primary schools, with 1,565 pupils; and two secondary schools, with 986 pupils. However, very few students continued beyond primary school (Sundiata 133). In 1988 it was estimated that only 55 percent of the population was literate (Sundiata 133). For this limited reading audience, writing became an instrument of affirmation of their cultural identity or, in Paulin Hountondji's words, "a certificate of humanity." That is why most of the early Guinean literary texts in Spanish were closer to ethnographic documents than to works of fiction. One such text is Leoncio Evita Enoy's *Cuando los combes luchaban: novela de costumbres de la Guinea Española* (When the Combes used to fight: A novel of customs from Equatorial Guinea), the first novel by a Guinean published during the colonial period. In *Cuando los combes luchaban,* the plot is just an excuse for the author to describe in a detailed manner the traditions, customs, and rituals of the Combe ethnic group.

In using an alien language—Spanish, the language of the dominant order— early Equato-Guinean writers wanted to break the silence, marginality, and invisibility to which the literature of the Spanish colonizers had confined them. Eventually, they meant to win recognition for their own culture. In so doing, they intended to give an authentic representation of Guinea, Africa, and Africans. Henry Louis Gates, Jr., writes: "The recording of an authentic black voice—a voice of deliverance from the deafening discursive silence which an enlightened Europe cited to prove the absence of the African's humanity—was the millennial instrument of transformation through which the African would become the European, the slave become the ex-slave, brute animal become human being" (11–12). Toward these ends, Guinean literature became an instrument of subversion and, in some cases, played a key role in the struggle for the liberation of Guinea from Spanish domination. However, literature for children and adolescents was not even considered a cultural project by the first generation of African writers.

During the colonial period, Spanish authorities had established a very tight policy of containment in order to prevent the spread of the nationalist movement that swept across Africa at the end of World War II. Furthermore, the linguistic isolation of the territory, as the only Spanish-speaking country in Sub-Saharan Africa, coupled with the comparatively late independence of the country in 1968 (nearly eight years after that of most African countries), contributed to the absence of children's literature in colonial, as well as in postindependence, Guinea.

In colonial Spanish Guinea, children were exposed to three kinds of literary products: school textbooks, religious books, and children's magazines (consisting mainly of comic strips, adventure stories, and mysteries) originally intended for Spanish metropolitan children. Commenting on a similar situation in a neighboring country, Nigerian author and critic Mabel D. Segun points out:

> In the late nineteenth-century, Nigerian children, like their counterparts in other parts of Africa, read books written, edited, illustrated and published in Europe by people whose cultures differed considerably from those of the countries they were writing about. Most of the authors had little knowledge of the countries and peoples in their books. Stereotyping and sensationalism were the order of the day for, first and foremost, the books were meant for audiences in their home countries who relished the thrill of reading about primitive, half-naked black people and the terrible things that went on in the "Dark Continent" such as cannibalism and human sacrifice. (25–26)

This situation applied to nearly all the former African colonies. The colonial ideology was evident in the titles and cover illustrations of the books published about this Spanish colony by Spanish authors, be they school manuals or texts. Literary products such as Donacuige's *Aventuras de un piloto en el Golfo de Guinea* (Adventures of a pilot in the Gulf of Guinea), Emilio Bonelli's *Un viaje al Golfo de Guinea* (A voyage to the Gulf of Guinea), José Mas's *En el país de los Bubis: escenas de la vida en Fernando Póo* (In the land of the Bubis: Life on the island of Fernando Póo), Joaquín Rodríguez Barrera's *Mobbe, un negro de Fernando Póo* (Mobbe, a black man from Fernando Póo), Eladio Antonio Rebollo's *Estupendos misterios de la Guinea Española* (Wonderful mysteries of Spanish Guinea), and Buenaventura Vidal y Torras's *La danza de los puñales: novela de aventuras africanas* (The dance of the daggers: A novel of African adventures), to mention but a few, fall within this category.

These texts had a very specific goal: to alienate and develop in the minds of Guinean children the psyche of colonized, inferior individuals who are meant to be dominated by European colonizers who had come to Africa to save their souls. This colonial literature was a cultural product Guinean children could not identify with because the stories, as well as the settings, were alien to them. It did not teach them anything about themselves, their universe, or their culture because, as Nancy J. Schmidt has pointed out, it was "aimed at Europeanizing and colonizing rather than satisfying their needs and interests" (quoted in Okafor 52). In other words, the Spanish colonial system of oppression was not only limited to adults; it also affected children. Spanish was the only language allowed in the colony, and children as well as adults were subject to punishment for using their native languages. In the historical novel *Las tinieblas de tu memoria negra* (The darkness of your black memory), Donato Ndongo-Bidyogo's narrator, a nameless child, poignantly reflects on his experiences in school: "You had the mere advantage that everybody spoke Castilian well at home, and that is why Sir Ramon never punished you by making you kneel on the heap of pebbles he had ready for children who spoke Fang at school, in his presence, or even outside school"[3] (30). Furthermore, the child narrator reminisces on how this strategy of alienation played a central role "in

forming a certain kind of subject, in presenting particular versions of the colonized" (Niranjana 2). According to the colonial version of history taught in school:
"Spaniards had come to save you from anarchy because your ancestors were
infidels, barbaric, cannibals, and idolaters that kept cadavers in their houses,
expression of their savagery. . . . It is natural that God send a superior and chosen
race to save the infidels, to christianize them and to win them for Civilization and
the True Unique Doctrine" (*Las tinieblas* 31–32). The colonial system of education
did not consider the transmission of African culture as one of its goals for Guinean
children; rather, it attempted to make children reject their own cultural heritage
and embrace that of the dominant Spanish order.

THE POSTCOLONIAL PERIOD

In Equatorial Guinea, a national children's literature in Spanish appeared much
later than in other parts of Africa—for example, in Senegal, Nigeria, or Ghana—
because of historical and political circumstances. As a result of colonial policy, the
territory was sealed off by authorities and no translated children's works by
Anglophone African writers was allowed in Spanish Guinea. After independence in
1968, the status of children's literature did not change immediately, and one could
say that it even got worse during the First Republic (1968–79), primarily because
Guinean children were still being exposed to the same kinds of texts they had read
during the colonial period: textbooks used in elementary and secondary schools,
the catechisms, and children's and adolescent publications imported from Spain.

Five months after independence, President-elect Francisco Macías Nguema
suspended constitutional rights and established one of the bloodiest dictatorships
in postcolonial Africa. Swiss historian Max Liniger-Goumaz describes the regime
as "Afro-fascist." He called the Guinean version of it *nguemismo* because it was a
monoethnic project organized around the Fang ethnic group, particularly the
Fang-Esangui subgroup from Mongomo, home province of Nguema, located in
the Río Muni (Continental Guinea).

The *nguemista* dictatorship (1969–79), coupled with the repression and perse-
cution of intellectuals and tight censorship, was a major obstacle to the development of a national literature in Equatorial Guinea. Since the strategy of the
nguemismo was to prevent the emergence of an alternative discourse, it tried to
neutralize Guinean society by marginalizing the remaining social actors—political parties, unions, cultural organizations, and the other ethnic groups—and by
destroying the scarce cultural infrastructure—library, theater, press—inherited
from the colonial period. Therefore, children's literature was still absent during
the years of the *nguemismo*.

With the fall of Nguema's regime in August 1979 began a process of cultural
renaissance that would affect all aspects of cultural life in Equatorial Guinea. In
1982 the Centro Cultural Hispano-Guineano was founded in Malabo, the capital,
with the mission of promoting and disseminating Equato-Guinean culture in the
country and abroad. The Centro Cultural established two libraries for adults,

children, and adolescents. Moreover, it introduced a literacy program that offered classes in Spanish and the national languages (Bubi and Fang) to children and adults; organized literary contests every year; started a publishing press, the Ediciones del Centro Cultural Hispano-Guineano; and published two magazines, *Africa 2000* and *El Patio.*

In the 1980s, because of the lack of children's reading material, the Centro Cultural Hispano-Guineano commissioned Spanish "cooperantes" specialized in pedagogy to write textbooks for elementary schools. Texts such as *Cayuco: método de enseñanza de la lectura* (Cayuco: a reading teaching method) and *Buenos Días: curso de Español para niños* (Good morning: a Spanish course for children), by Antonio Manso Luengo and Dionisio Rodríguez Jorrín, are being used as school readers. Though the books were not written or illustrated by Guineans, their content is oriented toward local needs; their authors have lived in Equatorial Guinea for many years and are familiar with the country. The limited number of writers and the scarcity of texts for children in Equatorial Guinea have also led authorities to encourage children and adolescents to read adult literature. Texts such as Ndongo-Bidyogo's *Las tinieblas de tu memoria negra,* María Nsué Angüe's *Ekomo,* Maximiliano Nkogo's *Adjá-Adjá y otros relatos* (Adjá-Adjá and other stories), Antimo Esono's "La última lección del venerable Emaga Elá" (The last teaching of the venerable Emaga Elá), as well as most of the publications of Ediciones del Centro Cultural Hispano-Guineano are also available to children and adolescents.

RAQUEL ILONBE'S SEARCH FOR AFRICAN ROOTS AND IDENTITY

Raquel Ilonbe's *Leyendas guineanas,* the first text published by a Guinean writer intended for children, must be placed in this historical, political, and cultural context. Ilonbe's collection of legends had its genesis in her desire to connect with her African roots.

Born on the island of Corisco, of a Spanish father and a Guinean mother, Ilonbe was taken to Spain before she turned one. There she spent most of her life in the cities of Burgos and Madrid. Many years later, after her marriage, she decided to travel to Equatorial Guinea in order to know the land where she was born and about which she had heard so much. She returned to Guinea several times after that first trip to explore her roots and to search for her identity. To this end she crisscrossed the country, the Río Muni, and the different islands to get to know the people and the land and to discover traditional literature as part of her cultural heritage. She collected several oral narratives from different ethnic groups such as the Fang, Ndowe, and Bubi. She writes in the preface: "I have always loved speaking with people of the different ethnic groups that live on the island and in the continent. I was interested in everything they told me and I took notes. They are extraordinary narrators who transmit their stories from father to son" (9–10). The result was *Leyendas guineanas,* which she dedicates to Guinean children and to the children of the world.

Leyendas guineanas is a collection of eight stories based on Guinean oral tradition and aimed at entertaining, but mostly at educating, young readers. A significant aspect of Guinean culture was designed to develop children's personalities by making them aware of their cultural and ethnic identity. Genealogies, historical legends, folktales, proverbs, fables, riddles, songs, and myths were some of its most important didactic instruments to educate and inculcate good moral values in children. In such an oral culture, the use of the spoken word went beyond mere communication; it was the symbol of knowledge and wisdom.

As is typical of Black Africa, the traditional literature of the Fang, Bubi, and Ndowe was a cultural product of the community, in both its production and consumption, making children's education a collective responsibility. Home was the first school children attended, and women (mothers, aunts, sisters, grandmothers) played a very important role in their early education. It was under the guidance of women that children were exposed to literature in traditional Guinean society, first through cradlesongs, followed by fantasy and magical tales. Children were subject to a double literary exposure: first within the extended family and then through their playmates with whom they shared physical and intellectual games. As adolescents their education would become more systematic, exposing youth to a more sophisticated and varied oral literature: songs, dance, mimicry, esoteric formulas, and symbolism of objects. It is during this period that they would go through rites of passage and initiation ceremonies such as circumcision, excision, and tattooing. The themes of these oral texts were meant to prepare adolescents for life in general and for their responsibilities as adults in the community. Traditional literature also reflects the duality of the universe as a site of the supernatural and the unknown as something normal. Since the supernatural and the natural coexist in traditional society, this world then becomes a place of encounter for the dead and the living, and for men and the spirits of the ancestors.

Oral literature played a central role in the education of children and young adults because, as Felix Boateng points out, traditional education was both acquired and lived. The younger generation was taught through its participation in sociopolitical and religious institutions that ensured what he calls "intergenerational communication" (110). Nigerian critic Emma Okey Nnabuko writes: "The essence of oral forms in children's literature is the awareness it brings on the future fathers as contented, liberated and patriotic members of the community prepared to knit a harmonious whole in their relationship with other members of the community. Thus, they are conscious of their environment, ready to promote and defend their culture" (197). *Leyendas guineanas* must be examined from the perspective of an environment where traditions and the ensuing process of acculturation that children go through are rapidly losing ground to so-called modernism. Therefore, Ilonbe's text is primarily geared to educating Guinean children, to making them aware of their rich cultural heritage, and to eventually developing "the skills for its upkeep" (Boateng 110).

The stories included in *Leyendas guineanas* can be divided into two categories. In the first category, the protagonists are children who must overcome adversity in order to triumph in their society. The second group consists of stories about animals that are portrayed with human qualities. The metaphoric use of animal characters allows the author to explore the human condition and its contradictions. The setting is also marked by two broad characteristics: in the former, it is the real and known human world to which children can easily relate; in the latter, the universe is characterized by fantasy, magic, miracle, and the unknown.

In the first group, except for the opening story, "Los sordos" (The deaf men), which is entertaining and amusing because it exploits a physical defect in order to provoke laughter, the remaining stories are intended to teach moral lessons to children as well as to adults. For instance, in "Los tres hermanos" (The three brothers), the author discusses issues related to hard work, conveying the message that the prosperity of a community depends on the dedication of its members and that work is always rewarding. Similarly, "El plato bailarin" (The dancing plate) and "Los dragones" (The dragons) reflect the importance of respect, discipline, and good behavior. The second group of narratives, consisting mainly of myths and legends, presents a universe in which magic, miracles, and the supernatural are essential to the unfolding of the story. In "Las dos gotas de agua" (The two drops of water), "La tortuga y el perro" (The turtle and the dog), "Los dos perros que dejaron de hablar" (The two dogs that stopped talking), and "La Señora del río" (The lady of the river), the Guinean version of the Cinderella story, the presence of magic contributes to a happy ending. The supernatural is central to the plot of "La Señora del río" as it is in the European version: when young Ilonbe is ill-treated by her stepmother and stepsister, a beautiful woman comes out of the river to help her with household chores and to attend the prince's dance. A shining star on her forehead, a symbol of her connection with the magical, helps the prince to find her later. While the story of Cinderella is generic and can be identified with any Western country, this version is culturally specific—in its names of characters, type of dance (balele) held by the prince, cultural details—to a small region of Africa, the Gulf of Guinea or Biafra. Underlying the magic world of the stories in this section is the didactic message that bad behavior will be punished and good behavior rewarded. They explore the positive dimensions of the individual's role in society, such as acceptance of responsibilities, good leadership, unselfishness, community values, and honesty.

The stories are written in a language simple enough to be understood by children whose mother tongue is not Spanish. Taking into account children's need for variety and their inability to sustain a long period of concentration, Ilonbe's stories are short and entertaining, using a variety of narrative techniques. She keeps the narrative to a minimum while focusing on a lively dialogue, which often helps accelerate the rhythm and action of the story. In addition to using stock characters, mostly animals of the area, associated with a certain type of behavior (greed, trickery, pride), Ilonbe sets the story in an environment familiar to the children and characters with names they can relate to. The book is very attractive to children because it integrates the text with the colorful aquarelle illustrations. Whether the pictures are inserted in the text or presented as full- or half-page illustrations, they are captivating and allow children to relate certain passages of the text to themselves.

RECENT DEVELOPMENTS

In the late 1980s, the Centro Cultural Hispano-Guineano initiated a project geared to recording the traditional literature of the major ethnic groups of Equatorial Guinea for general readers, including children. The Centro Cultural either commissioned or supported researchers and scholars, mostly Spanish assisted by Guinean nationals, in the collection, transcription, and translation of Ndowe, Bubi, Fang, and Annobonese texts into Castilian. One such text is Iñigo de Aranzadi's *El tambor* (The drum), based on the Fang oral tradition. Unlike the other texts discussed below—such as *Cuentos de los Ndowe de Guinea Ecuatorial* and *Cuentos de los Bubis*—Aranzadi's *El tambor* is a captivating story of men and animals, depicting a universe characterized by magic and wonder. The book is appealing because the colorful illustrations are well integrated with the text. The bright illustrations on each page depict the action or part of the action narrated in the accompanying text. The book begins and ends with colorful, full-page illustrations, and throughout there are either full-page color illustrations or the text and illustrations alternate on the page.

El tambor is organized in four parts: the first part is a Spanish translation with Fang words in bold in the text, with endnotes explaining the linguistic and cultural meaning of each word; the second part is a Fang transcription of the story in the international phonetic alphabet; the third part is a Fang transcription based on the Roman alphabet; and, finally, there is an interlinear and literal semantic translation of the Fang text into Spanish. This book is not only useful to children but also to adults who want to learn how to read and write in Fang.

In 1990, Jacint Creus published *Cuentos de los Ndowe de Guinea Ecuatorial* (Short stories by the Ndowe of Equatorial Guinea), a collection of short stories based on the Ndowe oral tradition.[4] Using several informants from Ndowe villages from the interior to the coast, Creus collected hundreds of stories and songs. With the help of Guinean collaborators, he then proceeded to determine the similarities and differences of each story and its variations. He later prepared a composite version of the texts based on cycles and themes. The book is divided into four parts, each one corresponding to a cycle. Part I is "El ciclo de los cuentos del Ndjambu" (The Ndjambu cycle); Part II is "Ciclo de los cuentos de animales" (Animal stories cycle); Part III is "Los ciclos menores" (Minor cycles); Part IV is "Cuentos no adscritos a ningún ciclo (Stories not belonging to any cycle). The stories are organized around four major themes: survival, sexuality, family relationships, and social relationships. There are a total of 106 stories characterized by didactic and social messages that are closely related to the daily life of the people and their place and functions within and obligations to the community. There is also an appendix entitled "Likano Ndowe" (version in Ndowe, that is, a transcription of the stories in the Ndowe language).

Finally, in 1992, Creus, María Antonia Brunat, and Pilar Carulla published *Cuentos de los Bubis de Guinea Ecuatorial* (Short stories by the Bubis of Equatorial Guinea) with the support of the Centro Cultural Hispano-Guineano. The text is based on the oral tradition of the Bubis of the Island of Bioko, collected from Bubi informants ranging in age from 10 to 73. Unlike the collection of Ndowe stories, the Bubi stories are not classified according to cycles because they are too diverse. Rather, the 106 stories are arranged thematically in five parts followed by an appendix with a transcription of the stories in the Bubi language: "Cuentos de los animales" (Animal stories), "Cuentos de la familia" (Stories about family life), "Cuentos de seres supranaturales" (Supernatural stories), "Cuentos contra las conductas indeseables" (Stories against undesirable behavior), and "Cuentos no adscritos" (Nonclassified stories). Though the main objective of the stories is to educate and prepare members of the community, mostly children, to be socially responsible and full participants in the construction of their society, the collectors also point out what they call the "lateral and complementary functions" of the stories, that is, their therapeutic value (12). The messages conveyed by the stories are also meant to prepare children to be mediators of conflict and healers of tension, in addition to teaching them a sense of justice so necessary to maintaining harmony in the community.

Most of these texts are principally meant for researchers and specialists, and hence are not illustrated. However, the beautiful production, relevant themes, and short length of the stories make them attractive to children, especially in a country like Equatorial Guinea where children do not have much choice in their reading material.

CHALLENGE TO GUINEAN WRITERS

The survey presented above indicates that there are only a few books accessible to children today. However, this is significant progress when the history of Equatorial Guinea and what the country experienced during *nguemismo* are taken into account. While this small body of literature does respond to the reading needs of Guinean children, the main problem in Hispanic African children's literature lies in its limited themes and genres. In Anglophone countries such as Nigeria, Ghana, and Cameroon, or Francophone countries such as Senegal and Côte d'Ivoire, where there is a relatively established tradition of fiction for children and adolescents, writers have begun to address issues and problems in the context of postcolonial developing nations (issues of identity, urban life, overpopulation, polygamy, and drugs). Yet Guinean literature for young people still relies heavily on oral tradition as a source of inspiration. Though these texts are valuable in terms of their moral teachings and sense of cultural identity, they are not relevant to the issues and problems of children living in a changing, technological world. This is the challenge facing the second generation of postindependence Guinean writers who must create relevant books for children. Nigerian writer Mabel D. Segun emphasizes the importance of a literature written specifically with the needs of children in mind: "Good children's books entertain, stretch the imagination, help a child to identify with others, make him understand the world in which he lives, and inculcate in him moral and spiritual values such as love, selflessness, devotion to duty and responsibility. The child is the father of the man and the influences of his childhood are bound to play an important role in determining what kind of man he will be" (159). The emerging children's literature in postcolonial Guinea is, despite its youth, not only engaged in a process geared to the rehabilitation of African cultural identity, but also actively seeks to develop a national Guinean identity.

NOTES

1. The term *adolescent* is used as the equivalent of the Spanish *juvenil,* covering ages 12 to 18.

2. In most African countries, between 45 percent and 55 percent of the population is under the age of 25.

3. Unless otherwise stated, all translations are mine.

4. *Cuentos en el Abáa* by Manuel Fernández Magaz (1987) and *Cuentos de los Fang de Guinea Ecuatorial* (1991), collections of stories based on the oral traditions of the Fang of the Río Muni, and *Cuentos de los Annoboneses de Guinea Ecuatorial* (1992), containing stories based on the oral traditions of the Annobon island groups, are part of that effort geared to recuperating and publishing Guinean traditional literature.

WORKS CITED

Aranzadi, Iñigo de. *El tambor.* Malabo: Ediciones del Centro Cultural Hispano-Guineano, 1990.

Barrera, Joaquín Rodríguez. *Mobbe, un negro de Fernando Póo.* Barcelona: Vila, Aleu y Domingo, 1931.

Boateng, Felix. "African Traditional Education: A Tool for Intergenerational Communication." *African Culture: The Rhythms of Unity.* Molefi K. Asante et al. Westport, Conn.: Greenwood, 1985. 109–21.

Bonelli, Emilio. *Un viaje al Golfo de Guinea.* Madrid: Fortanet, 1888.

Creus, Jacint. *Cuentos de los Ndowe de Guinea Ecuatorial.* Malabo: Ediciones del Centro Cultural Hispano-Guineano, 1990.

Creus, Jacint, and María Antonia Brunat. *Cuentos de los Annoboneses de Guinea Ecuatorial.* Malabo: Ediciones del Centro Cultural Hispano-Guineano, 1992.

———. *Cuentos de los Fang de Guinea Ecuatorial.* Malabo: Ediciones del Centro Cultural Hispano-Guineano, 1991.

Creus, Jacint, María Antonia Brunat, and Pilar Carulla. *Cuentos de los Bubis de Guinea Ecuatorial.* Malabo: Ediciones del Centro Cultural Hispano-Guineano, 1992.

Donacuige, pseud. *Aventuras de un piloto en el Golfo de Guinea.* Madrid: Tip. M. Minuesa, 1886.

Enoy, Leoncio Evita. *Cuando los combes luchaban: novela de costumbres de la Guinea Española.* Madrid: Consejo Superior de Investigaciones Científicas, 1953.

Esono, Antimo. "La última lección del venerable Emaga-Elá." *Africa 2000* 14 (1991): 24–27.

Gates, Henry L., Jr. *Race, Writing and Difference.* Chicago: University of Chicago Press, 1985.

Hountondji, Paulin. *African Philosophy: Myth and Reality.* Bloomington: Indiana University Press, 1983.

Ikonne, Chidi, Emelia Oko, and Peter Onwudinjo, eds. *Children and Literature in Africa.* Ibadan: Heinemann, 1992.

Ilonbe, Raquel. *Leyendas guineanas*. Madrid: Doncel, 1981.

Liniger-Goumaz, Max. *De la Guinée Equatoriale Nguémiste: éléments pour le dossier de L'afro-fascisme*. Genève: Editions du Temps, 1983.

Luengo, Antonio Manso, and Dionisio Rodríguez Jorrín. *Buenos Días: curso de Español para niños*. Malabo: Ediciones del Centro Cultural Hispano-Guineano, 1990.

———. *Cayuco: método de enseñanza de la lectura*. Malabo: Ediciones del Centro Cultural Hispano-Guineano, 1990.

Magaz, Manuel Fernández. *Cuentos en el Abáa*. Malabo: Ediciones del Centro Cultural Hispano-Guineano, 1987.

Mas, José. *En el país de los Bubis: escenas de la vida en Fernando Póo*. Madrid: N.pub., 1921.

Ndongo-Bidyogo, Donato. *Las tinieblas de tu memoria negra*. Madrid: Fundamentos, 1987.

Niranjana, Tejaswini. *Siting Translation: History, Post-Structuralism, and the Colonial Context*. Berkeley: University of California Press, 1992.

Nkogo, Maximiliano. *Adjá-Adjá y otros relatos*. Malabo: Ediciones del Centro Cultural Hispano-Guineano, 1994.

Nnabuko, Emma Okey. "Literature and the Nigerian Child: The Image of the Son as a Liberated Father of the Man." In Ikonne et al. 187–98.

Nsué, María A. *Ekomo*. Madrid: Universidad Nacional de Educación a Distancia, 1985.

Okafor, N. R. "Technical and Economic Problems of Writing and Publishing Children's Literature in Africa with Particular Reference to Nigeria." In Ikonne et al. 52–60.

Rebollo, Eladio Antonio. *Estupendos misterios de la Guinea Española*. Madrid: Agencia Española Librería, n.d.

Segun, Mabel D. "Children's Literature in Africa: Problems and Prospects." In Ikonne et al. 24–42.

Sundiata, Ibrahim K. *Equatorial Guinea: Colonialism, State Terror, and the Search for Stability*. Boulder, San Francisco, and Oxford: Westview, 1990.

Vidal y Torras, Buenaventura. *La danza de los puñales: novela de aventuras africanas*. Madrid: N.pub., 1925.

6

Babar and the French Connection: Teaching the Politics of Superiority and Exclusion

Claire-Lise Malarte-Feldman and Jack Yeager

The intersection of education and colonialism provides a fruitful entry point to explore children's literature from colonial and postcolonial perspectives. Coming-of-age and educational narratives told from the point of view of children or as nostalgic memoirs such as Joseph Zobel's *La Rue Cases-nègres* (Sugar Cane Alley), Camara Laye's *L'Enfant noir (The Dark Child)*, and Nguyen Duc Giang's *Vingt ans* (Twenty years) are, of course, one of the most important manifestations of literature from the pens of those colonized by France. In these thinly veiled autobiographical narratives, the indigenous childhood experience in a "colonial setting" may be presented from the vantage point of the insider. The socialization of the protagonist into the learning modes of the French school system, which contrast with those of the main character's culture of origin, begins what will become the never-ending process of psychological shift from one's native culture to that of the metropole, an unattainable destination. The effect is one of alienation and uprootedness, a feeling of being in-between, in, as Frantz Fanon would put it, the halfway house of culture.[1]

The dilemma of dual and conflicting educations lies at the heart of the experience of the colonized. Nowhere is this more evident than in Jean de Brunhoff's *Histoire de Babar, le petit éléphant* (1931; *The Story of Babar, the Little Elephant*), *Le Voyage de Babar* (1932; *The Travels of Babar*), and *Le Roi Babar* (1933; *Babar the King*). Jean de Brunhoff (1899–1937) began as a visual artist and only later turned to writing. Before his early death from tuberculosis at age 38, he published only four Babar books—the three aforementioned and *L'ABC de Babar* (1934; *Babar's ABC*)—leaving sketches for two other volumes, *Babar en famille* (*Meet Babar and His Family*) and *Babar et le père Noël* (*Babar and Father Christmas*), both finished by his son Laurent in 1938 and 1940 respectively. After his father's death, Laurent continued the Babar series; thus, most of the books in the series were written by Laurent, now in his seventies. The Babar idea has, over the years, spawned many imitations and given way to the commercialization of the "petit éléphant" in a variety of manifestations, some, it must be said, of disputable taste (Hildebrand xv–xvii). Still, the image that remains is the one created by Jean, Babar the king, an image easily recognized as French by French and non-French readers alike.[2]

READING THE COLONIAL NARRATIVE

Jean de Brunhoff's first three Babar books, the focus of this essay, appeared during the height of colonial repression in many French colonies and protectorates and therefore invite readings related to this context. In this light, the stories seem to be examples of assimilation and the force of the "mission civilisatrice" as discussed by the well-known theorists of French colonialism: Albert Memmi, Aimé Césaire, and Frantz Fanon. The "mission," the French version of the "white man's burden," assumed the superiority of French culture and sought the assimilation of the colonized while respecting their traditions. At the same time, as Memmi points out in *The Colonizer and the Colonized,* the French colonizer would also block the assimilation of the colonized, for it would remove the barrier of difference between the colonizer and the colonized, thereby ending colonial privilege. In Indochina, for example, Ho Chi Minh would find work as a cabin boy despite his education.

Several critics have pointed out the possible readings of these popular books from colonial perspectives. In the earliest critique, "Babar's Civilization Analyzed," the anthropologist Edmund Leach explains the hierarchy of the animals as reflected in the Babar stories. Patrick Richardson, in "Teach Your Baby to Rule," considers the Babar books as "a primer in power politics" (179), while a chapter in Ariel Dorfman's *The Empire's Old Clothes* explores the colonialist thinking in Babar's desire to civilize the landscape, suggesting differences between American and French views of childhood. The historian Harry C. Payne places his reading of Babar in the wildly shifting political landscape of France in the 1930s. And Herbert R. Kohl, to whom Jean Perrot responds (in this volume), is only the latest of these readers with his provocative 1995 collection of essays, *Should We Burn Babar? Essays on Children's Literature and the Power of Stories.*[3] Aside from Payne, and to some extent Dorfman in his references to French childhood, however, none of these readers connects Babar specifically and at length to a French historical context. Our goal, then, is to read Babar against the particular backdrop of the French "mission civilisatrice" in its colonies and protectorates around the globe.[4] We have limited this study to the first three Babar books, all created by Jean, because the lasting image of the elephant is fixed here.

THE EVOLUTION OF BABAR: LESSONS IN COLONIZATION

In *Histoire de Babar,* the "petit éléphant" loses his mother, shot by a hunter portrayed in the illustration as white and wearing colonial clothing, a plausible criticism of the violence of the conquest. In their article "Death in Children's Literature:

Taboo or Not Taboo," Lois Rauch Gibson and Laura M. Zaidman have pointed out that the death of parents in children's literature "is a plot device designed to place children in new, often precarious situations—or to free them for adventures" (232). Gibson and Zaidman refer to Babar and Bambi to illustrate the use of this plot device in animal stories. The orphaned Babar (he has no apparent father) then flees the "forest" of his birth, arriving in the city. In the illustration that accompanies the text, the meaning of this flight is clearly indicated: Babar's forest, a paradise of palm trees now disrupted by the presence of hunters, has become a place of disorder and danger, while the city seems to represent a civilized and ordered safe haven.[5] Clearly, the city that Jean de Brunhoff chose to illustrate is based on a French model: a church spire topped with the French rooster as focal point; the town square dominated by the imposing statue of an official-looking man in a top hat; buildings with red tile roofs and shutters; trees in the town square tamed in a very French fashion, positioned symmetrically, with a neat grating around each trunk; omnibuses and chauffered cars in the streets. Epcot's use of many of these same characteristics in creating its "typically" French cityscape clearly demonstrates the durability of this image as suggestive of urbanism in France. In this particular sequence, de Brunhoff portrays the reversal of the back-to-nature/nurture myth common in texts for children, such as Maurice Sendak's *Where the Wild Things Are*. Struck by the newness and activity of this different way of life, Babar is filled with longing and desire: "[T]hey are very well dressed. I would like to have some fine clothes, too" (10).[6] Discovered by "a very rich Old Lady," who out of her fondness for "little" elephants becomes his patron, Babar does in fact learn to dress in Western clothes, eat at a table, wash himself in a bathtub, and drive a car. His green suit is set off by white spats, an indication of his future status and success. The Old Lady treats her charge much as French parents treat their children. Gentle but firm, in later episodes she will never miss an opportunity to educate Babar in everything from good manners to civic responsibility. Her apparent objective, to integrate the individual into society, reflects the goals of French education, the "forming" of a moderate, reasonable, tasteful, "civilized" adult. The measure of Babar's educational progress in the transformational "clothing" episode is then fixed in a photograph; the little elephant-child who thought the elevator in the store was some sort of "funny box" and who upon repeated trips was scolded that the device was "not a toy" is now an adult, destined to become king of all the elephants. Babar's successes at school prepare him well to impress tony social gatherings, as if he were on display, proof enough of the effectiveness of colonial policy to "civilize" native populations. As Memmi points out, eventually the colonized will imitate the colonizer's "dress, his accent and his manners" (13).

Still, all is not well: between worlds, alienated in his way, Babar is nostalgic for his "forest" and his cousins and friends, the monkeys; and he is sad and tearful when he remembers his mother. After two years, his ambivalence is transformed into a desire to return home, a desire catalyzed by the arrival of Arthur and Céleste. Searching for their lost cousin, they spark Babar's return to the forest. But first, Arthur and Céleste must be clothed and schooled into the advantages of the city.

Promising never to forget the Old Lady, indelibly marked as he is by her culture, he bids her farewell. For her part, despite Babar's transformation, the Old Lady still sees him as a child, and as she bids him good-bye, she asks herself longingly: "When shall I see my *little* Babar again?" (33; our emphasis). Likewise Babar will always see her as the mother he has lost. In effect she has become the mother figure that the child reader needs to protect the child hero, the little elephant, in order to feel safe and build bridges to Babar's world.[7]

By virtue of his "progress" (he is dressed, driving a car, and educated), the elder elephants name him king upon his return to the forest: "My good friends [says the wise old Cornélius], we are seeking a King, why not choose Babar? He has just returned from the big city, he has learned so much living among men, let us crown him King" (38). The celebration of his marriage to Céleste completes the first panel of the story, a traditional fairy-tale ending. Again, this text would exemplify almost too neatly Memmi's observation that the "representative of the authorities [is] recruited among the colonized themselves," the "recently assimilated" (13). Dorfman concurs: "The new ruler must come from the outside, a native instructed in the ways of men" (20). The metamorphosis of an elephant remains, however, incomplete; the balloon sails into the distance, leaving de Brunhoff open to continue his story.

This he does, in *Le Voyage de Babar,* de Brunhoff's cautionary tale that will test the newly crowned king. The balloon rises and departs, a spectacle for the gray mass of elephants. Far away from their kingdom, Babar and Céleste fly over a city that could only be located on the French Mediterranean coast (cypress, olive, and eucalyptus trees; palms along the beach; vineyards encircled by low stone walls; wooden boats with lateen sails; and a whitewashed church topped with a cast-iron steeple [a universally recognized sign of Provence] and surrounded with Mediterranean pines). A storm ruptures the text, stranding the two hapless elephants on an island "by extraordinary good fortune" (7). Unaware of the importance their clothes will acquire later in the story, Babar and Céleste logically undress to dry them out.[8] An attack by the inhabitants of the island, "fierce and savage cannibals" (10)[9] separates the elephants from all that can distinguish them from the civilization they feel a part of, further reinforcing the determining theme of nakedness running throughout de Brunhoff's texts.[10] As Montaigne opined, one is always someone else's cannibal.[11] Here Babar and Céleste see themselves as civilized next to the "féroces cannibales." In the ensuing struggle, the elephants leave their clothes behind, lose their crowns, and escape. Once back in the land of human beings, the unclothed Babar and Céleste are no different from any other elephant ("Babar" is just one liquid consonant away from "barbare" after all) and thus are detained in the hold of a ship, unrecognizable as king and queen, and as luck would have it, end up in a circus once the boat arrives in what is easily discerned in the illustration as a busy Western port. They react with anger that no one would know who they are, that they would be indistinguishable from any other elephant. The circus, an ultimate humiliation,[12] recalls a previous spectacle, Babar holding forth at the soirée in the first book. Meanwhile, Arthur, "the scamp," precipitates a civil war between the elephants and the rhinoceroses, an evocation of tribal wars. Once again, however, the Old Lady saves Babar, takes him and Céleste into her home when the circus arrives in her city, gives them pyjamas, and puts them to bed, greeting them the following morning with a breakfast of coffee and croissants. Their identity restored, they enjoy a ski vacation with the Old Lady in the Alps. Shortly afterward, they return home where, of course, they find their land in the throes of civil war. In a display of barbarous vengeance, the rhinoceroses threaten to eat Arthur, recalling the threat to the cousins earlier in the book. This clear sign of a lack of civilization is counterbalanced by the Old Lady's taking on the role of generous nurse to heal the wounded elephants. In a grotesque disguise, the elephants are able to dupe the rhinos and win the war.[13] The book closes with Babar thinking about how to be a good king to his people.

Thus *Le Voyage de Babar* is but a phase of preparation. Babar, no longer a little elephant, learns to face adversity on his own and to play a new role as husband. This second volume tests the new monarch as a transitional step to *Le Roi Babar*, the apotheosis of the elephant king, dubbed by Payne "one of the most successful political ventures of the twentieth century" (96). With peace restored, Babar can set about duplicating his own transformation across the landscape of his "forest." A sage will lay out the street plan as imported tools and other Western merchandise (hats, records, clothes, brass instruments for the fanfares to come, trumpets that replace the elephants' own), ordered by Babar, arrive from the "pays des hommes." Many will serve as token but heavily symbolic gifts (suits, hats, cloth, paint sets, drums, fishing rods, pens, rackets), rewards for the hard work of having built the city: "With what joy they all strive to do their best!" writes de Brunhoff. "All the elephants are happy as he [Babar] is. They drive nails, draw logs, pull and push, dig, fetch and carry, opening their big ears wide as they work" (9). The colonial theorist would probably be quick to see happy elephants, seemingly ignorant of their own exploitation, working for games and food ("panem et circenses"), under the watchful supervision of their king.

Despite the negative reaction of the fish and birds,[14] the city, named Célesteville, is completed. In perfect layers, it represents the epitome of Cartesian order, a monument to the virtues of (school) work and play. Equal (democratic) opportunity, bestowed by the benevolent monarch, is conveyed in the identical houses.[15] Clothing the elephants (we already know the importance of the sartorial) fixes their identities, attached to the jobs they perform in this new city.[16] Though the loss of the past is evoked with some nostalgia in the old song of the Mammouths with its incomprehensible words,[17] the completion of Célesteville is cause for celebration. The preparations for the happy day are sumptuous: tending the gardens "à la française" or cooking elaborate meals in the kitchen. Even the pesky Zéphir will not prevent the festivities. The symmetry of French gardens (a clear representation of Versailles and what amounts to a conflation of the "fontaine de Neptune" and the "bassin d'Apollon") reinforces the order of this new way of life, and the Molière play and the musical trio, the height of culture and beauty, are presented humorously and memorably in de Brunhoff's illustrations. All the elephants will be educated as was Babar, again represented as children in elementary school. In the early 1880s, Jules Ferry guaranteed this right to a free and universal education, the same Jules Ferry who would push French colonial expansion in the Maghreb, Sub-Saharan Africa, and Southeast Asia. In the illustration the pupils are learning math (and thus Western science) from the Old Lady, now transformed into a schoolteacher. This educational enterprise "à la française" is further supported by the calligraphy of the books, which is similar to what was traditionally presented to all French schoolchildren as the proper way to write. One of the key components of French colonialism was, of course, education, a physically nonviolent way of forcing upon the colonized a past that is not theirs. For example, the school-children in *La Rue Cases-nègres* might very well repeat the leitmotif "nos ancêtres les Gaulois" (our ancestors the Gauls), a phrase deprived of any meaning that has become a cliché in referring to French colonialism. However, in Célesteville, as else-where, there is no hint of the possibility of more advanced work and higher degrees. Education will prepare the elephants to take their place in this highly organized society where everyone has a job to do, a duty to the common good and the efficient functioning of the well-policed city where street cleaning is a daily habit, as it is today in Paris. The combination of hard work and play is essential: tennis and "pétanque" for the adults, toy-boat sailing in the fountain for the children, recalling those of the Luxembourg and the Tuileries. Finally, the two episodes of crisis, a fire at Cornélius's house and a snake biting the Old Lady, seem to demonstrate the efficacy of this new society to take care of its own. The fire department saves Cornélius, and both he and the Old Lady are nursed back to health in the hospital. This important object lesson precedes a more abstract one. In a final dream sequence, Babar imagines evil vanquished by the values of this new culture. Learning, work, goodness, and perseverance overcome ignorance, laziness, cowardice, and fear by the sheer force of their moral power, recalling once again the underpinnings of and justification for the French civilizing mission. Happiness depends on "courage," at the core of a French system of values.

CONCLUSION

These seminal Babar stories, then, would seem to present a particularly French view of culture and civilization. Society is organized along strictly hierarchical lines. Order and symmetry prevail in this worldview where civilization is imposed on the disorder of nature or the perceived chaos of non-French peoples. Rulers are distant, impersonal, and aloof (remember Babar in profile on horseback observ-ing the parade as king at the end of the third book), an incarnation, it would seem, of Charles de Gaulle's own notions of power and governance, of mystique and mystery, as expressed in *Le Fil de l'épée* (*The Edge of the Sword*), also from the 1930s. The Frenchness of the stories on the level of values is reinforced by the outward material signs of French life in the 1930s (and it must be said in the 1990s), from croissants at breakfast to the schoolchild's "cartable" and a passion for vacations. The detail of French life saturates the texts, setting them apart as distinct products of Gallic culture.

In Babar's case, particularly, the first three books represent his education and coming of age, in colonial terms, the civilizing of the colonized. In turn, he, too, will educate, demonstrating the apparent triumph of what he has learned in the West. Célesteville becomes, then, a culture apart, different from the elephant's original life in the forest, different from France, in between.

At the same time, this model of ordered society is anything but stable and safe. Chaos and turmoil are only around the next corner, or as close as the turn of the page as Roger Sale has indicated (14). Zéphir can easily start a war in Babar's absence. A poisonous mushroom can bring down a king. A fire can land old Cornélius in the hospital. This, too, it would seem, is a particularly French view of power and government, indeed perhaps of life. One need only look at how a minority of civil servants brought Paris to its knees in 1995. The battles between the hyperorganized *énarques*[18] like Alain Juppé or Jacques Chirac on the one hand and the forces of defiance, individualism, and anarchy on the other remind us of the either-or view of society and politics presented in the Babar tales. In any case, these particular stories illustrate almost all too neatly what the French called their "mission civilisatrice." They also reflect French ideas of social organization, power, and authority.

NOTES

1. Fanon, *Black Skin* 20. Fanon actually refers to a linguistic and thus an implicitly cultural halfway house.

2. As an example, one need only listen to Peter Ustinov narrating a Babar video in English with a thick French accent.

3. Unlike Kohl, we do not suggest censorship of Babar, but rather a sensitivity to and an awareness of the subtle, embedded messages in the texts.

4. Dorfman also mentions that de Brunhoff had the "mission civilisatrice" in mind while writing the Babar stories (23).

5. Dorfman notes that, upon his arrival in the city, Babar stands erect for the first time. He adds: "Somehow, without losing his animal appearance, Babar will be transformed into a polite and decent human being" (18).

6. All translations are from the English editions of the Babar books, given in the list of works cited. Pagination in both the French and English editions is the same.

7. See also Dorfman 38.

8. "To wear no clothes is a mark of savagery," as Leach points out (16).

9. "Le cannibalisme est un 'must' des ouvrages pour enfants, et l'on en trouve des exemples dans des classiques aussi indiscutables que *Le Roi Mathias Ier, Le Voyage de Babar,* sans parler d'innombrables bandes dessinées où l'image du blanc mijotant dans la marmite est un cliché rebattu" (Mercier 99).

10. "Le noir aime s'habiller et surtout se déguiser. Ainsi dans *Le Voyage de Babar* les cannibales essaient les vêtements de Céleste" (Mercier 101).

11. "Sinon que chacun appelle barbarie ce qui n'est pas de son usage" (Montaigne I.307).

12. See also Sale 13.

13. Of this subterfuge, Dorfman writes: "It is the economic backwardness of the savages which has been the decisive element. They did not know how to close the technical gap

which separated them from the elephants who, with sophisticated weapons, demonstrated the importance of their link to the Western world. The adult world, too. For the rhinos are actually running from themselves: the backsides of their rivals are none other than great African masks. Those stupid animals can't even tell the difference between reality and its representation!" (35). Another way of looking at it, of course, is quite simply as an example of the elephants showing their backsides to the rhinos ("leur montrer le cul").

14. This negative reaction may be read as the perceived threat to the environment, unlike Dorfman's interpretation that the urban has "perfected" nature (39) or that the creation of the city, the sign of progress, has been carried out "without upsetting the ecological balance" (26).

15. Payne describes the city well: "Turning from the family to Celesteville as a whole, one is struck by the balance of work, play, and festivity. Our first view of the new city, the symbol of Babar's civilization, shows a world of play beneath a hill on which are perched four buildings. On the far right is Babar's house, larger than the rest but still modest, symbol of the nature of this rule. On the far left is that of the Old Lady, symbol of age, continuity, urbanity. At the center-right [sic] is the *palais du travail,* the Bureau of Industry, exactly counterpoised at center-left [sic] by the *palais des fêtes,* the Amusement Hall. [The *palais du travail* is in fact at center-left, near the Old Lady's house; the *palais des fêtes* is at center-right.] The world of play is not new; indeed our first view of Babar among other elephants in *Histoire de Babar* shows children at play much as they are in the world of Celesteville. But Babar adds more structured play, work, and fêtes to this world" (98–99).

16. Dorfman comments on this illustration: "Dozens of elephants entering a door, on all fours, wait in line to receive their gifts. Once they exit, the gray, amorphous mass disappears. Through the other door they emerge, dancing (like children? like blacks?) on two feet, half-dressed, present in hand" (38). Later, he likens this transformation to the growth and development of children (44).

17. Many have mentioned the loss of indigenous history, a kind of induced cultural amnesia. On this, Dorfman writes: "if Africa is to be Europe's equal, it has to assimilate Europe's history as well. So a new history must be invented to supplant the elephants' disposable past" (47).

18. *Enarque* is a colloquial term in French used to refer to a graduate of the Ecole Nationale d'Administration, France's leading business school. The word is based on the acronym ENA.

WORKS CITED

Brunhoff, Jean de. *L'ABC de Babar.* 1934. Rpt. Paris: Hachette, 1994.

————. *Histoire de Babar, le petit éléphant.* 1931. *The Story of Babar, the Little Elephant.* Trans. from the French by Merle S. Haas. New York: Random House, 1933.

————. *Le Roi Babar.* 1933. *Babar the King.* Trans. from the French by Merle S. Haas. 1933. Rpt. New York: Random House, 1963.

————. *Le Voyage de Babar.* 1932. *The Travels of Babar.* Trans. from the French by Merle S. Haas. 1934. Rpt. New York: Random House, 1985.

Brunhoff, Jean de, and Laurent de Brunhoff. *Babar en famille.* 1938. Rpt. Paris: Hachette, 1996.

————. *Babar et le père Noël.* 1941. Rpt. Paris: Hachette, 1995.

Césaire, Aimé. *Discours sur le colonialisme.* Paris: Présence africaine, 1955.

de Gaulle, Charles. *Le Fil de l'épée.* 1932. Rpt. Paris: Editions Berger-Levrault, 1959.

Dorfman, Ariel. *The Empire's Old Clothes*. New York: Pantheon, 1983.

Fanon, Frantz. *Peau noire, masques blancs*. Paris: Editions du Seuil, 1952. Trans. Charles Lam Markmann as *Black Skin, White Masks*. New York: Grove, 1967.

Gibson, Lois Rauch, and Laura M. Zaidman. "Death in Children's Literature: Taboo or Not Taboo." *Children's Literature Association Quarterly* 16.4 (Winter 1991): 232–34.

Hildebrand, Anne Meizen. *Jean and Laurent de Brunhoff: The Legacy of Babar*. New York: Twayne, 1991.

Kohl, Herbert R. *Should We Burn Babar? Essays on Children's Literature and the Power of Stories*. New York: New Press, 1995.

Laye, Camara. *L'Enfant noir*. 1953. Rpt. Paris: Plon, 1972.

Leach, Edmund. "Babar's Civilization Analyzed." *New Society* 12 (Dec. 20,1962): 16–17. Rpt. in *Only Connect: Readings on Children's Literature*. Ed. Sheila Egoff, G. T. Stubbs, and L. F. Ashley. Toronto and New York: Oxford University Press, 1980. 176–82.

Memmi, Albert. *The Colonizer and the Colonized*. Trans. from the French by Howard Greenfeld. 1965. Rpt. Expanded ed. Boston: Beacon, 1991.

Mercier, Jean-Pierre. "Image du noir dans la littérature enfantine de 1850 à 1948." *Notre Librairie* 2.91 (Jan.-Feb. 1988): 98–103.

Montaigne, Michel de. "Des Cannibales." Book 1, 31 of *Essais*. Ed. Pierre Michel. Paris: Livre de poche, 1972. 307.

Nguyen Duc Giang. *Vingt ans*. Vinh [Vietnam]: Les Editions de la "Nouvelle Revue Indochinoise," 1940; revised 2nd. ed., 1942.

Payne, Harry C. "The Reign of King Babar." *Children's Literature* 11 (1983): 96–108.

Richardson, Patrick. "Teach Your Baby to Rule." *Suitable for Children? Controversies in Children's Literature*. Berkeley: University of California Press, 1976. 179–83.

Sale, Roger. *Fairy Tales and After: From Snow White to E. B. White*. Cambridge and London: Harvard University Press, 1978.

Sendak, Maurice. *Where the Wild Things Are*. 1963. Rpt. New York: Harper Festival, 1992.

Zobel, Joseph. *La Rue Cases-nègres*. 1955. Rpt. Paris: Présence africaine, 1974.

7

The French Avant-Garde Revisited: Or, Why We Shouldn't Burn Mickey Mouse

Jean Perrot

"Should We Burn Babar?" asks Herbert Kohl in a provocative title. In the introduction to this book, Jack Zipes describes the author as "one of the foremost progressive educators in America" (Kohl 1). What is involved here is censorship, as it is practiced in China, where, if we are to believe an article in the French newspaper *Le Monde* for December 24, 1995, such bonfires still take place. It is therefore a burning question, and one that is defined from the outset in the preface to Kohl's book as "a tempting though equally troubling way to deal with a text whose content is objectionable" (x). Kohl tells us that when he is confronted by certain books, he does not hesitate to salvage one or two copies for the library and "to take the rest to the dump and bury them" (27).

There is no doubt that censorship is practiced here with the best possible intentions in order to defend a "literature that speaks out in the interest of children and communities" (2) and that is based on the antithesis between "education for democracy" and "education that institutionalizes privilege" (xi). As Zipes points out, Kohl "introduces the opinions of children and teachers and incorporates them in his own analysis" (1). This allows him to lay down the law using a subtle cocktail of personal opinions and views he reports, which support his ideological thesis. He offers us an example of an "oppressive tendency" that runs counter to the freedom of readers because it is based on "fear." As Perry Nodelman stated in a paper at the 12th International Research Society for Children's Literature (IRSCL) Conference in Stockholm in 1995, "To fear texts because they imbed children in ideology is to fear all of the social and communal aspects of human existence—and all the pleasures they offer" (11). It is true, one may object, that Nodelman is primarily concerned with texts similar to that of Babar, which are supposedly "innocent" and which constitute the bulk of children's reading. As he writes: "And it's also unquestionably true that powerful forces in mainstream culture work hard to impose these repressive and limiting ideas of themselves on children. Witness, as just one example, the ways in which Disney films continue to confirm decidedly dangerous ideas about what desirable girls' and women's bodies should look like. Girls who accept these images, most often unthinkingly, as the one and only way to be attractive and powerful work very hard to conform themselves to these supposed ideals, at great expense, and often at great danger, of their health" (11–12). We may well imagine that the same danger threatens girls who play with Barbie dolls, as Kohl, before condemning Babar, imagined for a moment as he watched his own daughters playing with such dolls and delighting in the game. Such fears have, however, proven groundless, since despite this menace, Kohl admits that they have grown into "confirmed feminists" (14).

CULTURAL LITERACY AND POLITICAL CORRECTNESS

My defense of Babar from the charge of danger to America is not simply as a Frenchman called to rescue his national heritage, nor indeed as one called on to defend one of the several cultural industrial products that have successfully penetrated the American market. Nor will I make any attempt to defend some of the outdated aspects of these books. The discussion I wish to initiate is in fact much more important and concerns the international responsibility of intellectuals and their duty not only to attempt to be "politically correct" in their own country, but also to grasp the implications of the ultimate presuppositions of the author's outlook, of which the reader may be totally unaware. However lucid this may be, it may mask the interests of a science which George Gebner tells us "is increasingly a by-product of mass marketing" (quoted in Moebius 62). The drive toward cultural literacy is the faculty of welcoming powerful emotions which expand our ability to feel empathy in the search for texts that reveal "those unifying, affirming, hospitable, time-tolerant values that every schoolteacher, librarian, and parent can endorse," to quote a forceful argument from Bill Moebius's plea (57). Apparently the success of *Babar* is based primarily on the general taste of American children and their parents, which Kohl, using a narrow range of opinions, draws on to attack the book. We will not, therefore, make use of this argument for the defense: we will simply ask ourselves whether American youngsters have adopted Babar as their hero as a result of collective blindness, or whether these books contain specific values which respond to the questionings of the child's mind? These values, which are far more important than the ideological weaknesses identified by Kohl, may explain why the children plump for a position that may be more "politically correct" than we realize.

Kohl's reading misses the more subtle aspects of a general humanism profoundly in harmony with the "symbolic exchange" that characterizes the truth and sanity of family life and of childhood communication. Furthermore, could the defects pointed out not be the result of an incorrect reading and of distortions that arise from the projections of the adult reader himself? Instead of relegating Babar to the museum, as Kohl would have us do, should we not perhaps learn to read these books properly, so that we can rediscover the creativity that has not been lost but masked by the prejudice of a certain aggressiveness of the adult critic? By doing so, can we learn a lesson America still needs to learn because the interests with which the text deals are far from being satisfied?

THE AVANT-GARDE OF THE 1930s

Let us now look at the text more closely. In 1931 Jean de Brunhoff published his *Histoire de Babar, le petit éléphant (The Story of Babar, the Little Elephant)*, the first of his Babar books. As Marc Soriano in his *Guide de littérature pour la jeunesse* points out, this book emerged in the postwar context, at a time when the development of publishing and literature for children and young people was strongly influenced by Paul Faucher, founder of the Atelier du Père Castor publishing house, a supporter of the New Education theories of the Czech educator Bakulé, and founder of the Collection Education series that in 1932 was to publish Paul Hazard's book *Des livres, des enfants et des hommes* (Books, children and men), a selection from a series of articles that had appeared in *La Revue des Deux Mondes* in previous years (Perrot 299). The Babar story, therefore, appeared in the context of a shift in French publishing expressed by the aims of the Collection Education series, which involved people as different as Roger Martin du Gard and the founders of Gallimard's Bibliothèque de la Pléiade (Soriano 232–33). *Histoire de Babar, le petit éléphant* was translated into 15 languages, and four million copies had been published by 1939, making it a world classic of children's literature. Until he was superseded in this role by Antoine de Saint-Exupéry's *Le Petit Prince (The Little Prince)*, written in New York in 1943, the little elephant was the official roving ambassador of French children. This success, it is true, was expanded by the family business set up by the author's son, Laurent de Brunhoff, who exploited his father's gold mine in cartoon films and in commercial merchandising in true Walt Disney style.

In 1931 the book in fact represented something avant-garde and was an early protest against the slaughter of elephants, which is depicted here in the killing of Babar's mother by hunters. However, this condemnation of the evils of colonialism and this "ecological" outlook are encompassed in a vision of the happiness of a group of children, as portrayed by the elephants, in what is surely a marvelous transportation of the "garden city," the utopian incarnation of a certain form of communal living. Jean de Brunhoff's story takes its cue from the story by Charles Vildrac, author of *L'Ile Rose*, which was written for children attending French state schools. This story is based on the theme of a holiday camp in a rural setting and indirectly echoes the debates taking place at the International Congresses for Modern Architecture—which took place in Paris, Amsterdam, and Weimar from 1928 onward—which were concerned with the relationship between town and country in town planning.[1] We know that the development of "garden cities" took concrete form in 1928 in the foundation in the United States of the town of Radburn (Choay 497, 498). These are important forces which shaped the post-World War I imaginative vision behind the Babar book, and which could still inspire architects who now have to contend with the question of inner-city ghettos.

The rural community of the elephants, where we see Babar gently rocked by his mother in a hammock or playing in the sand while the other elephants play a variety of games in an idyllic natural setting, presents the vision of the ideal child's garden. We should also remember the closing ball, after the wedding, when even though the clothes of the dancers seem to denote some sort of hierarchy among them, the dancers still seem to be united in spirit as a result of the wholehearted generosity with which they all "dance merrily."

Kohl does not mention any of this. Is the village simply a Rousseau-like mask? Is it just a way of sugaring the pill of the alienation of those who are exploited? Is *Histoire de Babar,* as Kohl claims, "my token for what is objectionable in children's literature," namely, "the colonialism, the implied racism and sexism of the tale" (16, 17)? Yet, if we take the arguments he puts forward one by one, we find that the facts are far from this simple.

PROJECTIONS AND COUNTERPROJECTIONS OF KOHL'S READING

First, let us begin with the issue of power to which Kohl seems to attach the most importance. It is not fair to say, as Kohl does, that the Old Lady's hold over Babar is "because of her money and its power over Babar" (7). The critic betrays some of his own projections when he writes: "In *Babar* the reader learns that there are different classes of people and the Rich Lady is of better (that is richer) class and that elephants are not as good as people, but might be if they imitated people. Was I aware of such distinctions as a child? Did I learn to admire the rich from reading the book? Did I also learn about the inferiority of creatures from the jungle (people included)? I can't be sure, but I do think that from my early reading I got the impression that people who served the rich weren't as good as the rich" (7). The distortion of this syllogism is obvious. Nothing in the text suggests that Babar "serves the rich." On the contrary, he is served by them, because the "very rich Old Lady" gives him everything he wants, like a fairy godmother. In fact, she plays the symbolic role of the "oral good mother" described by Mélanie Klein. In this sense, Kohl's speculations about the origin of Babar's fortune corresponds to a realistic outlook and is groundless, for Babar is not manipulative. It is also untrue to claim that when Babar treats his cousins quite well "they seem delighted to be transformed into imitations of people." It is true that "The three of them even go to a pastry shop and have some sweets" (Kohl 9), but the joy of seeing each other again, and the presumed age of the characters involved, surely justifies this little treat? Has Kohl never enjoyed a treat of this sort with his own daughters? This is astounding censorship, worthy of a truly puritanical attitude indeed.

About the charge of colonial expansion, should we see the book as "recruiting" for colonialism? Is Babar the lackey of humans? Absolutely nothing suggests this, because the human characters are totally forgotten once we return to the world of the animals. The story is based, instead, on the constant oscillation between the world of adults and that of animals and children, rather than on any contrast between the colonized and their colonial rulers. Nor are we told that the people of the jungle are in any way inferior to those of the town. Babar is, in fact, given the place of honor, when after dinner he tells the friends of the Old Lady about his life in the Great Forest. The expression "the Great Forest" is not used just to create a mystery, but to establish the symmetry between opposing values: Babar is valued as the spokesperson for the children of Nature and the countryside. What we witness is, therefore, his progressive enculturation, and Babar is less a slave than a "good student": he is learning good manners and buying new clothes as part of his general education, the importance of which in building up a social identity has been sufficiently highlighted by Claude Lévi-Strauss in *L'Homme nu (The Naked Man)*. With the teacher giving him these lessons, Babar "is attentive . . . and was a most promising pupil." If this "charming Babar" is a product of propaganda, as Kohl argues, then propaganda is not totally without merit for it helps to promote science, a field that can sometimes help us see more clearly areas that are clouded by ideology. Instead of highlighting the "powerlessness" of Babar, who is described by Kohl as being "as passive as a paper doll and as uncomplaining," I would stress his desire to learn (7).

Kohl's account also gives the impression that Babar is an involuntary emissary of the Whites, sent to propagate the virtues of an alienating civilization. However, if we take a closer look at the text, we will find that the little elephant leaves the town of the Whites because he is homesick for the authentic life of his origins and roots. He does not have any regrets: he is not the victim of feelings of alienation; he is free and we cannot say that "Babar is drawn home and has to leave the Rich Lady" (24). The text states clearly: "And yet Babar was not altogether happy, because he could no longer play about in the Great Forest with his little cousins and his friends the monkeys. He often gazed out of the window dreaming of his childhood and when he thought of his mother he used to cry" (n.pg.; my translation). The homesickness is intensified by the arrival of Arthur and Céleste, which "decides" the little elephant to leave. The tale consists of successive separations and liberation from material concern, and the love he bears for his old "magical" benefactress is a sign of his emotion. Babar does not give a second thought to the quality of the life he is leaving, and the Old Lady, the foster mother who is losing him, makes no attempt to restrain him. Babar may want to be like the grownups, but he is not materialistic, and we cannot share the stern judgment of Kohl when he writes, "Wanting things is a serious business in our society, and I feel uncomfortable with books that reinforce that obsession" (19). Babar is the innocent who has neither envy nor hatred; he is acute enough to distinguish between the cruel hunter who has killed his mother and the other members of the adult world who want to help him. This ability to forget, the inborn generosity that is characteristic of childhood innocence, is a quality no longer appreciated in societies marked by racial hatred and resentment. After this course in unselfish love, of the "symbolic gift" of forgiveness,[2] Babar is now fit for adult life. Kohl's comments on the symbolic significance of objects—notably that of the hat, as a sign of power—simply point out that it is absurd to state that "[t]he use of symbols and possessions to legitimize authority is dangerous and antidemocratic" (20). Kohl has apparently never read

Bruno Bettelheim's *The Uses of Enchantment,* or is he intending to burn all stories that use the image of the king and queen to represent father and mother, or those in which a change in clothing symbolizes an inner transformation of the hero? Is ideological blindness not here in danger of toppling over into bad faith? Nothing justifies the claim that Babar is "dependent on money," or that "[h]e is an exile, a stranger in a strange land and in his own land at the same time" (Kohl 24). There is no sexism in Babar, who in fact gives precedence to his wife when he announces that "Céleste and I got engaged." The closing scene indeed shows us Babar and Céleste communing in a baroque contemplation of Nature when night has fallen and the stars have come out—a mystical elevation of the spouses beneath the starry sky of the philosopher Kant. This elevation, which is also reflected in the adventures to come—in the honeymoon in a glorious yellow balloon, rising up to the "seventh heaven"—is an indication of a taste for adventure and not for material possessions. As readers we do indeed find Kohl's theories rather "far fetched," as he expected us to (24), and we will not have the cheek to follow him through the next chapter, in which he asks "What's Missing from Babar?" History cannot be rewritten, and if Kohl cannot recognize the image of the Father in Jean de Brunhoff's story, it is an indication of both an inability to read symbols and a search for evidence on which to base his own personal inventions.

FOR FRIENDSHIP'S SAKE BUY BOOKS, GIVE THEM AS PRESENTS!

Basta! Enough! as Collodi, the author of *Pinocchio* might exclaim. But then, he, too, is roughly treated by Kohl. Kohl's reading reveals several lacunae and some degree of national insularity in himself and in the models to which he refers. Kohl imagines that Babar has helped to hoodwink him and prevent him from questioning some aspects of maleness, thus "contributing to [his] not questioning many aspects of patriarchy earlier in life" (28). Does this male guilt, a new mental burden and modern stone of Sisyphus, lead to the even more serious blindness reflected in his reading? Happily, he tells us that his wife has remained more sensible and will not burn what she has loved. This is evidence of a maturity that has been able to learn from experience and put into perspective a more subtle approach that envisages childhood as the challenge and crux of correctness which gains as much from being "political" as "cultural." To conclude, I would like to return to one of the last phrases Kohl uses about this international children's classic: "I wouldn't ban or burn *Babar,* or pull it from libraries. But buy it? No. I see no reason to go out of one's way to make [it] available to children, primarily because I don't see much critical reading going on in the schools, and children don't need to be propagandized about colonialism, sexism, or racism" (28). "Buy it." This may be the final explanation behind the cultural imperialist struggle of which Kohl is the involuntary pawn. This is why I feel justified in having reread de Brunhoff's book. I am justified not just because it enabled me to counter Kohl's polemical arguments, but because this debate may promote the development of authentic reading in schools and critical exchanges across the seas in a cooperative spirit; and it may combat something that threatens the continuance of symbolic communication, free from market forces. To quote from Moebius's article, which tackles the issue of cultural literacy, "I would like to approach the question of cultural literacy as a matter of capitalized letters, capitalized in the sense that they stand tall in book titles and, in a quasi-economic sense, that they possess the potential for future investments" (57). This "capitalization" is not the exclusive preserve of adults in libraries, but should also be open to young readers who are used to making their own judgments about the works of an avant-garde who fifty years later may not yet have yielded up the full power of his message.

NOTES

1. This debate had been reinvigorated by the work of Le Corbusier (1887–1965), reflected in the magazine *Esprit Nouveau.*

2. This term was used by Marcel Mauss in his celebrated "Essai sur le don. Forme et raison de l'échange dans les sociétés archaïques," *Année sociologique,* 2nd series, vol. I (1923–24): 20–80.

WORKS CITED

Bettelheim, Bruno. *The Uses of Enchantment: The Meaning and Importance of Fairy Tales.* New York: Knopf, 1976.

Brunhoff, Jean de. *Histoire de Babar, le petit éléphant.* Paris: Hachette, 1931.

Choay, François. "Urbanisme: Théories et réalisations." In "Urbanisme." *Encyclopedia Universalis* 16 (1968): 492–99.

Klein, Mélanie. "Early Stages of the Oedipus Conflict." 1928. Rpt. *Love, Guilt and Reparation and Other Works 1921–1945.* New York: Delacorte/Seymour Lawrence, 1975. 186–198.

Kohl, Herbert. *Should We Burn Babar? Essays on Children's Literature and the Power of Stories.* Introd. Jack Zipes. New York: New Press, 1995.

Moebius, William. "Political Correctness and Cultural Literacy." *Lion and the Unicorn* 16.1 (June 1992): 57–65.

Nodelman, Perry. "Fear of Children's Literature: What Is Left (or Right) after Theory?" *Reflections of Change: Children's Literature since 1945.* Ed. Sandra L. Beckett. Westport, Conn.: Greenwood, 1997. 3–14.

Perrot, Jean. "La Littérature d'enfance et de jeunesse." *Précis de littérature comparée.* Ed. Pierre Brunel and Yves Chevrel. Paris: PUF, 1989. 299–319.

Saint-Exupéry, Antoine de. *The Little Prince.* New York: Gallimard, 1943.

Soriano, Marc. *Guide de littérature de jeunesse.* Paris: Flammarion, 1976.

Vildrac, Charles. *L'Ile Rose.* Paris: Tolmer (Enfants), 1924.

8

Vicarious Culture Shock: Children's Books about North Africa

Greta D. Little

This essay differs from others in this volume in that it concerns exclusively literature for an English-speaking Western audience written by English-speaking Westerners. The setting and characters are North African, but the perspective is not native. Writers speak with the voice of an outsider, an observer, whose purpose is to represent and explain in some fashion the region and people of North Africa to young readers. They display little of the nation-centeredness that we expect of postcolonial writing; instead, these books share more with the travel writing and adventure stories of earlier times than with emerging national literatures.

However, they cannot be called colonialist in the traditional sense of the word. The writers' investment in the cultures and economies of the countries they write about differs dramatically from the settlers of Frantz Fanon or the colonizers of Albert Memmi. As visitors—expatriates or tourists—in the postcolonial period, they do not have the protection of the colonial apparatus and its collateral military support. Their long-term plans rarely involve continued work or residence in the third world. More important, they have not been threatened by indigenous peoples in the same way that colonialists were. They have come to see, to learn, perhaps to earn as well, but their homes are elsewhere, and they do not intend to establish a new national identity.

In their books these expatriate and tourist writers rely on their experience living and working in the third world. They write books intended to educate their fellow countrymen about the geography, people, and customs of their erstwhile home. They present their stories through Western eyes, filtered through Western experience, and ultimately promoting Western values. Their intention is not large-scale exploitation; in fact, many are living and working at financial sacrifice, and they are often motivated by lofty ideals. Nevertheless, by their very presence, they often contribute to neocolonialist Western hegemony and domination in the region. And the books they write reinforce Western ways and values as the norm.

CULTURE SHOCK THEORIES

A number of differences separate postcolonial expatriates and tourists from colonialists. Both groups share an illegitimately high status, both socially and economically. But in newly independent governments, the administrative and political
machinery no longer keeps Westerners insulated from native populations and their
cultures. Without that protection, the attitudes and fears that had earlier plagued
European colonialists have been reinterpreted as a disease affecting travelers who
experience disorientation and uncertainty in unfamiliar environments. Culture
shock, as this disease is known, was first identified by Kalervo Oberg in 1958.[1] It is
a peculiarly postcolonial phenomenon. For travelers to suffer culture shock, their
confidence in the superiority of their own ways must be challenged; they must be
aware of and concerned about the reactions of the others whose societies they have
encountered. Since responses differ among individuals, it is difficult to identify a
uniform manifestation of culture shock. However, most experts agree that culture
shock occurs in a series of stages characterized by changing perceptions of the new
culture and one's relation to it. In the face of foreign values and new rules, a visitor
at first concentrates on finding the familiar in a strange world. During the second
stage, social and cultural differences intrude, making a visitor uncomfortable and
insecure. The third stage is characterized by increasing contact with the native culture and a growing understanding of it. The final stage is full recovery and acceptance of the unfamiliar land, people, language, and customs. More recent views of
culture shock focus on the personal growth and development that can result from
cross-cultural experiences and reject the label of disease.

   In "Culture Shock and the Cross-Cultural Learning Experience," Peter Adler
objects to the notion that those who experience culture shock are helpless victims.
He proposes an alternative model that emphasizes the learning that usually
accompanies the period of adjustment. Adler's version of culture shock explains
how individuals react to a new cultural landscape. The process is unique and personal to individuals who have been forced to examine themselves and all their
relationships through extremes of frustration and anxiety. Adler believes that they
must approach these situations through trial and error, comparison and contrast:
"The cross-cultural learning process, then, is a set of intensive and evocative situations in which the individual experiences himself and other people in a new way
distinct from previous situations and is consequently forced into new levels of
consciousness and understanding" (31). Adler's theory differs from other models
of culture shock in that it allows for positive outcomes as well as explaining anti-
social symptoms. It clarifies the identification and emergence of the phenomenon
in the postcolonial period, when a fuller range of interaction with native populations and cultures was possible. Groups like colonialists or military families who
lived on protected compounds rarely suffered from the full range of culture shock
symptoms or fully profited from the experience of living in another culture.

   Adler's model is also useful for explaining the different responses we find
among modern Western writers who have experienced North Africa and are trying
to share their understanding with readers. The overall attitude of these writers is

positive and meant to be sympathetic. They want to convey something of what they learned from living as an outsider, but the images they create often bear the imperfections of their own limited understanding. Some even reveal characteristics of latent hostility and insecurity. Readers who enter the fictitious worlds constructed by these writers may themselves experience a kind of vicarious culture shock. The discomfort, suspicion, and disorientation they may feel as they read can also inspire empathy in them and a desire to understand.

NEOCOLONIALISM: AN AFFIRMATION OF WESTERN VALUES

Turning to the literature itself, we find several stories set in North Africa but written by Westerners who have lived and worked there. In these works, culture shock operates at two levels, one conscious and the other unconscious. When Western tourists or expatriate families are protagonists, the writers exhibit an awareness of culture shock and its progression as their characters grow and develop in the context of a foreign culture. Writers can also unconsciously show effects of culture shock in terms of how they themselves view the lands and people they write about. This impact is particularly clear in early travel books when authors tell of their own discomfort, anxiety, and hostility. More recent books are less likely to dwell on negative aspects of the culture; nevertheless, Arabs are still seen as unfathomable characters, and their ways are often presented in watered-down versions to make them more accessible and more acceptable to Western readers. The most positive portrayals of North Africans are to be found in characters from the historically valued precolonial past and in modern products of Western education. The books focus on the thrill and adventure of a strange, exotic land populated by exciting, slightly sinister "others."

Walter Dean Myers's *Tales of a Dead King* is an example of these adventure stories. The protagonists are two American teenagers, John and Karen, who travel to Egypt to join John's uncle in an archaeological expedition searching for Akhenaton's tomb. Learning that John's uncle is missing, they track down his former guide, who leads them to a deserted Nubian village where they are held captive with the missing archaeologist. They manage to escape in time to welcome the Egyptian police who have been following them. The Egyptian setting provides exotic detail, but otherwise has little impact on the characters. There is little information about modern Egypt beyond brief descriptions and comments on native and Western dress: "The airport was interesting. Men in jellabas, the long robelike things that I had seen in so many pictures of the Middle East, were more common than men in western-style business suits" (3). The children's hotel is run-down, "on a wide street that was paved in most places" but with "patches of dirt" (5). They note these differences between Egypt and what they are familiar with, but they are not really affected by many of the differences.

Although their encounters with native Egyptians are rare, they are fairly unpleasant and convey a sense of insecurity if not outright danger. At the local market, where they go to meet a man who may have information about John's uncle, someone throws a dagger at them. As they leave they acknowledge the fear: "Outside the sun was as hot as ever. The only thing different was that all the mild-mannered shoppers in their long caftans had turned sinister, their faces half hidden in the shadows of their hoods" (58). Myers is more intent on recounting an adventure than he is on portraying an accurate picture of Egypt or explaining the reactions of two American children to the foreign culture in which they find themselves. Consequently his perspective reveals little information about Egyptian characters as individuals or how John and Karen adjust to Egyptian society. The local police who rescue them have only a minor role, and the pre-dominant image of Egyptians is greedy, violent, and unscrupulous.

The Cliffs of Cairo by Elsa Marston gives a richer picture of modern Egypt and of expatriate responses to the cultural adjustment. The heroine, Tabby Sherwood, is an American teenager living in Cairo with her parents and brother while her father is working under private contract. Tabby's passion is the Fatimid caliphs of medieval Cairo, which leads her to a ring of smugglers who are exploiting reli-gious fanatics to sell ancient artifacts outside the country. The family lives in a high-rise apartment building; the children attend a French school favored by foreigners; they have Egyptian servants and mix socially mainly with other expa-triates. Tabby, however, can speak some Egyptian Arabic and is comfortable mov-ing about Cairo. From her experiences she is learning about herself as well as about Egyptian culture. Her attitude is in marked contrast to that of her jaded parents, who have lost interest in the unfamiliar and are concerned only about their immediate comfort and plans to return home. The adult Sherwoods' culture shock is in a stage when it manifests itself not as tolerance and growth, but as cyni-cism and frustration.

In the annotation for her own novel in a bibliographical essay, Marston claims the picture of Egypt is accurate and authentic: "Scenes of home and non-American school life, encounters with many 'ordinary' Egyptians, street activity, and a rowing excursion on the Nile add to the authenticity of the setting. . . . To date this appears to be the only American novel for young people that accurately portrays life and cross-cultural experience in contemporary Egypt" ("The Middle East" 405). Yet this picture itself may bear the impact of Marston's own adjust-ment to Egyptian culture. The book offers a preponderance of the generalizations characteristic of expatriates suffering the negative effects of culture shock. Mr. Sherwood grumbles at removing shoes to enter mosques or Egyptian homes. He laments the necessity of worrying about pickpockets on the streets and in the markets, seeing the country as inefficient and corrupt, where one has "to tip half the population of Cairo just to look at some wall." Only Tabby seems to be truly interacting with Egyptians and the Egyptian way of life.

Part of the storyline involves Tabby's attraction for the opposite sex, played out in her relationship to two Egyptian young men—Nabil, an urban planning student at the University of London, and Hamed, her hairdresser. In addition to the obvious class differences in the two men, Nabil is clearly more westernized and therefore more acceptable in Western eyes than his rival. For this reason, Mr. Sherwood prefers Nabil as an escort for his daughter: "He seems a little more your type" (103). Nabil's virtues are those instilled by Western education, his lapses ascribed to his Egyptian commitment to family. When he does not call as promised, Mr. Sherwood reassures Tabby: "You know Egyptians—they love their sons." And Tabby is said to appreciate "her father's practical way of looking at the situation" (104).

Throughout the story there is an undercurrent of fear and violence at the domestic, grassroots level. Egyptians are presented as stereotypes rather than individualized characters. Hamed is attractive, romantic, but dishonest. His family is allied to the smugglers trying to steal Egyptian antiquities. The religious cult members are portrayed as irrational, completely duped by the smugglers, and described alternately as "woebegone and passive" and "wild-eyed and fanatical." Tabby is attacked by a workman who changes into a wild, insane creature bent on killing her. Ultimately only Egyptians who have been westernized to a significant degree have any place in the world of expatriate Cairo. It may be as Marston claims that her portrayal of life and cross-cultural experience in Egypt is accurate, but the view of the two cultures is far from balanced or equal. This society values West over East, more closely resembling the situation in the colonial past than in a newly independent nationalistic present.

Fear in Algeria by Marian Hostetler more explicitly affirms Western values while associating fear with the indigenous Algerian society. Told from the perspective of missionaries expelled from the country in 1969 and 1970, the story follows Zina, an American teenager, who has returned to the place of her birth to visit her aunt. Her visit takes her from Algiers and Constantine into rural Berber areas all the way to the edge of the Sahara desert. The account is reminiscent of nineteenth-century travel logs. Zina describes the scenery, relates basic information about the region's history, and gives limited ethnographies of the peoples she encounters. Every event is an opportunity for a lesson about the country, its customs, its people. Her observations include comments on religion, the role of women, the school system, changing lifestyles in the city. She pays little attention to politics, viewing everything in terms of religion.

Like her nineteenth-century predecessors, Zina recounts her adventures and impressions with apparent objectivity, but they nonetheless are colored by her Western orientation. When she visits the family her parents had worked with years earlier and decides to stay there overnight, her comments reveal her bias: "Mebareka and Salim's house, possibly because she had worked at the clinic, was cleaner than most of the others around. It must have taken constant effort on her part to keep it that way and to keep her children as neat and clean as they were" (76). The positive elements of the family's life are attributed to the influence of exposure to Christianity and the West. Islam is associated with superstition. On finding that the couple's son wears a Koranic charm, Zina remarks, "This was supposed to keep . . . evil away. I was surprised that someone who'd worked in a clinic would believe in such things" (84). Further evidence of the perception that Algerian ways are inferior appears when she tells readers that an anthropologist had explained that "Chaouia habits and customs had not changed much since the late stone age" (79).

In the other village she visits, Zina is introduced to Mozabites, a closed sect of Muslims who "are exceptionally clean and honest people, and also very strict—no tobacco, no games, no music" (108). Mozabites differ from Arabs; they have lighter skin and rounder faces, and do not wear turbans. Zina's depiction takes into account a diversity often lacking in Western views of North Africa, yet her description grants higher status to Mozabites, who are more like Europeans. Other than the Chaouians and the Mozabites, the only Algerians that Zina meets during her trip are students interested in Christianity. They are portrayed sympathetically, but they are all critical of traditional Islamic society and heavily influenced by their Western-style education. The Algerian government is represented by police enforcing expulsion orders and a mysterious man who follows Zina throughout her stay. Although they do arrange rabies treatment for her dog bite, the emphasis is on their irrational suspicions and the delay they caused.

Zina experiences little growth and development as a result of confronting Arab culture and Algerian nationalism. She remains at the first level of culture confrontation; she only looks for points of similarity between Algeria and her own world. She is far more interested in the light-skinned Mozabites than in other Algerians. Nevertheless, she can hardly be said to suffer the full impact of culture shock because, like the colonials, she never questions herself or her life. She remains convinced that Christianity and her Western home are superior to anything she has found in Algeria. Her understanding of the cultural and political differences she encounters is limited by a strong Western bias, probably tied to her implied religious beliefs. Consequently, readers are unlikely to gain increased understanding of Algerian culture from reading the book.

Despite the fact that the conflict is a religious one for the characters, the book does reflect postcolonial responses to continued Western hegemony in the region and the steps taken by the Algerian government to counter that influence. Hostetler does not advocate those views, but they do play a prominent role in the story. Further, Algerian nationalists may be faceless with no identity, but they are empowered and in the end they prevail.

It is interesting to note that in all three of these books, the only well-rounded, fully developed characters are Westerners, in fact Americans. The only North African of any depth is Nabil in *The Cliffs of Cairo,* but he is cast almost entirely in terms of his westernized character. Lloyd Norris's *The Village That Allah Forgot: A Story of Modern Tunisia* represents a departure from this pattern. Set in the wake of Tunisian independence, the story addresses postcolonial issues of establishing political stability, public education, and a sense of nationalistic independence by focusing on a young boy whose father was killed in the Bizerte riots of 1961.

After his father's death, 11-year-old Ali's life changes dramatically as he attempts the task of taking care of his mother and often-ill sister, Jamila. They live in Msalla, a small village several hundred meters off the main road. Without direct access to the road, the village has low priority for the progress promised by the independent Tunisian government. Word of progress arrives with Farhat, a university student whose family once lived in Msalla. Farhat explains the pressures that are delaying the government and promises to teach the children on Saturdays until a school is built. His visits help the villagers see the need for a road, and they determine to build one. The children divide into teams led by Ali and his cousin Schedli in a contest to see whose section of the road will be finished first. Ali's team has the lower half of the road that is separated from the main road by a ditch and unfortunately must be handled by a road crew. It falls to Ali to find the road crew and summon them to Msalla in order to finish the road. Completion of the road brings the outside world to Msalla, and with it Ali finds an understanding of his father's death. The story has additional subplots, involving the fractured relationship between Ali and his cousin and Ali's efforts to support his family.

Norris uses his knowledge of the culture to structure the events of the boy's acceptance of his father's death around the celebration of important Islamic festivals. As Ali emerges from his initial grief, he remembers a watch belonging to his father. He confronts his uncle about it during Aid-el-Khebir, the feast of freshly slaughtered lamb to celebrate Abraham's willingness to sacrifice his son at God's command. Ali misses his father reciting the Koran and vows that for the next year's feast, he will supply the sheep and recite the prayers. Ramadan, the month of daytime fasting to remind believers to have compassion for those less fortunate than they, marks the start of work on the road. At the end of Ramadan, Ali's uncle begins a reconciliation with the boy when he turns over the watch, which Ali thought he had sold. Finally, when Aid-el-Khebir occurs again, a matured Ali indeed has supplied the sheep for his family. Moreover, it is the product of cooperation between him and his cousin Schedli and represents the two families' reconciliation and Ali's readiness to assume his father's role. The structure highlights the importance of these events and weaves the significance of the festivities into the plot. Thus the readers' introduction to Islam is woven into the story, not set apart in its orientation.

Both boys are developed characters with whom readers may identify and empathize. In the aftermath of Ali's father's death, the two become rivals because neither boy knows how to deal with his feelings. In the year that passes before they are reconciled, each gains a sense of his own strengths and learns to respect the other. Still, misunderstandings and suspicion separate them until they join forces to buy the sheep for the feast and begin to talk about their feelings. Ali's efforts to support his family first place him in competition with his cousin, but as the boys mature, each develops his own potential. Schedli's physical prowess is established in moving stones to build the road. Ali's ingenuity and skill at bargaining allow him to purchase a chicken to produce eggs for the family. Later his artistic talent enables him to earn more money for his family.

Most of the book that is directly related to Tunisian independence is introduced through the university student Farhat and his interaction with the villagers. It is Farhat who explains why the government is delayed in filling its promises of schools and economic prosperity. He provides information about the local history of the village and the national history of the region as well. Farhat's stories help Ali understand that his father was a hero who died for his country. He also explains the role of the French in the country and in the death of Ali's father, telling how the Tunisians at Bizerte were patient until it was clear the French were not about to leave and it would be necessary for them to act. When Ali asks why the patriots did not just throw the French out, Farhat gives two reasons: "One is we couldn't win. Second is, we need them" (109).

In his treatment of the French, Norris reveals a Western orientation that belies his nationalist theme. With remarkable tolerance for the former colonialists, Farhat urges Ali not to hate them: "It's not the French you should hate. You can hate the idea that one country should rule another. Hate ideas, not people" (112). In fact the entire book is surprisingly positive about the French and their role in Tunisia, especially given that the story is ostensibly about the son of a Tunisian patriot. Almost every empowering event in the book seems to emanate somehow from the French and their continuing influence. The extra money that enables Ali to buy his chicken is given to him by French tourists, and later the first successful sale of his drawings is to a French buyer. Farhat gives credit to the French for motivating his initial visit to Msalla. Even the children's road is built with expertise learned from French colonial masters by the old men of the village. Norris thus portrays a positive role for France in nation building, accepting the position that Western colonialism served a pragmatic purpose in North Africa.

Further evidence of Western orientation can be found in the book's depiction of Islam and its code. While it is true that Islam is a religion encompassing a range of belief and practice, the version presented in the story is precisely that least likely to offend modern Western readers. The inclusion of girls in the village school, Farhat's declaration that they need not wear veils, Ali's acceptance of drawing the human figure,[2] and his mother's reluctance to reconcile herself to her plight as "Allah's will" are all affirmations of Western values and evidence of positive European influence. As an expatriate, Norris profited from an extensive knowledge of and experience in North Africa. In Adler's terms he has achieved considerable cultural understanding and appreciation. He is not judgmental in his presentation of Tunisians, but his understanding of the people and their culture is limited in ways that are probably predictable. As a Westerner, he wants to see a benefit from continued Western presence in the area, and he wants to believe that the national culture is only superficially different from his own. Thus, in spite of all he does understand and appreciate, his adjustment to and understanding of that culture remain incomplete.

Giggy Lezra's *Mechido, Aziza and Ahmed,* a collection of three stories set in Morocco, also features North African characters. However, there is little cultural authenticity in the stories themselves. Other than the Moroccan setting, Arab names, and a few exotic details, the stories are concerned with fairly universal themes of children growing up and discovering their role in life. For the most part, the book has little relevance to postcolonialism; contact with the West is not a meaningful part of any of the stories, nor is politics, religion, food, dress, or any other cultural artifact.

In the first story Mechido is expected to follow in his father's path and become a baker. The first step is being *tarah,* the baker's boy who delivers the bread and cakes. The story is accurate in the sense that Moroccan bakers not only bake bread but make their ovens available to customers for baking their own cakes and rolls.

A *tarah* both delivers goods from the baker and brings dough back to the oven for baking. Mechido is unsuited to the job of *tarah,* preferring to work with the local cabinetmaker. His father is piqued that his son wants to break tradition, refusing to allow him to use the beautifully inlaid bread box he has made instead of a tray, even though it is more practical and will keep the bread warm. Finally, he and the cabinetmaker, whose own son has no love for cabinetmaking, decide to train each other's sons. Both boys and their fathers are satisfied. Since the cabinetmaker's son is not from a long line of bakers, he can make use of Mechido's fine bread box.

The setting of Aziza's story is reminiscent of the gardens one finds especially in Marakesh, but other than the characters' names and the sultan of Aziza's reveries, there is little in the story to make it specifically Moroccan. Like Mechido, Aziza displays a fairly universal problem adjusting to her parents' expectations that she behave in a dainty and feminine fashion. Her father gets especially upset because he sees in her a resemblance to relatives he does not like. To neutralize his angry rages, Aziza's mother and her aunts stereotypically distract and appease him. An exuberant child, Aziza finds an overgrown miniature garden in the compound of her parents' new home. In her daydreams the garden is inhabited by a tiny sultan, his queen, and their court. They help her to adjust as she works to make the garden "gracious, intricate, feminine" (76). At last Aziza has found a way to satisfy her parents and conform to her gender role. This story has little overt cultural content, but in setting up the story, Lezra exploits her readers' unarticulated Western stereotypes of the submissive role for women in Arab society.

The setting for "Ahmed and His Uncle" is a village near Fez. Ahmed has gone to live with his uncle Kaddur, a bean dealer, so that he may discover what he wants from life. In this story, like the others, the theme concerns Ahmed's coming of age and finding his place in life. He does so by saving the life of his donkey with his quick thinking. The story's locale is its only specific tie to North Africa. The bean shop is clearly set up as a storehouse where customers choose what they wish to buy without entering the shop, a manner of commerce that is unfamiliar to Westerners, but widespread in the third world. In fact most of the details in all three stories are found in the underdeveloped world. Readers are encouraged to approach these stories by dedicating themselves to finding similarities throughout the world. They are not pushed beyond that early stage of a cross-cultural encounter. Very little of the difference that is unique to North African culture is included. Illustrations do not particularize the places; the characters' dress is never fully described; values are only implied in stereotypical allusions.

A disturbing aspect of these stories is the infantile image given to the adults. In each one, the children display more maturity and intelligence than their elders. Children's writers often employ such a device because it has great appeal for young readers; however, in a context where other perspectives are so limited, the negative impact is pervasive. When our children's impressions of the North African "other" are based on stories such as these, it is understandable that they conclude that these "others" are unequal to adults of their own group and not worthy of the same consideration.

The body of literature for children about the Arabs of North Africa discussed here presents an interesting case for postcolonial interpretation. Can we really claim that the literature here is in fact postcolonial? Does it provide a faithful picture of new nations struggling to establish themselves in the wake of independence? Most of the books I have considered were indeed written well after the end of the colonial period. The perspectives of these European or American authors, sympathetic though they may be, are nevertheless views from the outside, views of the "other." Indeed, the stories seem to have more in common with those written during the colonial period. Much of that literature consisted of travelogues written by tourists whose main concern was to observe the people and places of the world, to get to know the "elsewhere" and the "other." As Mary Louise Pratt observed, those early travel writings created spaces where disparate cultures met, clashed, and grappled with one another, "often in highly asymmetrical relations of domination and subordination" (4). The readers of these books were on a kind of vicarious journey themselves.

In many ways postcolonial books depicting North Africa also fit this genre of the travelogue. Young readers encounter new cultures with much of the same imbalance, in spite of the fact that official colonial rule expired decades ago. The message that North Africa is an exotic place with strange people who have bizarre customs is very strong. Readers may learn facts, but accompanying those facts are circumstances that titillate their imaginations and confirm their notions of cultural superiority. These books present for children a vicarious, first cross-cultural experience of visiting a foreign world. As literature that gives depth and character to the inhabitants of that world, they are less successful. Characterizations of cultural "others" lack sufficient substance for readers to feel they have lived their lives or come to understand anything about their ways. The depictions leave our vicarious visitors stuck in that early stage of culture shock where they focus on the familiar, on how alike children everywhere are. Differences appear at only the most superficial level; the really hard issues like the uneven distribution of wealth, Koranic law, or the role of women in Islamic society are never touched except to reaffirm Western values.

THE WESTERN READER AS "OTHER": A POSTCOLONIAL PERSPECTIVE

It should come as no surprise that so many views of North Africans and Arabs are biased. Children know that this "other" lives in the shadow. Arabs are almost always presented in the context of curious differences and spiteful violence. We live in an era where the words *terrorist* and *Arab* are almost synonymous. Arab terrorism is at the heart of an excellent book for older children, *Captives in a Foreign Land* by Susan Lowry Rardin, presenting the most nearly balanced cultural confrontation of East and West in any of the books I examined and consequently the only literature that I would call postcolonial.

This balance is achieved in part because the plot focuses on the terrorists and their relationship to the hostages. Thus individual characters are portrayed with sensitive, yet foreign, perspectives that allow Western readers to identify with them and sympathize with their dilemma. It is significant that almost without exception these are the most fully developed Arab/North African characters in the books I examined.

Captives in a Foreign Land is a hostage thriller involving Arab terrorists. Six American children are kidnapped in Italy, where their parents are attending a disarmament conference, and transported to a Beduin camp somewhere in North Africa. The terrorists are identified only as Arabs, members of a secret Islamic brotherhood. Their goal is to force the United States to make the first move toward nuclear disarmament. The story is told from the perspective of the children, who must use their ingenuity to cope with their predicament. The hostage-takers are depicted primarily as naive, Western-educated idealists who believe they are promoting world peace. The Beduin tribesmen who hold the children for them are traditionalists who impose their way of life on the captives. However, in both groups individual personalities emerge and forge relationships with the children. It is a strength of the book that these cross-cultural relationships are not stereotyped. The plot includes not only the children's efforts to escape, but their personal growth and development as they persevere and adjust to their new cultural milieu.

The children, four boys and two girls, are treated humanely, but required to follow the local customs of their Beduin hosts. They wear Arab clothing, learn to eat unfamiliar food with their fingers, and try to conform to the code of polite behavior. Despite the differences, they discover value in a way of life so unlike their own. In this cross-cultural confrontation under duress, the children experience the discomfort of being the outsider, the "other" in a world whose rules they neither understand nor accept. They also come to see the shortcomings of their own cultural values. When their captors taunt them about their ignorance of North African geography, history, and people, the children are embarrassed:

"This is awful," said Jessica, her voice tight with frustration. "Assad is right. We *are* ignorant." They looked down at the map, avoiding each other's eyes. Again Matt felt shame, and a returning undertow of helplessness. (133)

In addition, the children's religious beliefs are challenged, and they are forced to acknowledge the validity of that challenge. When Jessica arrogantly, although innocently, asks Assad if he knows about Adam, he responds: "The story of Adam is in the Koran, as in your Bible. Except that the Koran shows Allah forgave Adam for his disobedience and honored him. . . . Because Adam accepted for mankind the responsibility of knowledge. That is a good meaning. It is different from what your religions say. You—Christians and one Jew, yes?—you explain to me why you believe God did not forgive Adam" (76). They cannot provide an answer, nor can they prove that they know the prayers and scriptures of their churches. Even Sidney, who has been preparing for his bar mitzvah, cannot tell Assad the meaning of what he recites. Jessica falls back on an old colonial prejudice to excuse them all, "The way Assad came on, there was no chance to discuss things rationally." But Martha sums up the outcome of their cross-cultural skirmish: "He clobbered us" (80). The children are shown to recognize the value of their captors' point of view. This cultural encounter has the kind of impact that Adler described: "The greatest *shock* in culture shock may be not in the encounter with a foreign culture, but in the confrontation of one's own culture and the ways in which the individual is culture-bound" (34). Rardin uses the experiences of two children especially to demonstrate and interpret the impact of this cultural clash. Their responses, though not identical, are fully consistent with Adler's view of culture shock and its effects. Both profit from their experience, the younger boy particularly adapting to the new culture. Matt is the 15-year-old son of a U. S. senator and is concerned about nuclear proliferation; Steven is the seven-year-old child of a troubled marriage who suffers from asthma and a deep sense of insecurity. As the older, more politically involved boy, Matt feels greater responsibility for the group and also greater frustration at their situation. His observations and insights show the impact of his questioning and learning. The first day the boys are sent out to work, Matt looks around him and wonders "for the first time about the people who really lived in this dead place" (128). Later the same day he is corrected for eating with his left hand: "Matt felt ashamed—and then annoyed. Why be ashamed for breaking a rule he had never been taught?" (129). Matt's response to being corrected is embarrassment and frustration, not unusual for visitors no longer struck by cultural similarities, who are forced to acknowledge and accept the new and unfamiliar. Matt is also able to see that he and Assad share a belief that his father, the senator, can make the world safer. And later he can see and sympathize with the predicament of his captors when he observes, "*We* are the foreign land *he's* lost in. . . . He doesn't know his way out, either" (180). For Matt the experience in captivity is one of personal and political growth. He knows that he has changed when he returns to his family: "I am coming home changed, Dad. You liked what I was. Will you want what you're getting back?" (210).

While Steven is in North Africa, he too grows and matures. He gains physical strength and begins to see himself as a confident, capable boy who can cope with life. He returns a more secure child, able to face the disappointments of his parents' divorce. However, Steven has also had a much deeper cultural experience than the other children. Through his relationship with Bakhit, who was responsible for him on the work crew, Steven found a surrogate father and came to view himself as an Arab boy: "[People from home] would not know him. They would only see a Beduin boy—the stern eyes, shadowed by the kaffiyeh; the strong hands, deceptively thin; the brown legs flashing beneath the robe. . . . They would think, that boy is at home in the wild desert" (187). The children all changed during their captivity; they became more mature and more tolerant. Matt found an independent and meaningful voice from the increased awareness triggered by his cross-cultural experience. However, only Steven's adjustment is so complete that it leaves him ambivalent about leaving when the rescuers arrive. The deaths of Assad, Bakhit, and others leave Matt "stricken" (206), but Steven is disconsolate, "a newly rescued child who could only sob as though his heart would break" (208).

Through these two children, readers themselves encounter an unknown foreign land and individuals who are part of that land. They come to care for them and about them. Many will take the step of questioning their own behaviors and beliefs. Thus the book is a successful cross-cultural experience. In that sense *Captives in a Foreign Land* presents a postcolonial perspective in which the *reader* becomes the "other," both in the sense of being immersed in an unfamiliar cultural setting and in the sense of identifying with a protagonist whose values and ways are different. It is only in the context of a violent plot that the colonial past can be overcome, making it possible for characters to see one another as equally powerful. However, the terrorists' motive—to force the United States to disarm— reveals a continuing acceptance of Western hegemony. Rardin's Arab terrorists die, not for their own nations, or even their own religion, but in an attempt to get the attention of the neo-imperialist power, the United States. Ultimately the power and the authority rest with the West.

The books about North Africa that I have examined display another variety of colonial discourse rather than a bold and independent voice. In these stories, we find familiar themes: an emphasis on an exalted precolonial past, presentation of patronizing information about and surveillance of exotic others, as well as oblique justifications for colonialism. So far the accessible literature about North Africa has not provided a convincing cultural challenge from ordinary, nonviolent Arab others to Western characters and readers. Authentic North African voices articulating and celebrating differences instead of stressing similarities deserve more attention and wider distribution from Western publishers. Stories that protect readers from culture shock deny them access to the learning and enrichment of cross-cultural contact. Less instruction and more experience, even that achieved vicariously through reader identification with well-rounded, authentic characters, will challenge readers' views and values.

NOTES

1. Oberg is credited with first using the term *culture shock* when speaking before the Foreign Service Institute in 1958. His characterization of the phenomenon was that of a disease with a variety of symptoms. Later others adapted the concept and developed it into several paradigms; all share a perception of stages or steps experienced by those attempting to adjust to a new culture or cultures. A good survey of the scholarly literature available can be found in Paul Pederson's *The Five Stages of Culture Shock*.

2. Most Muslims consider representing the human figure to be forbidden by Allah.

WORKS CITED

Adler, Peter. "Culture Shock and the Cross-Cultural Learning Experience." *Toward Internationalism: Readings in Cross-Cultural Communication.* Ed. Louise Fiber Luce and Elise C. Smith. 2nd ed. Cambridge, Mass.: Newbury, 1987. 24–35.

Fanon, Frantz. *The Wretched of the Earth.* New York: Grove, 1963.

Hostetler, Marian. *Fear in Algeria.* Scottsdale, Pa.: Herald, 1979.

Lezra, Giggy. *Mechido, Aziza and Ahmed.* New York: Atheneum, 1969.

Marston, Elsa. *The Cliffs of Cairo.* New York: Beaufort, 1981.

———. "The Middle East and North Africa." *Our Family, Our Friends, Our World.* Ed. Lyn Miller-Lachmann. New Providence, N.J.: Bowker, 1992. 381–416.

Memmi, Albert. *The Colonizer and the Colonized.* 1965. Rpt. Expanded ed. Boston: Beacon, 1991.

Myers, Walter Dean. *Tales of a Dead King.* New York: Morrow, 1983.

Norris, Lloyd. *The Village That Allah Forgot: A Story of Modern Tunisia.* New York: Hastings, 1973.

Oberg, Kalervo. "Culture Shock and the Problems of Adjustment to New Cultural Environments." An edited talk. Foreign Service Institute, Washington, 1958. Cited in Adler.

Pederson, Paul. *The Five Stages of Culture Shock.* Westport, Conn.: Greenwood, 1995.

Pratt, Mary Louise. *Imperial Eye: Travel Writing and Transculturation.* London: Routledge, 1992.

Rardin, Susan Lowry. *Captives in a Foreign Land.* Boston: Houghton, 1984.

9

Beyond Illusion: Lessons of Morality in the Children's Narratives of Chinua Achebe

Karen Patricia Smith

Throughout his career Chinua Achebe has envisioned his responsibility as a writer to be an artistic conduit between the Nigerian people and the outside world, reflecting and illuminating their concerns through his works. These commitments are quite evident in his groundbreaking adult novel, *Things Fall Apart*, and in the other critically acclaimed works that followed: *No Longer at Ease, Arrow of God, A Man of the People*, and *Anthills of the Savannah*, as well as poetry, short stories, and essays.

In his 1995 study of African children's and youth literature, Osayimwense Osa comments that the major activity in the production of children's literature in Africa is currently centered in Nigeria (ix), and that because of his prolific output it is Cyprian Ekwensi who is considered to be the pioneer in the area of young adult literature (1). His study, with the exception of a brief mention of *Chike and the River*, does not discuss Achebe's children's works. In contrast, F. Odun Balogun, in an extended article published in *Journal of Black Studies*, analyzes Achebe's works for children and their similarities to his adult fiction.

While Achebe is not immediately associated with his contributions to Nigerian children's literature, his work in this area, though not prolific, is notable for its inventiveness, dedication to purpose, and concern and respect for children. Despite the appearance of simplicity, his four children's books—*Chike and the River, How the Leopard Got His Claws* (with John Iroaganachi), *The Drum*, and *The Flute*—offer young readers relatively complex and sophisticated narrative techniques designed to foster a sense of moral purpose. This essay specifically explores Achebe's use of fictional narrative and traditional folktales to convey messages to his youthful audience. However, Achebe avoids utilizing his books as mere "tools": his unique abilities as a writer endow these stories with interesting characters, dramatic incident, subtle irony, and a sense of environment. In effect, these works illustrate to young people that an artistically told story can be entertaining as well as instructive, and that it can be utilized to the advantage of both the individual and the group. The present essay examines each of the stories for internal construction, especially Achebe's use of Western narrative structure, biblical references, and the techniques of oral storytelling, relationship to the community, and Achebe's worldview.

PURPOSE AND DIRECTION

Achebe has stated that he wrote his children's narratives to counter the harm done to the younger generation as a result of the damaging European literature that depicted Africans in a negative way. However, the author, expressing his dualism as a result of colonization, sees the need for writing in both Igbo and English. "I can see no situation," he states in *Hopes and Impediments,* "in which I will be presented with a Draconic choice between . . . English and Igbo. For me, no either/or; I insist on both. Which, you might say, makes my life rather difficult and even a little untidy. But I prefer it that way" (61). The Igbo proverb, "If one thing stands, another will stand beside it," has evolved into a basic philosophy for him. While Achebe prefers to write for adults, he feels that it is the responsibility of the writer to provide moral sustenance for children through books: "I did it out of a concern for children because I would have been quite happy doing the adult things. . . . So there definitely was what I call a missionary drive to go and save the children" (Jussawalla and Dasenbrock 78). A sense of community is as much a part of his heritage as the opposing Western viewpoint, that of unabashed individualism. This stance is a direct outcome of oral tradition, growing out of a shared community of linguistic, artistic, social, and political concerns. Achebe has observed that oral tradition is really a complex of everything—all the language arts from fiction to history to politics (Baker and Draper 27). This circumstance is one explanation for the "late" entry of oral cultures into the print media; the influence of the "group" is perceived to be more significant than the needs of the "individual." This theme, the power of community and the manner in which it is negotiated with concerns of the self, is extremely powerful in Achebe's children's stories.

Achebe's dualism as a writer also involves coming to terms with traditional culture and Western civilization. It appears that to at least some degree he might still be working out for himself the rather difficult position of straddling two worlds. The son of Igbo missionary teachers, he attended the Church Mission Society School in Ogidi during his early years and was duly influenced by his upbringing (Swann 1). Yet, while he often alludes to the limiting effects of Christianity within Igbo culture, he stops short of openly condemning all aspects of Western civilization. On the one hand, he illustrates that corruption in Nigerian politics is due, in part, to Western influences, which, once introduced into previously group-oriented societies, is a powerful force that cannot be ignored. On the other hand, he points out that Nigerians were responsible for what happened to them after independence. If Achebe is critical of Western culture in Nigerian social and moral life, he does not absolve the individual who falls victim to temptations, because everyone suffers when corruption invades the human spirit. As we see in his children's narratives, some of Nigeria's difficulties are due to the inability of individuals to come to terms with moral precepts. Achebe states outright what he sees to be the materialistic aspects of Igbo society: "Anyone who has given any thought to our society must be concerned by the brazen materialism one sees all around. I have heard people blame it on Europe. That is utter rubbish. In fact the Nigerian society I know best—the Ibo society—has always been materialistic. This may sound strange because Ibo life had at the same time a strong spiritual dimension—controlled by gods, ancestors, personal spirits or *chi,* and magic. The success of the culture was the balance between the two, the material and the spiritual. But let no one under-rate the material side. A man's position in society was usually determined by his wealth" ("The Role" 11). C. L. Innes quite correctly notes in his comments on Achebe's adult works, such as *Things Fall Apart,* that Achebe's way of using the written word of the colonizers implies a paradox "that non-Christian tradition, its religion and culture, is in part validated for the western or westernized reader by indirect parallels with biblical tales" (35). Although he expresses concern over the use the colonizers made of Christianity to subdue Nigerians, he does not condemn Christianity; instead, he uses Christian symbolism and idiom to convey moral messages to young readers. Christian and Western references thus become an instrument of rhetorical and structural irony in Achebe's work, an irony that might very well have consciously eluded even the author at the time (Balogun, *Tradition and Modernity* 38).

CHIKE AND THE RIVER: A NOVELLA FOR CHILDREN

Chike and the River, Achebe's first excursion into children's literature, is a coming-of-age story in which an 11-year-old boy ventures into the world outside the relative security of his small family and village. Balogun calls it a novella because its format exceeds the scope of a short story, yet it is less than a novel in thematic scope, character development, and the selection and development of details ("Nigerian Folktales" 426). The story shows the attraction and influence of the peer group, the adolescent *need* for the group, and the Igbo tradition of identifying with one's age group.

When it was published in 1966 Nigeria had just lived through the tumult of an Igbo-led civil war. The following year would see the establishment of the Biafran republic. Achebe was strongly involved in the conflict through media-related activities: he had been working for the Nigerian Broadcasting Company since 1954 and was the founding editor of the African Writers Series for Heinemann Education Books in 1962. The political conflict also had an impact on Achebe's personal life. In 1966 his cousin, a military officer, was assassinated in a coup that took place in July. Achebe was soon to become a spokesperson for the Biafran cause, a mission that motivated him to travel throughout Africa, Europe, and North America (Innes xv–xvi).

While the political conflict is not essential to the story of Chike, the narrative reflects the author's interest in and concern for Igbo youth during a time of grow-

ing awareness of the world outside their immediate environment. Chike's travels
may be seen as an extended metaphor for Achebe's concern about the evolving new
order of things in Nigeria. The young boy leaves home in a state of high excitement
and anxiety. He is anxious and curious about what he will find in the town of
Onitsha, about which he has heard marvelous reports. While he is actually going
only a relatively short distance from Umuofia to Onitsha, the trip is a grand and
glorious endeavor, almost a window to the world: "He had heard many wonderful
stories about Onitsha. His uncle's servant, Michael, had told him that there was a
water-tap in the very compound where they lived. Chike said this was impossible
but Michael had sworn to its truth by wetting his first finger on his tongue and
pointing it to the sky. Chike was too thrilled for words" (1). Indeed, Onitsha has an
aura of its own. Located near the historic Niger River, it stands at the crossroads of
activity within Nigeria. A vibrant place where people mingled to trade and exchange
ideas, the city seems to reverberate with dualist overtones, and this is one explanation
for the town's distrust of "single-mindedness." According to David Carroll, it lacks a
well-defined tribal character—it does not have centralized institutions and powerful
chiefs. Instead, the town reflects the individualistic temperament of the people and
the impact of outside influences" (15–16). Gikandi observes: "As a place of exchange,
Onitsha rejects singular meanings; as a historical phenomena, the town stands as
the mark of the cash nexus that dominated the colonial economy, an economic system which weakened traditional Igbo modes of production, and yet sustained
essential mechanisms of this culture, including the extended family" (20). It is
ironic that Chike is going to Onitsha to live with a member of his "extended" family, namely, his uncle, who acts as the vehicle for his leaving Umuofia.

   Chike and the River embodies the ironic tension between the divergent pulls of
Igbo tradition and Western civilization. Within the framework of the fictional
narrative, Achebe infuses short, parable-like episodes intended to teach Chike in
his journey toward maturity, allusions to Western literary models, Christian references, and the African ethos and worldview.

   Achebe places readers outside the action, but involves them in the story through
the dramatic content and engaging characterization of Chike. Upon his arrival in
Onitsha Chike meets Samuel Maduka Obi, or S. M. O., who becomes his best
friend. Samuel quickly adds a "G" to his initials, thus becoming "S.M.O.G.," which
is considered a lucky nickname, since it is short for "Save Me O God," emphasizing
the Christian framework at work in Nigeria. Achebe employs both verbal and
situational irony to advance the story of Chike. For instance, Samuel's appellation,
S.M.O.G., once verbalized, also becomes "SMOG," implying a cloudiness (smoke
and fog) or pollution of the atmosphere. It is through S.M.O.G. that Chike comes
to have many learning experiences, not all of them good ones. Placing the biblical
cry for help ("Save Me O God") within the same framework as "cloudiness or pollution" is also an ironic context, especially when one considers that it is possible to
learn much (be saved) even as one finds one's way through the smog of confusing
experiences. It might even be argued that such an experience provides the *most
effective* learning vehicle.

Chike's arrival in Onitsha is but the start of a chain of possibilities for him, for on the other side of the Niger River is Asaba, and beyond that lies Lagos, the ultimate goal. Barely has Chike arrived in Onitsha when he becomes anxious to get to Asaba, which is for him "A Midsummer Night's Dream." This is no misplaced allusion, since Achebe read *A Midsummer Night's Dream* when he was growing up, and it signifies the impact of the British educational system on the upbringing of Nigerian youth. Further, the story does take place, for the most part, in Onitsha, which is known for its pamphlet literature. In his study of the subject, Emmanuel Obiechina states: "A major influence on the Onitsha pamphlet literature is the school study of English literature by the authors. This influence is expressed in a number of ways, ranging from simple allusion to a clear imitation of titles and content of literary texts. . . . Shakespeare is the principal author from whom popular pamphlet writers take their allusions, plots and occasionally, titles. . . . It is hard to go through a full grammar school or equivalent course of education without familiarity with a number of Shakespeare's plays" (72–73). His learning experiences are entirely consistent with the whims of youth, but inconsistent with what is really good for him. Achebe lets his youthful audience know through action, rather than lecture, that Chike has violated the rules of acceptable behavior. The moral tenets are brought home in a series of dramatic incidents presented in an interesting and artistically appealing fashion. In the chapter ominously entitled "Pride Goeth before a Fall," the audience is warned of near disaster through the use of the biblical reference from Proverbs 16. Certainly, Chike's riding an adult bicycle when he is only a beginner means that he will fall and his pride will be hurt. The inevitable occurs; the bike is almost ruined after Chike's spill. When confronted with the prospect of having to pay for the damage, Chike becomes devious, deliberately leads the irate bicycle owner up and down streets in a "search" for his house. Ultimately, when the angry owner accidentally bumps into a lady, scattering her groceries on the ground, Chike takes advantage of the ensuing confusion and runs off.

Chike's major goal is to get enough money to take the ferry ride to Asaba. In Achebe's view, he spends too much time considering ways of obtaining money to reach this goal. This includes asking a miser for it, as well as attempting to use supernatural means by going to a money doubler. In fact, the latter solution is considered to be such an affront to the work ethic that Achebe has Chike lose the little bit of money he has earned when the money doubler swindles him out of his threepence. The notice on Professor Chandus's door stands as an early warning to the audience:

Professor Chandus
Famous margician, and herbalists
A trial will convinse you. (31)

Of course, Chike neglects to see the warning signs. Indeed we, as the audience, are convinced of the charlatan nature of the "Professor," blatantly announced through the misspellings in his sign, as well as his poor use of English grammar. Achebe employs verse as an instrument of irony to show the duality of modern Nigerians, and it also subtly drives home the moral point.

The insertion of verse into the story also introduces an ironic commentary on Chike's situation. Balogun points out that Achebe's use of verse has nothing to do with traditional Igbo culture but is indicative of the total content of Chike's school education (which is European based) and its irrelevance to life in Nigeria ("Nigerian Folktales" 439). But the verse has specific applications as well. In chapter 6, Chike remembers a poem his teacher had written about a group of boys who had taken "brain pills" from a trader, believing they would become smart. They nearly died from the effects. The format of the poem is intended to be humorous and utilizes the rhythm of the limerick:

> There was a dull boy in our class
> Who swore: "At all costs I must pass."
> He read himself blind
> He cluttered up his mind
> With pills; and was bottom of the class. (19)

This verse foreshadows the trouble awaiting Chike in his desire to cross the river at all cost. Later, in chapter 14, as the mood becomes increasingly serious, Chike, feeling very grown-up at the thought of taking a ferry by himself to Asaba, whistles:

> Leave your wife and join the Army
> One more river to cross;
> One more river, one more river,
> One more river to cross. (46)

Interestingly, once he attempts to move within the adult sphere, the poetry becomes subtly darker. The refrain, "One more river to cross," emphasizes Chike's sense of purpose. Finally, on his way to Asaba, where he will soon discover that the place is vastly overrated, in fact dangerous, Chike whistles the popular children's rhyme, "Row, row, row your boat." Again, we note the use of the "dream" as an image. In fact, Chike discovers that life can be a nightmare. Achebe utilizes the idiom of traditional English rhymes within the Nigerian context to portend disaster through the repetition of "Row, row, row" and then "merrily, merrily, merrily." As Kierkegaard states: "Repetition is reality and it is the seriousness of life. He who wills repetition is matured in seriousness" (quoted in Snead 72). Through repetition, Achebe forecasts the difficulties to follow (which, of course, Chike cannot see), which will far outweigh the simple pranks and mischievous activities he and S.M.O.G. had previously engaged in.

We learn and suffer with Chike when later he is in the strange and alien environment of Asaba at night. Chike has an encounter with thieves and his well-being is seriously threatened. Though he learns too late to avoid discomfort and near danger, he emerges relatively unscathed. He is a young man who has learned the meaning of honesty. Chike redeems himself by exposing the thieves at the end of the story. His ultimate reward, and one that Achebe and any adult will approve of, is not getting a free trip to the exciting city of Lagos, but rather a scholarship to secondary school.

Such incidents in the story act as short parables for learning. While the endings may be predictable, the literary abilities of Achebe allow them to become defining experiences in the life of a very innocent young boy. The river symbolizes the passage of Chike's life as he strives toward acceptance into the group and copes with the pains of growing up. Achebe's ability to integrate Nigerian idioms within the framework of a colonial language displays his skill as an artist.

A LEOPARD, A DOG, AND THE STRUGGLE FOR POWER

In a 1973 essay, "Named for Victoria," in his collection *Morning Yet on Creation Day,* Achebe recounts a rather "unfunny" (as he calls it) inscription on a wall in an Amherst restaurant: "Take care of your boss / The next one may be worse" (124). It symbolized for him the specific struggles of the Biafran people in their attempts to free themselves of colonial oppression, only to be faced with internal upheaval and devastation. In *How the Leopard Got His Claws,* Achebe was experimenting with a picture-book format to offer young people the political lesson to unite in the spirit of cooperation, rather than separate into divergent factions. This fablelike story is, as Balogun points out, also etiological in construction ("Nigerian Folktales" 426). Published in 1972 with John Iroaganachi, two years after the surrender of Biafra, the story is a serious commentary on the state of affairs in Nigeria.

This story clearly straddles three worlds: folk narrative, contemporary Nigerian politics, and the Judeo-Christian context. At the time of its publication the interests of children were of great concern to Achebe. In an interview with the editors of *Parabola,* published in 1992, he recounts his unhappiness with the literature available to young children (his daughter was four years old) and says that *storying* is an important way to express oneself in a difficult and complex world ("If One Thing Stands" 21). Certainly, in *How the Leopard Got His Claws* Achebe uses the format of the animal fable to convey the complexities of the adult world to children, almost pleading that they not repeat the mistakes of their elders.

The opening, "In the beginning . . . ," places the story in a biblical context, when all the animals in the forest got along well and were satisfied with their wise ruler, King Leopard. The dog is quickly introduced as the antagonist. Unlike the other animals, he has sharp teeth, or formidable weapons. At first he is considered the oddity; some gentle jokes are made about the dog using his teeth to clear his farm. While the dog does not immediately retaliate, there is a hint of danger in joking about a potentially dangerous adversary. The dog is an interloper, never part of the group, but watching for his opportunity to take power.

The conflict arises when the animals decide they need a shelter from the rain, a decision that calls for group action. The dog has the most dissenting voice, and confusion follows when he opposes the plan. It is ironic that while the audience sees the potential for the dangers that will ensue, the characters in the story are too naive and caught up in details to perceive that danger. The rules of *storying* tell readers that disaster is imminent, since it is obvious that the group has not reached a unanimous decision. A violent storm sends the animals scurrying into their shelter; the dog enters the shelter uninvited, thus violating a principle of hospitality. A bloody encounter ensues as King Leopard and the dog fight each other. Since the dog has teeth—weapons stronger than those of anyone else—he wins the struggle, and the fickle animals immediately forget about their former leader and proclaim the dog as their new king. The fight between the dog and the leopard echoes the internal strife in Nigeria, especially the Biafran civil war. Toad (appropriately designated) creates a "new song in his praise":

> The dog is great
> The dog is good
> The dog gives us our daily food.
> We love his head, we love his jaws
> We love his feet and all his claws. (29)

The verse is a parody of an old children's verse often recited at the dinner table to offer thanks to God:

> God is great
> And God is good,
> We thank him for our daily food.
> By his hand we must be fed,
> Give us God our daily bread.

Such a parody gives unanticipated "bite" to the poem and offers another example of Achebe's use of irony.[1]

Midway through the story, the deer offers a prayerlike song to the heavens, begging for the return of King Leopard. Three phrases are repeated: "Where are you?" "The worst has happened to us," and "The cruel dog keeps us from [the shelter]" (23). The repetition is powerful and indicative of the African idiom. The cry and the intent behind it are also reminiscent of the Israelites crying out to God for assistance from their enemies in the Old Testament. The italics that accompany this cry for help separate it from the rest of the text, forcing the reader to take special note of it as a text within a text. The poem "Lament of the Deer," written by Christopher Okigbo, a friend of Achebe's who had been killed in 1967 during a military coup, gives further weight to the story as a metaphor for Nigeria's internal struggles and the cry against the injustices of the ruling system. The ellipsis at the end of the last sentence, "The worst has happened to us . . ." indicates that the worst continues to happen.

The leopard's decision to leave the group refers directly to the decision of Biafra to secede from the Nigerian state. Biblical references now shift from Old to New Testament as the leopard becomes almost Christlike in his humble behavior. The animals decide to bring him back forcibly. The act of throwing stones at the leopard serves as a pre-crucifixion scene. As an outcast, the leopard at first bears his pain stoically, but later becomes more and more bitter. In a surprise move, however, the leopard decides, unlike Christ, to bear no more afflictions. He appeals to a blacksmith—a man—for help and gets it in the form of teeth and claws. When he returns to the camp, it is as if a second coming of untold horror has arrived. The leopard, an extended metaphor for the Biafran state, reclaims his territory and leadership of the group by force. The dog, the cast-aside old power, leaves in anger and subsequently teams up with the hunter to kill the animals of the forest.

The story is wonderfully illustrated by Adrienne Kennaway. The facial expressions of the animals are carefully and effectively depicted in vivid watercolors. Closeups of the leopard and the dog depict the strength inherent in both of them, terrible power just waiting to be unleashed. The battle between them is a deathly struggle, mirroring the ideological struggle between the opposing factions of the Nigerian state. Toward the conclusion of the story, the toad tries to compose a song to celebrate the strength and victory of the leopard, thereby attempting to play the role of *griot,* or storyteller. His song is interrupted by a roar from the leopard, indicating that he no longer has any respect for tradition. The accompanying illustration shows the toad leaping into the air in a state of fright, dropping his drum in his haste to escape.

The encounter between the dog and the hunter is memorable: the hunter stands tall and proud and arrogant, while the dog cowers low to the ground. The hunter is a black African, indicating that many in the Nigerian government had been put into power and supported by colonial interests. The dog, in like fashion, offers to be the slave of the hunter and helps him seek out his fellow animals. Achebe emphasizes that this is a most unholy alliance, one that will destroy peace and equilibrium among the animals forever.

In *How the Leopard Got His Claws,* Achebe shows himself to be a master of understatement and irony. G. D. Killam has commented that Achebe's method "is based on allusion and implication which leaves much unsaid and thus his writing achieves a suggestiveness which communicates far more than he might achieve in long passages of explicit description" (11). Nowhere is this more powerfully demonstrated than in this children's fable.

THE DRUM AND *THE FLUTE:* INGENUITY AND MESSAGE

In 1977, five years after the publication of *How the Leopard Got His Claws,* Achebe published the folktale duo of *The Drum* and *The Flute.* The back covers suggest that *The Drum* may have preceded *The Flute.* Achebe experiments with yet another form of children's story, the traditional folktale. While *The Drum* contains more text than *The Flute* and is divided into chapters reminiscent of the structure of *Chike and the River,* the two stories are related in style and context. If *Chike and the River* and *How the Leopard Got His Claws* are placed within Western contexts through literary devices, *The Drum* and *The Flute* reflect Achebe's interest in preserving Igbo oral tradition through the written word. This is one of his strongest literary capabilities. What O. R. Dathorne has said of *Things Fall Apart* applies to these books as well: "Folktales and proverbs which help to give a flavor of authenticity to the writing and the conversations, do not simply exist as anthropological curiosities but are well integrated into the novel. Folktales aid in underscoring the action" (158). Both *The Drum* and *The Flute* evoke the supernatural forces of Igbo tradition. Spirits appear as the result of being visited and/or called up by characters who dare to defy the spirits through individual avarice.

Tortoise, the West African trickster figure, appears prominently in *The Drum.* He is a greedy and selfish character, and even when he is not actively plotting to

take more than his share, his self-seeking motives are never far from his consciousness. In *The Drum*, Tortoise's desire for palm fruits causes him to make two trips
to the spirit world, one by accident and the second on purpose. The setting is
dramatically described by Achebe: "One day Tortoise set out from home in the
early morning in search of wild fruits and berries. By noon the sun was beating
down on the earth without mercy and Tortoise, tired and sweating, had not found
even one berry. As he trudged along the burning footpath, nothing stirred or made
the slightest sound" (3). This may be the only time in the story when we feel any
sympathy for Tortoise. Achebe's prose style, though sparse and economical, makes
readers envision the harshness of the parched land and the desolation of the
environment. Tortoise is a victim of his circumstances. Readers internalize his
hunger: we know that food will be very important and directly related to the building of families and community. Roger D. Abrahams states: "Nothing strains the
web of culture so much as the threat of starvation. We see such matters under constant discussion throughout these [African] tales. Bonds are repeatedly strained or
broken because someone steals food, or because children are neglected when crops
fail. Therefore, no theme is more important or receives more attention, than the
building of families and of friendship ties to provide that strength which, even in
the face of natural disaster or perilous human responses to it, ensures a community's survival" (3–4). As in Achebe's previous children's books, verse and repetition
are effectively used in these books to convey meaning and define structure. In *The
Drum* poetry appears in all but one chapter (chapter 5). On the very first page we
hear the echo of Tortoise's footsteps on the sand: "Aja mbene / Mbe mbene / Aja
mbene" (3). Two pages later the monotonous refrain is repeated when Tortoise
becomes increasingly aggravated and tired of searching for fruit, only this time
with exclamation marks: "Aja mbene! / Mbe mbene! / Aja mbene!" The text tells us
that "The sands grew hotter under his feet. And the sound of his tired walk became
louder and louder in his head" (5). Later, Tortoise curses the land. Somehow readers know that even though he is tired, hot, and hungry and perhaps justified in his
grumbling, he will most certainly pay for his impertinence.

Tortoise's visit to spirit land is fascinating. In his efforts to find a fallen palm
fruit, he digs his way right into spirit territory. The inhabitants appear to be
benign figures. The spirit boy who has accidentally eaten the palm fruit responds
as would any well-behaved young child at being chided by an adult: "I am sorry
sir" (8). This incident is reminiscent of the story of Persephone, who ate the
pomegranate and as a result had to spend six months of every year in the underground world of Hades. Here, however, Tortoise is totally unintimidated by
having arrived accidentally in the spirit world, and he threatens to take the spirit
boy back to his own country.

The drum is given to him as an object of appeasement, or perhaps it is a trap.
A familiarity with folktale structure foreshadows that Tortoise's appetite is insa-
tiable and that he will be driven by greed to return to the land of the spirits. This
he does, although the catalyst is an overzealous elephant who destroys the drum.
When the drum is beaten the first time, it makes an impressive sound:

Kpam putu! kpam putu
Igba nni n' ofe!
Gidi gada! gidi gada!
Aneli nn' anu! (10)

The demonstration is repeated for the benefit of the animals when Tortoise returns to his own country. Once the animals have experienced the power of the drum to bring feasts, they too become greedy and begin to see Tortoise as a savior of sorts. This proves to be a mistake, since the bounty was actually provided by the spirits. The animals chant insistently, rudely demanding to be served:

WE! WANT! OUR! KING!!
WE! WANT! OUR! KING!!
OUR! KING! OF! KINGS! (18)

The state of affairs becomes dangerous, as Achebe subtly lets his audience know, because the animals have gone to excess in their praise: they equate Tortoise with a king and then with "the King of Kings," a direct reference to Christ in the New Testament. Punishment must follow, and it does.

Because his second trip to the spirit world is purposely conniving, the reader knows that Tortoise will get his comeuppance. Indeed, when he breaks the first drum the spirits give him in return for not forcibly taking away their child, we know he will not be given the benefits of a second magic drum, because he tricks the child into eating the palm fruit. Instead, evil demons appear from the second drum and beat Tortoise almost senseless.

But he has already promised the forest animals another magic feast. Rather than be honest with them, he plots to have someone else beat the second drum while he takes cover, thereby allowing the unsuspecting animals to be beaten. The animals are no better than the perpetrator of the hoax: despite the fact that they were at first innocent victims of Tortoise's manipulations, their motives have changed to outright greed; they are willing to sell their souls to anyone for food, and for this they must pay. Achebe concludes the story with: "As for the animals, what they saw that evening has never been fully told. Suffice it to say that they dragged themselves out of Tortoise's compound howling and bleeding. They scattered in every direction of the world and have never yet stopped running" (31). Thus the story is etiological in nature, for Achebe offers us an explanation for why animals are to be found in so many different parts of the world, rather than in one area. The animals pay a stiff price for their behavior when they are attacked by the spirits at the conclusion of the story. Achebe's message to his youthful audience is to be properly thankful for what they receive, never be greedy, and to act in moderation.

Anne R. Nwokoye's illustrations for *The Drum* are exceptionally colorful and dramatic. Particularly noteworthy are the changing expressions of the anthropomorphized sun, who oversees the drama below. The sun is shown on six different occasions, each time bearing a different facial expression, from sour and critical as it surveys the greedy Tortoise; to exasperated as the long-winded Tortoise tells a group of starving animals how he obtained the drum; to smiling in a satisfied manner as the hungry animals eat their first magic feast and then become overzealous in their praise for Tortoise; to dismay as Elephant accidentally breaks the drum by beating it too strongly. By the last illustration, the sun's response is clearly disappointment as it surveys the scene where Tortoise cowers with his wife under a rock in an effort to hide from the enraged spirits. The illustrations not only complement but enrich the text, thereby highlighting the dramatic context.

The spirit figures in *The Flute* are clearly less benign from the start. The plot concerns a young boy who, upon forgetting his flute in the yam fields, returns to retrieve it after dark, when the spirits claim the fields. The boy is challenged by the spirits. They show him several flutes and ask him to select the one that belongs to him. When he does so, they ask the boy to play for them. As in *The Drum*, verse plays a significant role in the structure and meaning of the tale.

> Chief of spirits, undisputed
> Lord by night of this estate!
> Father told me death awaited
> All who wandered here so late.
>
> "Please, my son, please wait
> till morning," cried my mother,
> But her warning fell unheeded.
>
> How could I contain myself
> and sleep till dawn
> When my flute beneath the sky
> Lay forsaken and forlorn? (10)

The sentiment of this Victorian morality poem is pleasing to the spirits; they approve of a boy who is properly contrite, admits to not having listened to his parents, and confesses to his adolescent rashness. At first it might appear that Achebe is valorizing Victorian literary models, which he was obviously exposed to in his schooling. However, upon closer examination one notices that he uses the form as both rhetorical and structural irony. The poem conveys an acceptable message: it is a tool to show his audience that the spirits are looking for evidence of a humble spirit. The spirits are so delighted that they give him the gift of a magic pot. He is permitted to choose between a large and a small one. The boy selects the smaller of the two and is permitted to leave in peace.

Once home, it is discovered that the pot has the wonderful ability to conjure up riches of all kinds, including food. Greed, however, prevails once more in an Achebe tale. It is not long before the senior wife of the family makes her own son go to the farm and *purposely* forget his flute. The boy is rude to the spirits and comments on how they smell. Given the opportunity to select a flute, he chooses one of gold, which is clearly not the one he claims to have lost. Further, he plays a song for the spirits that tells of his disgust for them.

> King of Spirits, he stinks
> Mpf! Mpf!
> Old Spirit, he stinks
> Mpf! Mpf!
> Young Spirit, he stinks

Mpf! Mpf!
Mother Spirit, she stinks
Mpf! Mpf!

Father Spirit, he stinks
Mpf Mpf!
Seven rivers water their town
Mpf! Mpf!
But nobody knows as much as to wash
Mpf! Mpf! (20)

The spirits are silent, but readers sense that such an affront will not go unpunished. When the boy is given the choice of a pot, he chooses the largest one. This time, however, when the pot is broken, "Immediately leprosy, smallpox, yaws and worse diseases without names and every evil and abomination filled the hut and killed the woman and all her children" (24). The story ends on a very dismal note, particularly since the diseases escape from the hut and infiltrate the world outside. This is also an etiological tale and the grimmest of the four children's stories. It bears strong resemblance to the myth of Pandora who, upon opening the forbidden box, allows evils to escape into the world. Where *The Drum* has moments of humor, *The Flute* has none. The very presence of the forbidding spirits in the cover illustration signals a far more dangerous story.

The Flute is also less literary in presentation than *The Drum*, yet it is a powerful tale in its brevity and almost frightening in its unadorned sparseness. It reminds the child audience to be polite, to tell the truth, and to be grateful for what they are given.

CONCLUSION

Through his children's stories Chinua Achebe illustrates his distinct ability to communicate with young persons and to experiment with form and context. While he has indicated that he is most comfortable when writing for adults, he deems it the writer's responsibility to meet the literary and cultural needs of the young. Contemporary critics express concern over didacticism in children's books, and their claims are often justified by an author's condescending attitude toward the child audience. Achebe, however, has created literature with strong moral messages that is at the same time a literature respectful of young persons.

Though three of the four stories are set within the realm of fantasy, they are real nonetheless in their ability to evoke the Nigerian landscape, social and political conditions, and a Nigerian worldview. They have the capability of firing the imagination, while also delivering an identifiable message. They are stories that can also be appreciated by children living in places outside Nigeria. While, as Nancy J. Schmidt has correctly noted, "it is common to decontextualize African folktales to make them easier for Euro-American children to read by removing unfamiliar features of the African sociocultural context and natural environment"

(130), these tales require no such tampering. One can only hope that Achebe and other African writers will continue to furnish the world with these authentic and meaningful tales.

NOTE

1. It must be noted that the text was written by both Achebe and Iroaganachi. It is not indicated which aspects of the tale each author is responsible for. However, Achebe's literary stamp on the story seems clear.

WORKS CITED

Abrahams, Roger D., ed. *African Folktales.* New York: Pantheon, 1983.

Achebe, Chinua. *Anthills of the Savannah.* London: Heinemann, 1987.

———. *Arrow of God.* London: Heinemann, 1964.

———. *Chike and the River.* 1966. Rpt. Nairobi: Heinemann Kenya, 1990.

———. *The Drum.* 1977. Rpt. Enugu: Fourth Dimension, 1979.

———. *The Flute: A Children's Story.* 1977. Rpt. Enugu: Fourth Dimension, 1979.

———. *Hopes and Impediments: Selected Essays.* New York: Doubleday, 1989.

———. *A Man of the People.* London: Heinemann, 1966.

———. "Named for Victoria, Queen of England." *Morning Yet on Creation Day.* Garden City, N.Y.: Anchor-Doubleday, 1975. 115–24.

———. *No Longer at Ease.* 1960. Rpt. London: Heinemann, 1987.

———. "The Role of the Writer in a New Nation." *African Writers on African Writing.* Ed. G. D. Killam. Evanston, Ill.: Northwestern University Press, 1973. 7–13.

———. *Things Fall Apart.* 1958. Rpt. London: Heinemann, 1986.

Achebe, Chinua, and John Iroaganachi. *How the Leopard Got His Claws.* 1972. Rpt. Nairobi: East African, 1976.

Baker, Rob, and Ellen Draper. "If One Thing Stands, Another Will Stand Beside It: An Interview with Chinua Achebe." *Parabola* 17.3 (August 1992): 19–27.

Balogun, F. Odun. "Nigerian Folktales and Children's Stories by Chinua Achebe." *Journal of Black Studies* 20.4 (1990): 426–42.

———. *Tradition and Modernity in the African Short Story: An Introduction to a Literature in Search of Critics.* New York: Greenwood, 1991.

Carroll, David. *Chinua Achebe.* New York: St. Martins, 1980.

Dathorne, O. R. *The Black Mind: A History of African Literature.* Minneapolis: University of Minnesota Press, 1974.

Gikandi, Simon. *Reading Chinua Achebe: Language and Ideology in Fiction.* London: Currey, 1991.

Innes, C. L. *Chinua Achebe.* 1990. Rpt. Cambridge: Cambridge University Press, 1992.

Jussawalla, Feroza, and Reed Way Dasenbrock, eds. "Chinua Achebe." *Interviews with Writers of the Post-Colonial World.* Jackson: University Press of Mississippi, 1992.

Killam, G. D. *The Novels of Chinua Achebe.* New York: Africana, 1969.

Obiechina, Emmanuel. *An African Popular Literature: A Study of Onitsha Market Pamphlets.* Cambridge: Cambridge University Press, 1973.

Osa, Osayimwense. *African Children's and Youth Literature.* New York: Twayne, 1995.

Schmidt, Nancy J. "Resources on African Literature: Children's Literature." *The Teaching of*

African Literature. Ed. Thomas Hale and Richard Priebe. Washington, D.C.: Three Continents/The African Literature Association, 1989. 125–47.

Snead, James A. "Repetition as a Figure of Black Culture." *Black Literature and Literary Theory.* Ed. Henry Louis Gates, Jr. 1984. Rpt. New York and London: Routledge, 1990. 59–79.

Swann, Joseph. "Chinua Achebe." *Contemporary Literary Criticism.* Vol. 75. Detroit: Gale, 1993. 1–31.

Myth of the Golden Age: Journey Tales in African Children's Literature

Michael Scott Joseph

"There's a dim, misty outline of the story that's told so often, of how man once lived in a golden age . . . how that world was lost, and how we some day may be able to get it back again" (Frye 20). Writing *The Educated Imagination,* Northrop Frye calls this outline the "framework of all literature" (21), although his considerations do not extend to children's literature. We may begin addressing the question of how African children's literature of the postcolonial period may be related to Frye's metastory of the loss and eventual return of the golden age by briefly looking at *Nyumba Ya Mumbi: The Gikuyu Creation Myth,* narrated for children by Kariuki Gakuo:

In the evening, when the flocks came home from grazing, the sound of pounding pestles filled the air. The voices of the nine daughters, rich with the melody of grinding grain, carried over the trees and onto the plains. After many moons had gone by, the nine girls grew into beautiful women who rippled with the beauty of the full moon. Their eyes twinkled like stars in the moonlight, while their breasts, full and ripe, stood proud as the dazzling peaks of *Kirinyaga.* Their enchanting laughter was like the sweet chorus of birds and their milky teeth glittered like white doves in flight. When they walked, the melody of the beads around their waists rose to the sky, deep, sombre and enchanting. (19–20)

Thus does Gakuo lyrically evoke bucolic aspects of the golden age: extolling nature, sensuality, labor, and continuity. In Gakuo's poetic depiction, so indistinguishable from nature are the nine daughters of Gikuyu and Mumbi (the original procreative human couple) that their physical endowments are actually interchangeable with natural forces, and their simple activities—such as laughing, grinding grain, or walking—are transposed into a form of music making, both literally and metaphorically harmonizing with their natural surroundings.

The picture of lost perfection drawn by Gakuo occurs fleetingly but persistently in African children's literature, particularly within traditional narratives that evince a preoccupation with ritualistic activities that determine how the golden age dissolves and returns, or mediate the transformation from mythical time to historical time. Traditional African societies—such as the Igbo, Yoruba, Ga, Igede, Dogon, Hausa, Fon, Gikuyu, Bushongo, Shona, Venda, Lovedu, and Asante, among others—have formed the predominant culture of Africa well into modern times. In 1962, Willie E. Abraham speculated that "something like ninety percent of Africa must surely be traditional" and described an "old elite" that dwelled in "a sort of suspended animation in the villages" (301).

The cultural avant-garde, as represented by postcolonial African authors, are significantly influenced by the "old elite," whose myths and legends are widely disseminated as part of traditional African religion, of which John Mbiti writes: "Its influence covers all of life, from before the birth of a person to long after he has died. People find it useful and meaningful in their lives, and therefore they let it spread freely. They teach it informally to their children through conversation, proverbs and myths, as well as through practice" (13–14). The children are directly involved in perpetuating communal traditions, and the oral culture is reiterated.

The nature and significance of ritual activities inhering in the myth of the golden age form the crux of Mircea Eliade's *The Myth of the Eternal Return*, which, in his preface to the 1959 edition, he termed "the most significant of my books" (xv). Eliade's research on myths is seminal to the formulation of his theories on the relationship of the sacred to the profane and the myth of return. What Eliade calls mythical time occurs routinely in African children's literature and forms an essential part of it. Normal time is suspended or radically altered, while characters commune with fabulous beings: spirits, ancestors, supernatural creatures, or gods. Eliade's focal point is the boundary between cosmos and history. A traditional society[1] he says, "tolerate[s] 'history' with difficulty and attempt[s] periodically to abolish it" (36) and to return "to the mythical time of the beginnings of things, to the 'Great Time'" (ix). Accordingly, traditional or archaic societies (as opposed to modern, historical societies) engage themselves in a "ceaseless repetition of gestures initiated by others," in "acts posited *ab origine* by gods, heroes, or ancestors" (5, 6). Far from being merely commemorative reenactments (the insipid period-dress pageants of our own society), these repetitions are believed to be prima facie annulments "of concrete time" (85).

Marriages, feasts, the construction of houses, births, medical treatments, and similarly fundamental activities in African children's literature savor of ritualistic behavior focused on the effacement of time, as do the actions and language of magical beings. Within the rigorously patterned traditional narratives woven into three basic tale types evident in African stories for children—the Dangerous Journey story, the Double Journey story, and the Jealous Stepmother story—time-effacing behaviors play a central and determining role.

THE DANGEROUS JOURNEY: *THE DIAMOND RING*

A typical Dangerous Journey tale, *The Diamond Ring*, by Kenyan author Asenath Bole Odaga, tells of Rapemo, a young boy who one day decides to visit his "grandfather, the great chief, who live[s] many miles away across a wide stretch of thick forest" (7). Protected from the wild animals in the forest by magical charms, at first Rapemo is confident and excited, but soon, lost in "the thickest part of the forest," he becomes very frightened. Roused from "horrible dreams" by "dwarfs" who angrily shout at him to leave their territory, Rapemo proves his innocence, and they finally present him with a horn made from ash to magically ward off "snakes and other reptiles." Straightaway, Rapemo comes to an ominous "high iron gate" that he recalls, just in time, marks the "home of hundreds of large, poisonous snakes, [that] stand straight up on the tips of their tails and . . . reach the sky" (21). Licking the ash wand, Rapemo anxiously hurries away, shuddering at the thought of being "turned into a horrid black snake." He continues down a narrow track, through the "middle country," and, on the seventh day of his journey, arrives safely at his grand-father's house.

Rapemo's wish to see his grandfather is tellingly urgent: Rapemo's grandfather— unnamed and thus incompletely assimilated into the mundane world—is the object of each of the story's first four sentences. If *The Diamond Ring* is a coming-of-age story, then this fundamental, perhaps definitive, act of childhood is essentially about expressing and yielding to the irresistible. Rapemo's fixation on his grandfather— an embodiment of age, wisdom, power, and detachment—corresponds with the initial premise insisted upon by Eliade that traditional societies feel an irresistible need "for a periodical return to the mythical time of the beginnings of things" (ix). The forest Rapemo enters suffices as a context for such a return, as well as its sym-bol. Indeed, symbolizing the return to mythical time is a function forests serve throughout African children's literature. Another element of such a return is the coupling of spatial and temporal displacement to a lessening of personal identity, as is illustrated in the passage describing Rapemo's awakening after his first night in the forest: "when Rapemo awoke, he could not remember where he was or why he was alone. For several minutes he lay still, lost in the shadows of the forest. He did not feel frightened. He was thrilled with the beauty of his surroundings" (13). The dramatic sense of isolation and sensitivity to natural beauty (reminiscent of the Gikuyu golden age) emphasizes that Rapemo's loss of self should be understood as a benign transformation, a liberation. On this point, Eliade notes that traditional societies oppose the "transitoriness" of human identity, finding therein an "individ-uality whose creative spontaneity . . . constitutes the authenticity and [therefore the] irreversibility of history" (46). As he enters the forest, then, Rapemo steps from the inhibiting world of identities into what Alfred Schutz calls "the world of pure ances-tors" (quoted in Masuzawa 170) and initiates a process of reembodying his grand-father's transcendent characteristics.

Rapemo's encounter with the fearsome snakes is the most exciting moment of the first half of his journey, although understanding Odaga's elliptical rendering requires familiarity with African creation stories, which prominently feature snakes. In the Fon creation myth, for example, the serpent preceded the Creator and carried the Creator everywhere in its mouth, with the Creator making the world as it went along (Parrinder 24). Eliade implies links between creation stories such as that of the Fon and ancient Egyptian New Year celebrations when the community reenacted the paradigmatic struggle between the hero Marduk and the cosmic serpent, Tiamat. In Eliade's reading, these primal celebrations constitute rituals of self-renewal, empowering the celebrants to halt the normal flow of time, first by summoning the chaos before Creation—represented by the serpent, Tiamat—then by dispelling it. In dramatizing Marduk's victory, the community would take part in Tiamat's defeat and Marduk's creation of the cosmos from the torn pieces of her body. By this rite, the veritable instant of the Creation—*illo tempore*—would be reenacted (Eliade 56).

The affinity of the ancient Egyptian icon of primordial night with Odaga's vision of "hundreds of large, poisonous snakes" blotting out the day argues for a shared ontology. Rapemo's dread of being "turned into a horrid black snake," consistent with his recollection of his mother's warning to avoid the "large poisonous" snakes, boldly reasserts the story's essential transformative nature and functions. Although to what extent Odaga shares in its meanings is difficult to know, the structure and imagery of the myth remain unchanged.

The story's framing of duration reveals the mythological source of Odaga's tale: Rapemo's journey to his grandfather's cottage lasts seven days, as does his visit. The seven-day visit, framed between Rapemo's twin passages through the forest, repeats the figure of interrupted time—the overshadowing motif of the myth of eternal return—and becomes the occasion for a figurative re-creation of the story as Odaga gives *The Diamond Ring* a "new beginning."

The number seven recurs throughout African children's stories with extraordinary persistence. In "Too Much of Indulgence," by Amos Tutuola, it is the number of gourds that can change night into day and so invigorate the evil spirit; in Chinua Achebe's *The Flute*, seven is the number of rivers the boy must cross to reach the haunted site of his lost flute; in Achebe's *The Drum*, it signifies the number of "giant steps" leading to the spirit world, and the number of "days and nights," as well as rivers and grasslands, that must be traversed to reach it; in Kola Onadipe's *The Magic Land of the Shadows*, the wicked stepmother is punished by seven diminutive spirit women, who, Eumenides-like, pursue and persecute her. These mutually illuminating occurrences seem to be similarly intended to exemplify characteristics of the Creation, such as its fixed, and therefore permanent, duration, and its auratic detachment from the mutability of history, although, of course, the sense of seven as a symbolic figure exceeds any specific function it has as a signifier.

Asked by his grandfather and *grandmother*—whose unpredicated addition conspicuously subverts the story's continuity—why he has attempted such a dangerous trip, Rapemo weaves an apocalyptic tale that only touches upon his journey once, in its brief and sudden conclusion: "The new village was built before I set out on my journey" (27). Rapemo's explanation lacks apparent functionality: it does not advance a basis or motive for his adventure, nor imply its inevitability. Instead, it praises the heroic vision of another newly introduced character, M'Kong, the chief of Rapemo's village, and connects his own leave-taking to M'Kong's construction of the village.

In the chapter entitled "The Regeneration of Time," Eliade asserts "A 'new era' opens with the building of every house" (76), whose foundations must be sunk in *illo tempore*. By replacing the "buildings of sadness and sorrow," M'Kong intends to uproot the lamentable history of the community, just as would happen during the New Year's celebration, and Rapemo's journey serves as a tool of its uprooting. All new constructions must be built above the head of the snake that supports the world, in Hindu lore. A mason drives a wooden peg deep into the earth where the snake's head is divined to rest and thus secures both snake and world; here, at the world's center, the cornerstone of the house is placed. By analogy, Rapemo's anxious encounter with the snakes assumes a magnified importance; not only is it the dramatic high point of his journey, but the journey's express aim. By performing a codified ritual (whose metaphor is the journey), Rapemo will forcefully evoke mythical time, summon and subdue the ebony serpents, and dependably ensure the security of the new village.

Rapemo's grandfather and grandmother accentuate the boldness of Rapemo's quest in their immediate and generous response: "'You're a brave boy,' they tell him over and over again" (27). Such a hearty response may expose the bloodier implications of the self-sacrifice Rapemo's journey involves: construction rituals demanded human sacrifice. According to Eliade, the building of the sacrificial altar "is conceived as the Creation," representing the cosmogonic act, when god "created the cosmos from his own substance" (78). The cosmogonic act, as configured in the sacrificial altar, and in other examples of sacred architecture, symbolically links together the underworld, the earth, and the heavens. Rapemo's journey also links the three worlds: he first descends into the underworld (the thick forest, the dwelling place of the snakes), reemerges from the underworld to earth ("the Middle Country"), and ascends to the heavens, the home of his grandfather (the dislocated "great chief"). The snakes standing "'straight up on the tips of their tails to touch the sky'" are an icon of precisely such a journey.

Rapemo's journey thus "restore[s] the primordial unity, that which existed before the Creation" (Eliade 78). His self-renunciation, revealed by his sense of loss upon waking within the forest and his symbolic descent into the underworld, reenacts God's creation of the cosmos from his own substance. Arranging a sequence in which the Creation (represented in the construction of the sacrificial altar) precedes the moment before the Creation (the sacrifice) ignores the logical order of succession. So does the structure of Rapemo's explanation: "The new village was built before I set out on my journey" (27). As the sacrifice that engendered the cosmogonic act, Rapemo's departure would logically have preceded construction. By once again flouting logical narrative development, Odaga reasserts her story's congruity with the myth of return. As an embodiment of the myth, the Dangerous Journey creates and commences in an atemporal afterlife, evokes primordial chaos, and reenacts the Creation of the cosmos. One vital element of the Creation is the fresh instant in which it occurs, its self-created temporal quality. It is this quality, the undisturbed ripple on a still pond, that is the moment of the golden age.

No matter how the middle of *The Diamond Ring* shifts the premise for Rapemo's journey (in effect abolishing its own history), the suspension of profane time and the reenactment of the cosmogony remain the story's primary theme. Its prevailing concern for the golden age is demonstrated repeatedly, no less at the story's conclusion, in Rapemo's grandfather's plaintive song expressing the collective dismay at the fall into history, which is all the more poignant for its plainness and brevity:

"Those days seem far away now," said his grandfather. "We only had to cultivate a small piece of land to produce enough food to feed the whole family. The land was young and untouched, but now it is old and tired. . . . The strongest of magic does not work as well as before. Life was happier in the olden days. We wanted little. We had plenty of time to enjoy our wealth. We lived and changed with the seasons. If we felt hot, lazy and sleepy in the dry season, we took life easily. When the rains came we felt strong and active and ready to work. (Odaga 51–52)

THE DOUBLE JOURNEY: *THE ADVENTURES OF TORTI*

The plot of the Double Journey, with its self-referential second journey serving as self-parody, makes the ritualistic structure of the Dangerous Journey more apparent. *The Adventures of Torti: Tales from West Africa,* a traditional tale retold by Okechukwu K. Ugorji, begins as Torti the tortoise departs. As in Odaga's story, time ceases when Torti enters "[t]he dense rain forest": "The moon was out that night, and it lit the jungle with authority as Torti wandered. He walked for what seemed like eternity. The more he walked, the more he wanted to walk" (55). Access to the spirit world rewards his persistence, which, in Ugorji's telling, is an otherworldly cliché, consisting of a gate balanced in the mist, an ancient gatekeeper with a "white sheet wrapped around him," whose feet float "about six inches above the ground," and, opening behind him, a sepulchral space "one could not see into or through" (55). Here is the divide between the land of the living and the abode of the dead.

Like Rapemo's quest to "peg down" the serpent's head, Torti's journey to the world's end implies self-sacrifice and is similarly turned to the common good. The spectral gatekeeper, whose powerful voice "roared like an earthquake," dispatches him homeward with a magical drum of gold and leather, which he must never wash.[2] Ugorji highlights the mythic outlines of Torti's journey by having his absence from home extend seven days. As Torti beats upon the magical drum, food pours from it and fills his house. "Bananas, apples, oranges, rice, beans, tomatoes, bread, cassava, yams, and many other delicious foods" (58) materialize an era of plenty. Torti refuses to be crowned king (the preference of the tortoise in other "magic drum" stories, such as Achebe's *The Drum*), but chooses instead to enjoy the peace, the abundance of food, and the good feelings his transport has wrought. Thus the first part of the Double Journey culminates in social renewal, the golden age returned.

The underlying structure of Torti's journey reveals the following seven elements:

1. private or communal suffering
2. provokes heroic quest
3. which *inadvertently* repeats a magical formula
4. in which mythic time is evoked

5. and a passage between dimensions created
6. which results in a boon from the spirit world
7. which ushers in a stable era of plenty: a golden age.

We can easily map this to the ritual myth of the eternal return articulated by Eliade, wherein the passage from chaos to cosmos is reenacted, effacing the historical gap between mythical time and the present moment of perception (79). Eliade identified the following archaic pattern in these myths:

1. calamity, celebration, or intolerance of history
2. requires ritual purification
3. for which the actions of exemplary models are copied
4. by which mythic time is evoked
5. and primordial battle joined
6. wherein the cosmos is recreated
7. and the instant of Creation regenerated.

Clearly the literary infrastructure noted in Torti's story not only resembles but represents the archaic pattern, from which the story derives meaning, force, and coherence.

The parodistic second part of the Double Journey makes this correspondence both more complicated and more plain. What appears to destabilize the relationship between literary infrastructure and archaic pattern actually represents it anew. When Torti finally violates the gatekeeper's admonition never to wash the magic drum, he finds it has lost its potency, and so, without pause, he goes off after another. A second journey (epitomized by Torti's wishful belief in a multiplicity of magical drums) pantomimes the difference between ritual and routine, reducing each of Torti's original virtues to its ridiculous opposite. Rather than approaching the unknown with circumspect fear and self-abasement, Torti behaves complacently. He hails the forbidding gatekeeper with callow and sophomoric smugness. When the gatekeeper calls out, "Who comes there?" Torti impudently replies, "Who is asking?"; then cloyingly, "This is your friend! Torti!" The gatekeeper answers, "The dead have no friends, my son, only beneficiaries" (59). But Torti fails to comprehend the dreadful implication and weakly repeats, "This is Torti!"

He then attempts to deceive the gatekeeper by claiming to have lost the drum, and the gatekeeper rewards him with a seeming replacement that does, indeed, resemble the magical drum but turns out to contain bees and wasps instead of food, which pour out of it "as if they had been waiting for years to be set free." They sting Torti "and his family so badly that their faces swelled beyond recognition" (60), resulting in painful disfigurement. When Torti shares his new drum with the community, the second part of the Double Journey culminates in disaster, the loss of the golden age, and the onset of history.

By repeating the journey framework while reversing its contents (the way a mirror will both preserve and reverse the image it reflects), the parodistic journey emphasizes its importance and its subtlety. But the relationship of the perfected Double Journey framework to the archaic paradigm has altered with the addition of four facets to the original seven:

1. private or communal suffering
2. provokes heroic quest
3. which *inadvertently* repeats a magical formula
4. in which mythic time is evoked
5. and a passage between dimensions created
6. which results in a boon from the spirit world
7. which ushers in a stable era of plenty: a golden age
8. introduction of novelty destabilizes golden age
9. which provokes heroic quest
10. repeats magical formula inaccurately
11. and elicits further suffering.

As the term Double Journey is intended to suggest, structural facets repeat: this synchrony restates, in the most fundamental way, the basic belief that repetition thwarts or annihilates time. According to the above plot outline, the second or doubling encounter with mythical time assumes greater stature and complexity, ending in facet 11, the point at which the spiral of cause and effect seems to culminate, which repeats and deepens facet 8, which is itself a version of facet 1. Interestingly, the second journey's correspondence with previous facets, and hence its structural validation, conceals the fact that facet 11 strays from the progression of derivations immediately preceding it. Its lack of correspondence with facet 4 asserts a kind of syntactic break—a catastrophe structurally demonstrating the kind of catastrophe described by the text. As realized by the Double Journey structure, the dynamic of eternal return (the pattern within the framework) systematically mitigates normal narrative sequencing. As anticipated by Rapemo's puzzling explanation—the midpoint revision—of Odaga's Dangerous Journey narrative subverting the order of time, the sense of the story does not "'begin at the beginning' . . . 'go on till . . . the end: then stop'" (the saturnalian King of Wonderland's simplistic advice), but, rather, it begins in a multiplicity of textual positions and runs in several directions at once, resisting the logic of origination and intentionally subverting the persistence of time.

Inasmuch as the framework of the Double Journey recapitulates the universal myth of eternal return—which, after all, is about ritualistic repetition—the presence of an additional, complex, repetitive structure can be neither accidental nor insignificant. Perhaps its function and its significance may be discussed with reference to the figure of suffering, which—by dint of the various droughts, floods, epidemics, fires, and storms—quietly haunts traditional children's stories. Eliade posits that resolving why people suffer is vital to traditional society, for whom nothing may be absurd or inexplicable (36). Parrinder makes a comparable observation about death in Africa: "death is never natural, but always [ascribed] to the malice of some person" (65). As soon as the sorcerer or the priest can discover who or what is responsible for "causing children or animals to die, drought to continue, rain to increase, game to disappear" (Eliade 98), traditional peoples can begin to accept and endure. Specific instances of suffering, once defined, become part of a rational system, within the scope of which is a primary rationalization for universal suffering, which it necessarily conceals. It would seem a dilemma of traditional societies that they must explain a pernicious phenomenon, the gap obtaining between themselves and "the great time"—what might be compared to the concept of The Fall and the loss of Eden—without counteracting the very point and purpose of their rituals, which is the constant negation of that gap. The additional, mimetic structure that defines the Double Journey both reveals and hides the explanation, positing it as a cause for laughter and hope as well as lament.

Telescoping out of the original representation, the mimetic "doubling" structure details how the sufferings of the community commence with the introduction of a novelty, a fabrication, an unexampled behavior. We might question, with reference to the strapwork-like pattern of the Double Journey, whether a similar deviant act also provoked the suffering that was present at the outset of the story. The omission from the plot structure of a first deviation hints at its anxiety-producing nature, as does its delayed representation within the mimetic projection of the contaminated journey (which safely muffles it within satire and picaresque buffoonery). The dramaturgical designs of story are served, too: the imaginative act of inferring a momentous original event from its reoccurrence mirrors (or re-mirrors) the operation by which the golden age will return, lending such a return the texture of inevitability. This imaginative operation is reinforced by the story's structure as well. By forcing a part of the narrative to substitute for a missing part of itself, the story winds into a circular shape, leaving readers at the story's "end" looking toward another successful quest into mythical time, an annulment of history, and a re-creation of the golden age. The Double Journey acknowledges the intolerable condition of history while intimating an occasion for hope.

THE JEALOUS STEPMOTHER: "THE POT FROM THE RIVER"

Although structurally analogous, the Jealous Stepmother tale modifies the Double Journey by contrasting the behavior of two opposing characters. The first character represents the self-sacrificing hero, such as Rapemo in The Diamond Ring, who establishes a golden age. The second character, venal and contumacious, is the defining agent of the Jealous Stepmother category. The journey the jealous stepmother provokes her child to attempt (or, in some tellings, such as in Onadipe's The Magic Land of the Shadows, attempts herself) bears disastrous consequences because of her disobedience and scorn. As in the Double Journey, the first journey elicits a golden age, the second dispels it; but the Jealous Stepmother goes beyond the Double Journey to introduce death into the world.

In The Great Elephant Bird, Cyprian Ekwensi includes a crisp retelling of the Jealous Stepmother tale, "The Pot from the River." After a man and his two wives discover they have run out of water, they send one of their daughters to fetch a potful from the river. Because "it is forbidden to go for water on an Eke day" (18), she finds her path blocked in turn by various menacing animals: scorpions, snakes, and leopards. To each she chants a song explaining that her mother has authorized the forbidden errand, and the animals allow her to pass. When she comes to the river, her song magically calms the flood tide that rushes "towards her in a terrifying wave" (19). As the wave subsides, two young men appear and, taking her "by either hand . . . lead her into the river, right down into the water" (19). There they remain for six days and nights. "On the morning of the seventh day" they release her, giving her two black pots to carry back home. They warn her of the hazards she will face on her way and how she must break the pots to avoid them.

The girl breaks the first pot, as instructed, avoids the evil entity threatening her, and continues along in safety. When she breaks the second pot, she beholds the lonely forest instantaneously transformed into a thriving community: "more than a hundred men and women, busy at the smithy, making pots, farming and feeding the goats" (20)—the condition of worthwhile labor celebrated by Gakuo and whose loss Odaga laments. When she reaches home, the girl discovers that her mother and father have become "very rich" and "everybody [is] very happy." Thus the first part of the Jealous Stepmother concludes in tranquility.

But Ekwensi's "everybody" does not include the jealous stepmother, who prods her own daughter into repeating the dangerous excursion. This daughter also encounters three waves of adversaries, but unlike her stepsister, to these she "[speaks] rudely, telling them to clear out of her sight" (20). She also is met by the magical young men who lead her down into the river depths, where they detain her until the morning of the seventh day. She is somewhat differently instructed to take a single pot home and to break it only after her mother has swept "the whole place . . . clean." Her mother merely "hastily [sweeps] a few patches in the courtyard" in her eagerness to acquire the wealth she imagines the pot contains. The second part of the Jealous Stepmother ends as the daughter breaks the pot unleashing an epidemic: "Ibos call it *Nchiche*. The disease ate off the noses of mother and daughter" (20).

Several details indicate that the dutiful daughter's behavior describes an invocation of mythical time: her magical incantations suggest what S. H. Hooke terms the *dromenon,* or spoken words and chants, whose "magical efficacy was an essential part of the ritual . . . [to] secure those conditions upon which the life of the community depended" (12–13). That her symbolic death by drowning and her correct reenactment of the supernatural script—an adherence to an exemplary model—are components of the heroic sacrifice is self-evident. The prosperous culture she miraculously manufactures and the inexplicable happiness of her family are therefore minted in the instant of the Creation.

In Hooke's taxonomy of myths,[3] the first part of the Jealous Stepmother suggests a "cult myth" in which a commemoration of the genesis of a specific group—here the descendants of the industrious peoples brought into being by the shattered pot—employs language that signifies the cosmogony. Ekwensi's cultic/cosmogonic symbolism combines with symbolism that connotes childbirth. Eliade acknowledges the correspondence between birth and the sevenfold archaic paradigm: "a new era begins . . . with the consummation of every marriage [and] the birth of every child" (81). The fundamental and complex relationship between childbirth and the Jealous Stepmother is attested in a cognate myth of the Ronga of Mozambique. A girl breaks "her pot on the way to draw water" (Parrinder 68) and magically ascends into heaven, where, after several trials, she is rewarded for her obedience and aptitude by being sent home with riches and a newborn baby. The Ronga myth's birth imagery casts light on the same imagery in Ekwensi's story: the daughter's seclusion, her watery encapsulation, her ability to create a new society (bear life), and, of course, the broken water-pot, an obvious symbol of the amniotic sack that ruptures at the onset of labor.[4] Thus the first part of the Jealous Stepmother ritually celebrates childbirth, implying that the birth of every child repeats the founding of the community in mythical time and restores the golden age.

The second part of the Jealous Stepmother parodies the cosmogonic ritual to give an origin of epidemic or death. In Achebe's *The Flute*, a version of the Jealous Stepmother, epidemic and death dramatically conclude the story. As the jealous stepmother expectantly breaks the magical pot, "leprosy, smallpox, yaws and worse diseases without names and every evil and abomination filled the hut and killed the woman and all her children" (26–27). The horror of such an ending, in marked contrast to the story's breezy tone, signifies how essential an explanation for such disasters is to the life of the story and the culture it inhabits. Achebe's and Ekwensi's stories relate to a family of myths (such as the Pandora's Box myths of Western folklore) told throughout Africa, whose salient characteristic is explaining the origin of death (Parrinder 32, 59). Within the setting of the Jealous Stepmother, the forcefulness of the explanation springs from its congruence with the ritual explanation of the origin of life.

The Pandora's Box element of the Jealous Stepmother imitates the preceding segment of cultic origin and birth by perverting it:

1. personal jealousy and greed
2. provoke a parodistic heroic quest
3. which negatively repeats a magical formula
4. by which mythic time is evoked
5. and a passage between dimensions created
6. which results in a curse from the spirit world
7. which invokes death, the beginning of history, and banishes the golden age.

Thus the introduction of death concludes the Jealous Stepmother story, which began with the Creation of life. But, unlike the Double Journey, the story elements are never integrated: disease, drought, darkness, and death do not eclipse hard-won providence (although to a modern mind death necessarily follows and derives from life); instead, the narratives coexist independently. They are concurrent and dynamically conditioning. The bearing of death into the world reinforces the start of life (or of the cult or of one's family), by formally reenacting (although with other contents) the same archaic paradigm, the ritual myth of return. Just as the structure of the Double Journey represses the terror of a paradigmatic violation, so that it may return, comically transformed, as a symbol of hope, the Jealous Stepmother ensures that the origin of death, because it is cast from the same matrix, echoes and affirms the preeminence of life. For instance, in Onadipe's *The Magic Land of the Shadows*, jealous Taiba's unique punishment for arrogantly disobeying the instructions of the Shadow People results in her premature aging and disappearance. This symbolic overtone of a first death, or lapse into history, reoccurs as gossip, or oral tradition, in "Happily Ever After," the supererogatory chapter: "The town was once again quiet, but for a long time people talked about Taiba and her little women. The people remembered Taiba dressed in rags. They remembered also the little women and their baskets of rags and strings of cowries. They laughed and said that wicked Taiba deserved this punishment" (57). In terms of the structure of archaic mythology, death and history are analogous: both alter, and are alternatives to, the paradisial golden age. Thus the golden age of which the chapter title portends originates in the townspeople's memories of Taiba, whose rags contrast with the protagonist, Ajua's, lovely clothes; whose "little women," with Ajua's helpful Shadow guide; and whose worthless "strings of cowries," with Ajua's precious jewels. Her story, although perverting Ajua's invocation of the golden age, nonetheless becomes subsumed as an aspect of its exemplary source. Upon the example of Taiba, the townspeople can reactualize the golden age.

RITUAL MYTH OF THE ETERNAL RETURN

The three kinds of ritualistic imitation repeated within African children's stories can be differentiated as follows: in the Dangerous Journey, an exemplary model is correctly imitated, constituting an *imitatio dei;* in the second or Double Journey, the imitation of an exemplary model constitutes a mere impersonation. The inadvertency characteristic of original acts, which the authentic *imitatio dei* embodies, is conspicuously lacking in the determinedly self-conscious or impersonative quest which fails to annul time. The third type of ritual imitation, found within the Jealous Stepmother, also inauthentically doubles the heroic quest, but perversely, manifestly deprecating (not merely ineptly copying) the exemplary model. Accordingly, while the impersonative quest fails to recover a transpersonal benefit, the patterned annihilation of the ritual warrants divine retribution of the gravest sort: the introduction of death into the world. However, by dint of its malevolent aspect, the perverted ritual serves to focus attention upon the possibility of a better and fuller way of being. Each of the three types of ritualistic imitation found in African children's literature of the postcolonial period provides the story with its direction and force, and, indeed, each divulges numerous points of correspondence with Eliade's theory of the ritual myth of the eternal return, or with the "framework of all literature," posited by Frye.

The persistence of ritualistic material in postcolonial African children's stories may illuminate attitudes toward childhood as well as suggest relationships between story and growing up or belonging to a community. Ritual, with its built-in system of metaphors and its own stringent grammar and syntax, might provide an excellent introduction to text, serving as an instrument of interpretation, a magical code with which to dissect and arrange: like Marduk, to make sense of the primordial chaos. Perhaps, in contrast to the historical concept of "growing up," the traditional view, as it is embodied in the prevalent myth of the eternal return, identifies a need to rehearse and reverse the process of growth repeatedly: to individuate and surrender one's individuality, to resurrect and defeat the jealous stepmother annually, cyclically, repeatedly—to grow up everlastingly.

NOTES

1. Obviously, the people who produced the texts under discussion are far from traditional, in the monolithically archaic sense Eliade develops. While it resembles actual traditional societies, the traditional society posited in *The Myth of the Eternal Return* serves Eliade as a hermeneutical construct for stabilizing his critique of historicism.

2. This taboo affords an interesting comparison with a New Year's rite mentioned by Arthur Christensen, in *Les Types du premier homme et du premier roi dans l'histoire légendaire des Iraniens, II* (Stockholm, 1917): on the day of Nawroz, God resuscitated the dead "and he gave them back their souls, and he gave his orders to the sky, which shed rain upon them, and thus it is that people have adopted the custom of pouring water on that day" (147). Compare also the taboo against going for water on *Eke* day in "The Pot from the River" as another example of water-taboos in African children's literature.

3. Etiological myths, cult myths, prestige myths, etc., have, for Hooke, a lesser importance, and derive their significance from the "magical efficacy" of ritual myth (12–13).

4. It is tempting to read further birth imagery into the first part of the Jealous Stepmother: the authorized violation of *Eke* day suggests the communal suspension of a sexual taboo; the watery seclusion suggests a period of lying-in; the civilization in the wood suggests the proleptic illumination of a projected future: the girl's posterity within an age of everlasting peace. An obvious rearrangement of elements would illuminate the underlying myth: the tribal mother, herself once an obedient daughter, once undertook, out of dire necessity, a hazardous errand and thereby founded a golden race, presumably the progenitors of those recounting the myth. This would be the ritual myth (comparable to the girl's magical song) with which each expectant mother of the community brought forth her child, reactualizing at the instant of childbirth the parturition of the tribal mother in *illo tempore*. The survival of her child would prove its legitimacy as a child of the Creation.

WORKS CITED

Abraham, Willie E. *The Mind of Africa.* London: Weidenfeld, 1962.

Achebe, Chinua. *The Drum.* 1977. Rpt. Nairobi: Heinemann Kenya, 1988.

——. *The Flute.* 1977. Rpt. Nairobi: Heinemann Kenya, 1990.

Ekwensi, Cyprian. "The Pot from the River." *The Great Elephant Bird.* 1965. Rpt. Nairobi: Heinemann Kenya, 1990. 18–20.

Eliade, Mircea. *The Myth of the Eternal Return: or, Cosmos and History.* Trans. Willard R. Trask. 1949. Princeton, N.J.: Princeton University Press, 1971.

Frye, Northrop. *The Educated Imagination.* Toronto: Canadian Broadcasting Company, 1963.

Gakuo, Kariuki. *Nyumba Ya Mumbi: The Gikuyu Creation Myth.* Nairobi: Jacaranda Designs, 1992.

Hooke, S. H. *Middle Eastern Mythology.* Harmondsworth: Penguin, 1963.

Masuzawa, Tomoko. *In Search of Dreamtime: A Search for the Origin of Religion.* Chicago: University of Chicago Press, 1993.

Mbiti, John. *Introduction to African Religions.* London: Heinemann Educational, 1975.

Odaga, Asenath Bole. *The Diamond Ring.* 1968. Kisumu: Lake Publishers & Enterprises, 1989.

Onadipe, Kola. *The Magic Land of the Shadows.* 1970. Ibadan: African Universities Press, 1990.

Parrinder, Geoffrey. *African Mythology.* New York: Bedrick, 1982.

Tutuola, Amos. "Too Much of Indulgence." *Yoruba Folktales.* Ibadan: Ibadan University Press, 1986. 21–27.

Ugorji, Okechukwu K. *The Adventures of Torti: Tales from West Africa.* Trenton, N.J.: Africa World, 1991.

11

QUEST FOR SELFHOOD: THE FEMALE HERO IN AMOS TUTUOLA'S *THE BRAVE AFRICAN HUNTRESS*

Judy Anne White

The enduring popularity of oral literature, or orature, in the classroom lies partly in its function as a model of psychological development, a model that reflects what Carl Jung calls the process of individuation: the instinctive, lifelong attempt to achieve absolute self-knowledge. The epic or mythic hero—the man who quests, who endures, and who at tale's end reaches a higher level of self-knowledge, or even attains immortality if he dies—has been shown by Erich Neumann, and later by Joseph Campbell, to represent what we might call the "I" figure of ego consciousness. In one Amos Tutuola story after another, the hero, representing the ego or "I" figure, also ventures forth on a quest. He fights monsters or ghosts; he rescues countrymen in danger; he returns triumphant to his town, where he is adored. By meeting challenges, negotiating with entities human, divine, and in-between, and sometimes failing before eventually succeeding, the hero learns something new about his psychic strengths and limitations with each adventure. His journey stands as a metaphorical example of the psychological process of "becoming" through experience. Tutuola's heroic tales engage adolescent readers in order to teach them how to conduct themselves honorably once they become adults.

Tutuola is widely recognized as an authority on Yoruba and other tribal folklore, sometimes grudgingly; his critics often point to his vast knowledge of Yoruba orature when confronting him with the enormous ethical questions that surround the adaptation of traditional orature and the appropriation of characters and motifs for a newly created written work. Of course, the influence of these traditional narratives on Tutuola's writing is unquestioned. Bernth Lindfors, for example, describes the hero of *The Wild Hunter in the Bush of the Ghosts* as "a composite of the most popular folktale protagonists—hunter, magician, trickster, superman, and culture hero" (335). He also notes that the description could certainly apply to any one of Tutuola's protagonists. Lindfors goes on to suggest that Tutuola's most common motifs—especially those with supernatural elements—are grounded in oral tradition as well. Indeed, Tutuola seems to be adept at refor-mulating traditional elements, particularly those that combine the real and the fantastic, into a "modern" tale.

As adolescent boys and girls read these tales, they learn what is acceptable behavior, often because the monsters demonstrate what unacceptable behavior is. More important, they learn that maintaining a sense of honor and developing psychological toughness, and maybe even learning to acknowledge personal weak-ness, are all important skills for a man to grasp if he is to function in this world.

CAN THE MONOMYTH ACCOMMODATE A FEMALE HERO?

Since the hero is traditionally male, it follows that his behavior reflects what is acceptable, even noble, for man. Neumann asserts that "only with the hero myth does the ego really come into its own as the bearer of masculinity" (137). This point is not lost once we begin to consider the hero's actions in light of indivi-duation, for Jung acknowledged in the early years that his theories were based on a male psychological model.

Therein we have the crux of the problem. If the totality of a hero's actions reflect the development of the masculine psyche, then how are we to analyze the totality of the hero's actions when the hero is female? In sum, what are we to do with the female hero Adebisi in Tutuola's *The Brave African Huntress?* What are we to make of the clearly heroic quest she undertakes? Does the story of her adven-tures teach a young woman of her culture how to grow, psychologically, as the tra-ditional epic teaches a man how to function as a male in his culture?

In *The Brave African Huntress,* young Adebisi takes on and completes the ardu-ous task of rescuing her four older brothers from a villainous band of pigmies. On her way to the pigmies' village, she outsmarts or outfights a multitude of manlike monsters and fantastic creatures. As she goes deeper into the jungle, the danger increases: each monster is smarter and less vulnerable than the last. Despite this, Adebisi, relying on her own strength, cleverness, and magic, is able to enter the dark-est part of the jungle and free not only her brothers but also thousands of other cap-tive hunters in the process. She returns home to a hero's welcome and rewards.

Adebisi's adventures may be divided into distinct phases, each of which corre-sponds to stages through which the male hero moves in a traditional epic. Her movement into the deepest, densest part of the jungle is analogous to the tradi-tional hero's temporal movement toward and physical descent into an underworld. Her ordeal in the village of the pigmies and the surrounding jungle initiates her into the mythic or heroic world; and her emergence as a hero and triumphant return mirror that of mythic heroes, who return home secure in themselves. Transpersonally, this pattern constitutes the hero aspect of the monomyth; in per-sonal psychological terms, however, it reflects the process of individuation, which begins as the mature ego comes to realize that inferior or undesirable elements of the personality are emerging, one at a time, from the unconscious, only to appear as projected images in the external world, that is, as a cluster of personal characteristics the ego recognizes in another person. Once the ego accepts that these archetypal images are in fact part of it, it must make peace with that part of its personality. The hero gains his reputation by dispatching these images, which we often call monsters. The process of reintegration, or recognition and confrontation, continues throughout life, ultimately leading to a greater self-understanding.[1]

At the same time, though, Tutuola has invested the narrative with what might be called the persistent consciousness of feminine presence. This manifests itself in two ways: with constant reminders that the heroine's behavior is atypical of her gender, and in repeated confrontations between the heroine and monsters or people who symbolically reflect varying configurations of the construct of masculinity. Adebisi's father finds his little girl's announced intention to rescue her brothers hilarious. Once she reaches adolescence, however, he finds her plan not amusing, but infuriating; he initially denies her permission to go hunting in the Jungle of the Pigmies, announcing that "the hunting profession blong [sic] to men only" (17). In terms of epic convention, weakness or worthlessness sometimes marks the childhood years of the hero; here Adebisi understands her destiny at an early age, yet is discouraged from fulfilling that destiny by her father, who wonders aloud how she can expect to succeed where male hunters have failed.

The villagers, too, are worried by Adebisi's intentions. Though her father has reluctantly agreed to initiate her into the hunting profession, her friends and relatives, aware that she is entering into a man's world, still fear for her safety. And while she tells us that she does not listen to them, as the hunting dress and jujus have made her "wild," she later shows that she is constantly aware that she is perceived in terms of gender. To any monster who confronts her on her way, she either explains or boasts: "I am a huntress on my way to fight in the Jungle of the Pigmies."

Male heroes do not have to defend their decisions to do battle, nor must they prove themselves against an assumptive charge of weakness. But Adebisi must confront a considerable tide of cynicism on the part of her family and village even before her true battles begin; then, once in the jungle, she must reestablish her identity—although she is clearly a hunter, in possession of a shakabullah gun and other hunting equipment—before everyone she meets. This suggests to young female readers that they must be prepared to justify their own actions in the event that they choose other than traditional roles.

Tutuola has also created a consistent dichotomy between Adebisi, as huntress, and the phallically related "other." The numerous ogres she confronts represent another type of primary archetypal image, the Animus, the contrasexual element of the personality—the masculine "other" in the case of Adebisi. Tutuola purposely sets his heroine against a host of masculine images identifiable through their phallic associations.

As hero-ego, then, Adebisi must wrestle with a set of problems unknown to male heroes. This suggests that the trials of the female hero cannot be considered apart from consideration of her gender, and thus intimates that a female hero, in the metaphorical role of hero-ego, undertakes a different kind of journey from that undertaken by her male counterparts. The central question, then, is whether

Adebisi's experiences lead her to confrontations with what Jung terms the Shadow, Animus, and Self archetypes, or whether a new pattern of egotic-archetypal conflict emerges within the conventional epic frame established by Tutuola.

ADEBISI'S HEROIC JOURNEY: OVERCOMING THE PHALLIC "OTHER"

The first supernatural being Adebisi encounters indeed seems to serve as a Shadow-figure, an archetype that functions as a reflection of the dark side of the host personality. Its characteristics are derivative of both personally undesirable and socially unacceptable personality traits. Odara, the "cyclops-like figure" (25) confronted by Adebisi, proves to be childlike and impulsive, a challenge to the heroine only because she does not yet realize how strong or clever she is.

Odara is at once humanoid and animalistic. He is tall and hirsute and covered with knots and scars. While his followers speak, he shouts; although he wears trousers adorned with cowries, those shells are full of rotten blood and the feathers of birds he has killed. On his shoulder he carries a bag of poisonous cudgels, his only weapons. Adebisi's encounter with him, though frightening, barely taxes her physical or psychic strength; it does, however, allow her to see how self-destructive infantile, bullying behavior can be, and thus sends her on the metaphorical road to maturity.

Odara's behavior reflects that of the immature warrior. He is human enough to be wearing trousers, yet cannot articulate his threats or desires. His only mode of communication is a "great fearful shout" (27), a mode that here can be considered preverbal. He runs about through the jungle trying to catch all the warriors at once; Adebisi comments that "he had forgotten that a person who chases two rats at a time would lose all" (30). The ogre's actions reflect both an indiscriminate lust for conquest and an ignorance of any societally determined rules for engaging in combat. And as Adebisi herself relates, Odara's greed ultimately sinks him, literally; though he has captured one man, perhaps for his dinner, he is so intent on capturing more that he follows the other hunters in the jungle heedlessly over a narrow stick that is serving as a footbridge across a river and falls into the river when the stick breaks under his weight. Like that of Beowulf's adversary Grendel, who functions as an anti-warrior and shows the tale's audience all that a warrior should not be, Odara's behavior suggests that he represents the infantile self—a self-centered, demanding "I" that perceives everyone and everything in the world to exist only to fulfill his needs. And for a young, unproven warrior, his image is a perfect Shadow image.

Adebisi's actions and reactions imitate Odara's behavior in one sense. For what seems like hours, she runs aimlessly from one hiding place to another, planning no attack, depending on the randomness of Odara's movements to carry him away from her and toward the other hunters. She, too, shouts, although she clearly states that she shouts for assistance from the others. Through magical intervention, neither can harm the other with a weapon. While the two are physical opposites, in intention and action they are in fact very similar.

There is a suggestion that Adebisi is learning how not to engage in combat, how *not* to engage in a hunt. Until she realizes that action is necessary for her survival, she allows her intense fear to control her: her uncontrollable shaking in her hiding place atop a tree draws Odara's eye; and her running and shouting make her an easy target. She survives only because Odara himself is unfocused in his pursuit. For much of the time, she has no focus or intention; she relies on instinct rather than advice or intellect.

After an initial period of inaction, Adebisi does show that she can be prepared, that she has the ability to act in the face of fear. Poisons from Odara's cudgels do not injure her because she has taken juju before she left home. At one point, she says, she does not think about where and how she is running, and runs zigzag through the trees. She also takes care to keep her gun, her hunting bag, and the cudgels she collects with her, so that she is prepared to face the next challenge. Her final action, throwing cudgels back at Odara so he cannot clamber up on the bank, shows both that she is perceptive in her assessment of a potentially dangerous situation and that she has at last found the courage to attack. In facing the Shadow, Adebisi proves that she has potential to be a great hunter.

After Adebisi's encounter with the ogre, she follows the surviving hunters to their town, the Ibembe town. There she encounters a much more dangerous creature than Odara—a giant half-human, half-bird, who breaks through the roofs of the houses and carries people away. She greets the villagers and the king of the town, both of whom are curious about her profession. Her arrival gives the reader of the tale a chance to see exactly how much psychological strength she has gained through her encounter with Odara.

As the hunters are taking Adebisi to meet their king, a host of villagers emerge from their houses and follow her, asking one another, "Is this a young lady huntress?" (32). She says that they were filled with wonder, as they had never heard of a female huntress. The king also asks her the question, and her response is notable: "Yes," she says; "I am a brave lady who is a huntress" (32). At this point, she is not boasting, but taking ownership of these new or genuine feelings; the hero-ego she represents has been strengthened through her experience with the ogre. The villagers, suspicious of the stranger, are unable to fathom the existence of a female hunter, and so turn on her. As one, they inform her that if she is a huntress, she must be "a wicked lady who would turn into a witch in future" (33). Adebisi remains undaunted by the villagers' collective judgment and unmoved by either the king's attempts to intimidate her or to change her mind through flattery. Her psychological strength, here suggested both by her determination not to be dissuaded from her mission and her focus on it, will help her to survive the next hunt or the next battle.

The semibird, as Adebisi calls him, is lethal in a way that Odara was not; the half-human bird monster pierces people to death with a supernaturally long, sharp beak. He is focused in his attacks, targeting specific houses—those in which lights were burning or people conversing—and carrying off their inhabitants. In contrast to the ogre, who was master of a land uninhabited by humans, the semibird, in terrorizing the town, takes control of a unit of human society and disrupts the daily lives of the villagers. He also threatens to disrupt the social order by undermining the power of the king and his chiefs. The creature provides a greater challenge than did Odara, yet also provides the opportunity for Adebisi to develop her hero skills more fully.

The bird also speaks: he tries but fails to frighten Adebisi with outrageous claims about his origins and his invincibility. The ritualized boast is a complex and conventional means of either announcing one's intention to fight or engaging an enemy in combat. As a hero, Adebisi immediately recognizes the exaggerated nature of the boast; she responds with one of her own. The bird, unaccustomed to the challenge, decides to attack.

This time, Adebisi begins to understand how fear can work for her. She first shoots the diving semibird with her gun, but all this does is keep the bird from carrying her away. She is alarmed, then, but not paralyzed, nor made witless by fear; she decides to use the cudgels she has taken from Odara. She finds that the cudgels, which are part of the same supernatural world as the bird, rob the creature of the ability to fly. And although she is once again frightened by the immediacy of the bird's presence, she gathers courage and stamina to wrestle the creature, beating him meanwhile with the second cudgel. The fight lasts for two hours until the bird finally dies.

There is also a sense that Adebisi has come to understand the variables involved in fighting. There are changes in weapon, from gun to cudgel; changes in venue, from the air to the ground; changes in method, from a targeted attack to a wrestling match. Through all of this, Adebisi remains determined and aggressive. These qualities, which she is developing through her experiences, will serve her well in the Jungle of the Pigmies.

The semibird is also discernible as a Shadow-figure. Like Adebisi, he is a dangerous foe, focused and confident in his abilities, but also in his identity, as his boasts suggest. The process through which he decimates the village is more complex than the process by which Odara protected his territory; at the same time, the process through which Adebisi defeats the beast is also more complex than that which she used in Odara's defeat. The question of whether Adebisi must adopt a masculine stance, or *persona*, comes into focus here; creature and human assault each other with phallic weapons. The bird pierces Adebisi again and again with beak and with thorny wings; the hero, in turn, beats the creature with a clublike cudgel. The stakes have been raised for the young hero; in turn, she learns more about her own strengths.

Clearly, Adebisi encounters this second Shadow-figure on a more complex level; but a second set of archetypal images—Animus-figures—yet awaits her. The first Animus-figure will engage her abilities in more enigmatic ways than either creature she has defeated thus far.

After leaving the Ibembe town, Adebisi takes her direction from a "juju-compass" given her by her father; within a day she comes within sight of the Jungle of the Pigmies. First, however, she has to confront the gatekeeper of the jungle. He is strangely squat and muscular, with arms "thick at about two feet diametre" (50) and a head so large he could literally butt another creature to death. He is further distinguished by a long beard. He is a pigmy, yet his appearance suggests that he has been touched by the supernatural.

The gatekeeper initially presents a distinctively psychological challenge to Adebisi. "Who are you?" he immediately asks upon seeing her coming down the road. "Where are you going?" (50). When she states her purpose and destination in a quavering voice, he responds with this paradoxical statement: "All right," the gate-keeper says, "come and lay your head on this rock and let me cut it off. You do not need yourself or the rest part of your body [sic] but your head" (50). Certainly, this statement is chilling in its matter-of-fact cruelty, but when considering it in metaphorical terms, it is clear that the creature's statement carries an important message for Adebisi. The intellect—the head—is the central concern of the ogre; he seems to be saying that Adebisi's survival will depend not on her physical strength, but her mental strength and intelligence. This is borne out by his subsequent action.

The pigmy seems to hypnotize the young hero, at least temporarily. "Willing or not," she states, "I was first going to him as he commanded me." His control here depends not on his physical strength, but on a combination of his intimidation and her fascination with him. After yielding briefly to the creature's influence, Adebisi finds that her fear is stronger than his will, that it sets in motion a mental process through which she reclaims her identity and courage and moves toward confrontation. She begins to focus on the purpose of her journey: to rescue her lost brothers and bring them back to their parents. At this point, her bravery returns and she considers that, as a huntress deemed powerless by the pigmy, she will be able to succeed in taking him by surprise. She steps forward and asks to be granted passage into the jungle.

The pigmy is no different from many of the other humans in the tale. As Adebisi expects, he fails to take her seriously. In a scene eerily similar to that played out between the child Adebisi and her father, the pigmy "simply bursted into a great laughter and he said—'I believe you don't know where you are yet. To open this gate for you or what do you say now?'" (52). He proves the hero right; she has been observing his arrogance and has recognized it as the source of his weakness—thereafter, he can only lose the battle to her.

Even so, the pigmy turns out to be a far more formidable opponent than any Adebisi has encountered thus far. He tries to beat her with the massive cudgel he carries about; he nearly crushes her to death with his bare hands; he holds her high above his head and dashes her onto a rock. Only a bizarre occurrence—Adebisi's foot getting tangled in the pigmy's beard—leads to her eventual victory. She is able to climb a tree with the pigmy hanging from her leg, and to hang on until the pigmy drops to the ground, his head and neck injured. She then jumps down and beats him until she is sure he is dead.

The gatekeeper represents a particularly aggressive masculine archetype, and a single aspect of the Animus. Several of the signs and symbols of masculinity figure prominently in Tutuola's description of the pigmy: his oversized head, thick, hirsute body, and prominent beard, the thickness of which leads to his downfall; his Svengali-like means of controlling by intimidation; his arrogance, which is a hard-edged version of Adebisi's father's failure to take her seriously; even the bludgeon he carries, a "heavy cudgel with a big round head" (51). He is not interested in a fair fight, but in total control and domination. His behavior toward Adebisi is a twisted variation on courting behavior, and it can even be said that his physical relationship to her, that is, her becoming entwined in his beard and literally bound to him, is what results in his death. This particular Animus-image might be called the Seducer.

As Adebisi makes her way through the Jungle of the Pigmies, she encounters a series of human and supernatural creatures who also represent various aspects of the Animus image. The first one she meets, a pigmy she calls "obstacle," has as his occupation the capture and detainment of any hunter who comes into the jungle. He wrestles with her until she becomes exhausted and then cuts her left foot off before she can get away. This act is especially disturbing because Adebisi describes the effect the mutilation had upon her: "When he cut it off I fell down at once and I was crying loudly for pain . . . at last when I could no longer bear the pain I shouted greatly for help because I believed . . . I might die" (63). Even more disturbing, though, is the pigmy's reaction; he stands over her laughing for at least half an hour—laughing like the ogre she met earlier and like the father she left behind.

The act of cutting off a body part, especially one of the extremities, is often symbolic of castration. However, it usually involves the hero's decapitation of a monster. Here the tables are turned, and this is an important clue to the relationship between the pigmy and the female hero. It is clear that he is, as Adebisi says, "the keeper of the jungle," and that his job includes following the masculine imperative of territorial domination and the punishment or bringing into submission of the transgressor. No act other than castration so completely symbolizes total domination; no other act so completely strips a man of identity. But the female hero, Adebisi, cannot be castrated physically; so the Animus-figure, who might be called the "Land-Guard," performs the symbolic act in order to establish his dominance.

This makes even more sense when the reader realizes that "obstacle" eventually reattaches Adebisi's foot so that she can walk into town with him. It then becomes clear that his intent is neither to kill her nor to maim her permanently, but to show her how powerful he is. When she is finally able to kill him by shooting him in the head, she is reestablishing her control over herself and her own life. This episode contains an important lesson for the young women who might read this story; it functions as a warning that a woman must be vigilant against unwarranted intrusion, literal or figurative, by a male who is threatened by her very presence, for such a man may wish to wrest control of a woman's life away from her.

An animal that represents yet another aspect of the Animus-figure emerges as Adebisi continues her journey. Several days after she kills "obstacle," she finds herself confronted by a strange and wonderful "super-animal" that resembles a woolly mammoth. "It was as big as an elephant," recalls Adebisi, with a beard "that covered his chest and belly as well" (66). He also had horns "long and thick as cows' horns" standing upright—symbolically phallic—in a cluster on his forehead. But his most amazing characteristics are his eyes; they shine as if they were torches or lamps. Adebisi uses physical strength and mental agility to subdue him, despite his size.

And when she is sure he is dead, she decapitates him; cleans out the skull, leaving the eyes intact and trimming the horns; and puts the skull over her own head, using it both as a helmet and a light. As she did earlier with Odara, she strips the dead creature of symbolically masculine objects—here the creature's eyes—and takes them as her own.

Why are these shining eyes associated with masculinity? The answer is that light is associated with consciousness; and in transpersonal terms, in myths and religions throughout the world, such a light is attributed to specifically masculine consciousness. In the Bible, for example, God is "the Light"; in Greek mythology, Apollo, not Diana, is associated with the sun; in Egyptian mythology, Ra, not Isis, is the Sun deity. In the creation episode of the monomyth, when the World Parents split, the World Father becomes one with the sky, light, and consciousness, while the World Mother becomes one with the earth and its enclosing darkness. Thus does Adebisi take on the masculinity associated with light when she puts on the head with the illuminating eyes.

The last otherworldly being the hero confronts drags her literally into the heart of the Jungle of the Pigmies, the pigmies' town. The pigmy who captures Adebisi is notable for the way he justifies his taking her prisoner. To him, Adebisi is a thief, intent upon taking all the animals from the jungle by killing them. At first he seems to resemble Odara, who is obsessed with protecting his territory; but it is clear that this pigmy is a more complex, more sophisticated version of the ogre and of "obstacle." In fact, he seems to be a combination of the two earlier Animus-figures, but with a prominent feminine cast.

Paramount in this episode are the moral ambiguities of the pigmy's words and actions. Adebisi relates that the pigmy visited a host of sadistic punishments upon her, all the while claiming his moral imperative to do so: "As he was following me along and flogging me repeatedly, it was so he was shouting horribly on me— 'Thief! thief! thief! I catch you today!'" (77). Later, she says, the more she begged for mercy, the more severe her punishment became. It is hardly surprising that she felt she would be dead within a few days' time.

Yet the pigmy is also notable for his outsized navel, five feet in diameter, which hangs in front of him as a second belly might do. On a transpersonal level, the navel is widely associated with the innermost part, or the origin of the world— and with the earth mother. The size of the pigmy's navel is also suggestive of this association, since an oversized belly is associated with pregnancy. The suggestion that the pigmy is androgynous becomes even more plausible after considering Adebisi's description of her trek into town with the pigmy: "Uncountable of wild animals . . . were full along this road . . . when they saw that it was this pigmy who was pushing me along, they would not do anything to me" (78). The overbearing, protective character, human or otherwise, who protects the hero from immediate external danger only to harm him at a later time is usually female; Grendel's mother does this to Beowulf. Indeed, Jung states that it is woman, not another man, who is man's "greatest danger" (9, ii: 24). In addition, the fact that the pigmy wants to protect the animals from Adebisi's gun suggests that he wants to preserve a balance in the jungle—a balance between nature and humans, and even between killing indiscriminately and killing for food. Of course, it is woman, not man, who is part of the earth and of nature. A particularly androgynous figure, the sadistic pigmy provides evidence that a female hero might encounter an Anima-figure, in a positive or negative light, as well as an Animus-figure.

The culmination of the hero's journey usually involves a confrontation with the Self archetype, a confrontation that leads to the reconciliation of all the disparate elements of the personality, both conscious and unconscious. Confrontation with the Self, or the archetype of wholeness, also involves taking an honest accounting of one's strengths and limitations. The hero may recognize his own physical or mental weaknesses during a moment of self-reflection; but more often, he comes to terms with these in the course of his last battle and his return home. What is interesting is that Adebisi as hero-ego does not meet a projection of the Self archetype in her travels, but instead experiences the emergence of the archetype within her own psyche.

Adebisi's struggle to emerge as whole begins with her capture and confinement in the pigmies' town, in a huge prisonlike building she calls "custody." There she is shoved into cramped quarters with thousands of other hunters, all of whom have been given up for dead by their families back in their respective towns. There she experiences several changes of identity which, taken together, indicate that the hero-ego she represents has undertaken the reconciliation of opposites.

First, Adebisi endures the horrifying experience of being branded. The stern pigmy, who had already beaten and whipped her earlier, now finds it a satisfying task to hold the hero's arms while the chief brands the captured thief's face with the sign of three Xs. Scarification often reflects either the accomplishments associated with initiation or adult status in society. Here it causes a physical transformation, in the sense that Adebisi will never look the same, nor have the same psychological perspective as she had before the experience. The branding also binds her to the other captives, creating a bond that in fact connects her to their collective past. This ordeal is merely the first in a series of transformations that symbolize Adebisi's encounter with the Self.

When Adebisi has spent some days in the custody, doing hard labor and trying to avoid getting beaten, the chief keeper sends for her. He gives her a position as servant and housekeeper, in effect rescuing her from the work yard. None of the pigmies knows Adebisi is female. Thus, as the healthiest and best-dressed captive, "he" is brought in to work. After months and months of having others qualify her hunting abilities, and her thinking abilities to a lesser extent, because she is female, Adebisi finds herself in a position where her work is appreciated without qualification, and both her cleverness and sense of humor are valued. This proves beneficial as she regains enough confidence in her abilities to create a plan by which she will be able to destroy the town. Metaphorically speaking, what she experiences here is a reconciliation of male and female characteristics; she dresses as a man, is treated as a male servant, yet claims her individual sense of self as a woman.

The next part of her transformation involves the principle of rebirth. Just as the traditional epic hero is sometimes brought close to death in battle, yet lives on, transformed by the experience itself and encouraged by the brief nod toward immortality, Adebisi's experience in the chief keeper's office leads to a different kind of rebirth.

When the keeper discovers Adebisi sampling liquor from his cabinet, his rage overcomes him immediately, and he throws her out of the room, causing her to hit her head on the stone floor. He then rings for his assistants and orders them to take her and beat her to death. As they carry her back to the custody, she concocts a plan to avoid further torture: she pretends she is dead. "When I stopped to breathe," Adebisi recalls, "these pesters thought that I was already dead on the way to the custody and by that they did not attempt to beat me" (93). They throw her into a mass grave and go back to the custody; no one witnesses her escape. "I stood up and thanked God greatly," the hero comments, "for I came out of this custody safely" (93).

Adebisi's figurative suicide is reminiscent of narrower escapes experienced by male epic heroes. She "dies" paradoxically, in order to preserve her life, in the same way that a male hero dies and in the process gains a heroic reputation that lives on in legend. At the same time, though, her "death" also causes a rebirth, a literal arising from the grave, and a figurative reclaiming of heroic purpose. This transformation also suggests that Adebisi's encounter with the Self is a result of her own experiences.

Adebisi's greatest act is to set the town aflame, liberating the captives in the process. Eventually, she finds her brothers, all of whom have managed to survive their years of captivity. They return to the town, where a party is held in their honor. Adebisi sells the precious metals she has collected in the jungle and begins a new life as a rich woman. Adebisi's heroism becomes the stuff of folklore, as the tale itself reveals.

THE FEMALE HERO: SOURCE AND BENEFICIARY OF HER INNER STRENGTH

For the female hero, Adebisi, there is a pattern of psychological development similar to those of male heroes. There are a few differences, however. First, the contrasexual presence is a constant in every encounter the hero-ego has with an enemy, even though the contrasexual archetype—the Animus—may himself only appear once or twice. In addition, the female hero is faced with the dilemma of whether or not to take on some of the trappings of the masculine world in which she functions. It should also be said that the female hero is challenged in a way the male hero is not: she must constantly reassert her twin identity, as woman and hero together, or else be discounted as a hero.

The world through which Adebisi journeys is not a peaceful one, yet she accomplishes the task she has set out to perform. If the female reader can look at the hero's journey as instructive, she might conclude that although the matter of gender is always present, a clever woman who is willing to take risks will always find the means through which she can satisfy the urge toward further growth. This is an especially vital message for adolescent female readers, who must take to heart the following premises: the world is male and appears hostile to women largely because of its "otherness"; that world may seek to relieve a woman of the responsibility of achievement and thus discourage her from reaching her goals; a woman can be successful if she looks to herself as both source and beneficiary of her own inner strength.

NOTE

1. The "outline" or potential form of each archetypal image is universal and reflects a basic human instinctual process or relationship; the fleshing-out or completion of that image is personal and derives from the experience of the individual. In all cases, however, the host personality, of which the egotic "I" is the conscious center, evolves throughout life from childhood to old age and in the process seeks to answer a number of questions. "Who am I?" it might ask in early adulthood. "Why am I here?" is its concern as it reaches midlife. And as it reaches old age and prepares for death, it may ask itself "How well have I lived my life?" Every person instinctively embarks upon the quest to know himself or herself completely and does not relinquish it until death intervenes.

REFERENCES

Campbell, Joseph. *The Hero with a Thousand Faces*. 2nd ed. Princeton, N.J.: Princeton University Press, 1968.

Collins, Harold R. *Amos Tutuola*. New York: Twayne, 1969.

Jung, Carl G. *The Collected Works of Carl Jung*. Trans. R. F. C. Hull. Princeton, N.J.: Princeton University Press, 1953–71.

Lindfors, Bernth. "Amos Tutuola." *Dictionary of Literary Biography 125*. Detroit: Gale Research, 1993. 332–46.

Monick, Eugene. *Phallos: Sacred Image of the Masculine*. Toronto: Inner City, 1987.

Neumann, Erich. *The Origins and History of Consciousness*. Bollingen Series 42. Princeton, N.J.: Princeton University Press, 1973.

Robertson, Robin. *C. G. Jung and the Archetypes of the Collective Unconscious*. New York: Lang, 1987.

Tutuola, Amos. *The Brave African Huntress*. New York: Grove, 1970.

———. *The Wild Hunter in the Bush of the Ghosts*. New York: Grove, 1970.

———. *Yoruba Folktales*. Ibadan, Nigeria: Ibadan University Press, 1973.

Walker, Steven F. *Jung and the Jungians on Myth*. New York: Garland, 1995.

12

Stories of Passage, Stories of Crossings: Trends in South African Youth Literature from 1990 to 1995

Miki Flockemann

It has become common practice to identify landmarks to "measure" the extent to which South Africa has transformed itself since the first democratic election held in April 1994. A useful landmark for looking at developments in the literature produced for children and more particularly young adults is the period following Nelson Mandela's release from prison in 1990 to postelection. However, the state of publishing and readership for youth literature should be seen against what librarians, critics, cultural theorists, and writers have said the literature "should" do and what it has been doing in the past, in order to gauge whether there have been any discernible changes. To avoid simplifying the complex appropriations and transformations in a period of political and social transition, it is necessary to situate this discussion in the context of broader cultural processes. Three anecdotes concerning writers whose work is aimed at a young (and adult) audience indicate the diversity of voices and positions characterizing some of the material that is currently being written, performed, heard, and read.

During a recent radio talk show about storytelling, Gcina Mhlophe, writer, playwright, and performer, spoke about radio as a powerful medium for reaching audiences in both rural and urban locations, suggesting a syncretism of oral traditions and media technology. A listener urged Mhlophe to keep telling "pure" traditional African stories, untainted by "modern ideas," and this points to the debate on maintaining African traditions in an urban setting. As the following anecdote suggests, traditional African stories will gradually, one hopes, become part of a South African heterogeneous urban culture. Claiming that she is on a mission to familiarize African children with their heritage by telling stories that involve characters that come from the continent, like Nkonjane the bird or Ufudokazi the tortoise, Mhlophe described the response she encountered when visiting an integrated school in a suburb of Johannesburg: "I was amazed, I was performing at a school . . . and I started singing, (sings) *"Ylitye likantunjambini alivulwa ngabantu, livulwe yizi nkonjane"* (Nobody can open the stone but the bird), those children started singing with me, all four, five hundred of them. I was so pleased. And this is a mixed school. So yes, the message is getting through. There are some children who are really beginning to be in touch with where they are." Another perspective on a rather different aspect of South Africa's heritage was offered at a panel discussion on literature for children and young adults, "Transforming South Africa: The Power of Imaginative Writing."[1] Commenting on the difficulty participants had with visualizing the future in their writing, a delegate suggested that part of moving forward is moving back into the past. For instance, Dianne Case read an extract from her young adult novel, *92 Queen's Road,* set in the 1960s. The extract describes an incident where the six-year-old narrator strays onto an uncrowded "white's only" beach, where she plays with another girl until she is chased away by the girl's red-faced father: "'And you children get away from here,' he roared glaring directly at me. 'You coloureds have your own beach. Go on! Shoo!' he said, and gave me a shove with his foot" (45). The personal trauma that results from this racist encounter has a profound effect on the child: "I . . . wanted to plunge myself into the surf and sink to the depths of the ocean and emerge again—cleansed of this coloured-thing—white as snow" (47). Case explained that she chose to read this extract because it is important not to gloss over the personal cost of apartheid and its long-reaching effects, particularly on children and families. Postelection does not yet mean postapartheid.

Case's anecdote reveals the need to confront the past. As cultural theorist Neville Alexander argued in a radio program on racism, South Africans must talk frankly about the details of racial prejudice on a deeply personal level before they can attempt to participate in a nonracial society. The fact that today black and white children play together on that same beach in Cape Town does not undo the obscenity of the past when they were prohibited from doing so. At the same time, it could be suggested that the anecdote is revealing in another way, for before the ubiquitous "father" came and separated them, the children were playing together—unconsciously—as if in preparation for a nonracial future.

A very different response to the past was suggested by Marguerite Poland, a prolific and well-known writer whose stories range from historical romance for teenagers to re-creations of stories of San origin for children. In doing research for her novel *Shades,* she visited a mission station to retrace her family's history, which included an ancestor who was involved in labor recruitment practices in the nineteenth century. Here, in 1990 she encountered a returned political exile who had come to the mission, just as she had done, to pay his respects to his "ancestral shades"—no doubt victims of those very labor recruitment practices. On discovering the names of her ancestor and his placed side by side in the mission's baptismal register dated 1890, she interpreted this fortuitous meeting as a reconciliatory one. These anecdotes by Case and Poland should be seen in the context of current debates in the media on reconciliation and the establishment of a Truth Commission that will expose the crimes of the past. Mhlophe's anecdote, in contrast, indicates a shift from the previously expressed concern that an emphasis on traditional African folktales bought into ideologies of racial and ethnic difference, and that this helped to maintain the apartheid policy of cultural separation (see Jenkins, *Children* 23). At the same time, a healthy trend is emerging in that more South African texts are gradually being introduced into schools where previously the curriculum had been strongly Eurocentric. The fact that local writers are interested in using other media such as radio and television, graphic novels, cartoons, and theater will go some way toward overcoming the inequities of the past. Moreover, the different situations from which writers like Mhlophe, Case, and Poland speak are indicative of the diversity that marks the terrain at present; this very multiplicity of voices is appropriate and indeed necessary for a literature produced during a transitional period.

ADOLESCENT LITERATURE

As adolescence is itself a transitional phase, it follows that literature for and about adolescents produced over the past five years could be seen as a barometer for some of the social and political changes taking place during this time. There appears to be a discernible shift from a cautionary critical discourse about what youth literature ought to represent to a more hesitant, descriptive attitude toward what is emerging in the postelection phase, and how this is articulated with the processes of political transformation. For instance, at the first national symposium on children's literature, held in 1987 at the University of the Western Cape, Manana Nhlanhla referred to the need for "a form of correctional literature in which women are not given inferior roles and blacks are no longer reflected as subordinates, nameless, poor, aggressive" (164). Beverley Jansen asked that "writers should prepare our children for a class free South Africa" (92), while Andree-Jeanne Tötemeyer, who has done important work on racist stereotyping in South African literature for children, claimed: "It is time a new kind of children's book emerged, to meet the challenge of a new, nonracial South Africa, in which inter-personal and inter-racial understanding, will, we hope, prevail" ("Towards Interracial" 87). Despite the fact that the new curriculum for a unitary education system is not yet in place, it is fair to say that a new kind of youth literature is gradually emerging.

In a recent report in the *Mail & Guardian*, Phillippa Garson comments on the flood of books for young adults that are being "churned out" by local (predominantly white) writers, dealing with the social and political issues confronting contemporary South African teenagers. She quotes two researchers on the contemporary young adult novel in South Africa, Ann Smith and Claudia Mitchell, who argue that young adult novels should receive more attention from academics for the way they "explore issues of identity-formation and the process of 'becoming' [thus playing a] unique role both in terms of the South African literary arena and in terms of social change within the country" (quoted in Garson, "More Than Just" 3).

One of the features of the "new kind" of youth literature has been a shift from a corrective to an interventionist strategy. Referring to work produced in the period leading up to the election in April 1994, Denise Newfield comments, "Writing about the sensitive and crucial issue of racism is particularly difficult in this interregnum as, all about us, rampantly racist behaviour is evident, even though anti-racism has ostensibly become hegemonic" (39). However, the work she describes being done by, for instance, the Storyteller group, who write cartoon material based on future (nonracial) situations of "what can be," suggests a shift from a corrective role to what is described as "effective intervention," where the aim is to "impose competence" using the forms of popular culture that young people are familiar with: "The promotion of reading, concern for the environment, and the theme of social reconstruction are all major ideals. Propagation of these ideals does not take the form of protest or strident assertion, but the matter-of-fact presentation of a non-racial world which is then naturalized" (58). This is a far cry from aspects of South African juvenile literature predating 1990, which Tötemeyer described as symptomatic of various "syndromes," such as the "avoidance syndrome," where racial problems are ignored; the "dehistorisizing syndrome," in which historical events are seen from a white perspective; or the "apartheid syndrome," where "the dissolution of interracial friendships through educational (separate schools), social and economic segregation, is accepted without criticism" ("Racism" 174–75). More recently, in his book on South African children's literature, Elwyn Jenkins has claimed that while "some youth novelists have young people explore the historical aetiology of apartheid . . . [and capitalism]," and "show concern for the processes of victimization as well as for the victims themselves," these texts still fail to deal with political transformation (*Children* 150). Commenting on the paucity of nonrealist, nonlinear narratives, he continues that, with some exceptions, local writers on the whole cannot manage "confronting the handling of change in the centre of consciousness" (150). Could it be argued that part of this "failure of the imagination"[2] is the result of having no clear picture of the future during the interregnum? Is this vision of the future any clearer now? What about the observation made by Karen Press, herself a writer and publisher, that while white authors are increasingly looking at black experience, "what is not being written about is what it is like to be 'me' in an ordinary black environment" (quoted in Garson, "More Than Just" 3).

CROSSINGS: NEW TRENDS IN YOUNG ADULT FICTION

A useful point of departure for discussion of some of these questions is offered by a recently published anthology of stories appropriately titled *Crossing Over: Stories for a New South Africa*, published in March 1995 and aimed mainly, but not exclusively, at a young adult readership (with a teacher's guide also available). The compilers, Linda Rode and Jakes Gerwel, asked for stories that dealt with the experience of young people entering adulthood in the new democracy, to be submitted in any of the South African languages. Interestingly, all the entries were in English or Afrikaans, by writers from a variety of cultural backgrounds. Significantly, only one of the stories used a nonrealist style, and one can speculate that more experimental nonmimetic modes, including fantasy, might become more prominent in the future, as the grip of the past begins to loosen.

In view of the multiplicity of voices characterizing the transitional period, this anthology seems aptly suited for a discussion of the development of trends in writing for young adults. However, as the cover jacket claims that the anthology "should appeal as much to older readers as to young adults," one can identify several features more commonly associated with adult than young adult fiction. How, for instance, are the generally recurring themes of adolescent literature adapted to the South African condition, namely, "changing bodies and the initiation of sexual exploration, the push and pull of family relationships, the search for a coherent identity in thought and deed and the desire for a functional morality" (Weiner and Stein 134)? In her discussion of debates around the definition of what constitutes young adult literature as a genre, Isabelle Holland argues that it is important to keep the boundaries of young adult literature fluid, for "I think today's adolescent deals with his and her multiple and (to me) bewildering options by receiving them . . . on different levels" (35). This comment is interesting because this anthology manages, in its attempt to be representative, to give voice to just such a fluidity and incorporates a multiplicity of levels in terms of intended audience. The contributors include well-known writers for children and young adults and those publishing for the first time. As Gerwel points out in his foreword, the anthology "bears the stamp of the transition to a democratic South Africa"; the liberating effects of this event extend far beyond the obviously political.[3]

The title of the anthology indicates a shift from "stories of passage" describing the initiation or entry into adulthood (a common theme of the literature of the interregnum),[4] to stories that are concerned with what I term "crossings." In other words, there is a shift from a focus on an entry into adulthood to an emphasis on crossing boundaries, real or perceived. "Entry into" suggests moving into a determined socialized space, whereas "crossing over" or beyond suggests a more fluid transgressing or bridging of established boundaries. Stories of passage, then, are associated with works set in the "old South Africa," whereas stories of crossings are suggestive of the new. As suggested in Gerwel's foreword to *Crossing Over*, there is a strong emphasis on the way political processes impinge on personal relationships. While several of the stories in the anthology recall the abuses of the old enemy, the apartheid regime, others expose a new and pervasive enemy, crime. This is a subject that much preoccupies South African society at large in this transitional phase as expectations are not met and unemployment rates are high.

In choosing a selection of stories from *Crossing Over* to discuss trends in young adult fiction, some questions need to be asked. How do these texts relate to prevailing discourses of identity including cultural and gender identity? Or, as Gerwel puts it, how do they present "a window on the worlds of others?" What strategies are used to deal with the issues of reconciliation and the past? How does this anthology provide "a fresh outlook on all cultures" as well as a fresh outlook on the future, which Sylvia Engdahl describes as a distinctive feature of young adult fiction (42)? How is this literature related to oral traditions and popular culture, if one takes the view that "people are born into a world—into a culture—which is not a 'heritage,' a culture that did not exist twenty years ago" (Stevenson 115–16)? Finally, how do these stories, read in relation to one another, approximate the fluidity of the adolescent condition, and to what extent does this represent a significant aspect of a South African literature in transition? Here it might be useful to look at two recurring features in the anthology: first, the use of the child's perspective as narrative strategy; and second, the exploration of youthful cross-cultural relationships.

NARRATING VOICES

One of the most striking aspects of the anthology is the way "differences" are transgressed in the adoption of voices that move across the writers' own class, gender, and race situations in their choice of narrative point of view. Significantly, the number of male contributors still outnumbers female by a small margin, fifteen to eleven, though of these only four are white males. However, for obvious historical reasons only three are black women.[5] Of course there is nothing new in such an appropriation of the voice of others, but while in the past this has often been seen as another form of colonization—particularly when white writers attempted to speak for blacks—more recently this "transgression" has been interpreted differently. For example, when Njabulo Ndebele was asked why he adopted the voice of a woman in his story "Death of a Son," he replied that this was a deliberate attempt on his part to put himself in the situation of an "other," seeing this as part of a broader project of attempting to understand whether blacks can speak about whites, and vice versa.[6] Identification with others has been described as an important aspect of young adult literature. Youth educators have used the adolescent reader's tendency to identify strongly with fictional characters as a strategy for challenging a variety of cultural stereotypes, using a technique called "hot-seating," where the students are placed in the position of one of the characters and have to "speak for them" (see Naidoo 106). While there is undoubtedly a need for more black writers to describe black youth experience "from within" (such as found in adult fiction by writers like Njabulo Ndebele, Mbulelo Mzamane, Miriam Tlali, and Ahmed Essop), these crossings of voice should also be seen as an integral part of the processes of political transformation.

A recurring motif in the stories is the common trope in young adult literature of the adolescent's preoccupation with a growing awareness of "self" as distinct from family and community. Frequently, this manifests itself in a sense of not belonging, of being an outsider, and a concomitant urge to escape perceived family constraints. Kenneth Parker suggests that white South African fiction tends to focus on the individual, whereas in black writing the individual is seen in relation to community (quoted in Jenkins, *Children* 126–27). Generally speaking, in young adult fiction being an "outsider" and the urge to "escape" are seen as part of a process of initiation or learning, a transition from childhood to adolescence or adult society. However, the child protagonist's sense of alienation and urge for escape can also serve as a critique of adult society, and it will be interesting to compare the stories in terms of closure. Moreover, when comparing the use of a male or female child as narrating consciousness, some interesting differences emerge.

Both Kaizer Nyatsumba's "Streets of Hillbrow, Here I Come" and Michael Williams's "Red Sports Car" use an angry young township boy as narrating consciousness. There is a suggestion in both stories that the child's anger, which is directed at the parents, is deflected from the "real" political and historical source or target that is beyond the child's control. This deflection of anger has become a cause of concern for social workers in black communities. In Nyatsumba's story the child, perhaps appropriately named Justice, is furious with his parents for their decision to divorce and for their attempts to make him choose to live with one of them. When asked a question in court about his parents, with childlike but shocking intensity he claims of his mother: "I hate her. I hate her with all my life" (139). Speaking directly to the reader he says, "I know you will probably not take me seriously, and dismiss me as an angry twelve year old who has yet to experience life. Just like my former parents did. But I tell you. I will never trust anybody again for as long as I live" (138). This outburst gives voice to an aspect of black experience not often spoken about. The story does not present the child as helpless victim, but allows Justice to voice his anger at the familial disintegration that has disrupted his world. Justice also shows that he can hurt his parents in turn when he refuses to choose between them and opts for life on the streets of Hillbrow. "I came out of that court swearing. I was determined to embarrass my former parents. I swore louder whenever we came near people as we walked out of the court building" (141). He refers to his "former parents," as he calls them, by their first names to indicate his rejection of their rights over him, and more seriously (in terms of traditional values) his kinship relation to them. However, the reason for his anger is that his parents have destroyed his comfortable childhood securities: he longs to return to times when they called each other "lovie," attended soccer matches as a (nuclear) family, wearing their Orlando Pirates tracksuits, or watched videos at home. There is a suggestion that the breakup of the parents' marriage is caused by the pressures of middle-class aspirations. Ironically, the reason for his escape to the streets of Hillbrow, Johannesburg, is not political oppression, violence, or neglect as is often the case, yet it is a neglect of a new sort. The story focuses on the effects of urbanization and upward social mobility on African family life. Like Huck Finn before him, he drops out of "this world controlled by adults. Adults with experience who understand *nothing*" (145).

In contrast, the narrator in Michael Williams's "Red Sports Car" directs his anger at his mother, not at the womanizing Mr. Nzule. He describes his rage in self-dramatizingly physical terms as he "escapes" by jumping out of a window: "I want to be tossed and bruised and feel the cut of the stones and broken bottles that litter the roadway as I hit the earth" (1). The use of the present tense here captures the "inner life" of the child and encourages identification with his emotional turmoil. As is typical of the genre, the child articulates his feelings by projecting them onto material objects that cause physical pain, like "broken bottles," thereby externalizing his sense of confusion. We note the apparently contradictory desire for "lots of money," which is merged with an existential longing to be "beyond everything, naked, skinned and dead." After a near accident with a red sports car, he goes to a bathroom and observes himself dispassionately in the mirror. Looking into the mirror does not provide a reassuring sense of identity, and he plans an escape through the bathroom window. However, the sound of music intervenes and he hovers between flight and music: "I could run. I could. But then I hurry to wash the dust from my face and listen to the music. The window will be there later" (4). This decision results in his being chosen to join the rehearsals, and the suggestion is that he has entered a new phase of his life. Unlike Nyatsumba's story, his initiation results not in a rejection of the adult world, but an articulation with it through the activities of song and dance.

The way the two boys respond to cultural forms, popular and traditional, is significant: these appear to provide a sense of identity that the mirror does not. When the boy in "Red Sports Car" first hears the music, he does not know the songs, "but the music is familiar" (4). For his audition he sings "The Sorrow That Is Soweto," which turns into the highstepping toyi-toyi dance usually associated with political defiance; however, here it becomes a transformative action. He says, "I feel my anger turn to joy as we chant and bounce to the rhythm of the toyi-toyi," the "we" indicating a newfound sense of community (5). In Nyatsumba's story, however, Justice "mirrors" his behavior in court on the popular American television program *L.A. Law* when he skillfully evades the lawyer's questions (140). The ending of Nyatsumba's story suggests that it is aimed more at an adult than a youthful audience, for, as VanderStaay and Jenkins point out, in young adult fiction, serious subjects (like street children) do not generally end in such "bitter triumph" (VanderStaay 49; Jenkins, "Letters" 17). The ending to Williams's "Red Sports Car," where the boy's anger is transformed through the communal activity of music and performance, offers a more conventional closure.

In two stories using the voice of a young girl, by Miriam Tlali (whose work has received considerable attention) and Riana Scheepers, it seems significant that the focus is on a mistrust of men, rather than adults or parents per se. While the child's experience in Tlali's story is mediated through a reflective adult narrator, Scheepers employs the immediacy of the child's own experience as narrative strategy, providing an apparently naive account that is then interpreted by the reader rather than the narrator. Tlali's story, "A Second Look," concerns the young child's first recognition of the fallibility of adults, when, on her deathbed, her grandmother suggests that her son might ransack her house looking for money after her death. This is a traumatic moment for the child: "in that short time, I had ceased to be the 'baby' I had been all my life. My Nkhono's [grandmother's] illness had ushered me, very painfully, into the world of profound uncertainties and the fear of the selfishness of others" (136). However, in a coda to the story, we discover that the grandmother's suspicions were unfounded, and the protagonist's faith in her beloved uncle is restored. The story of initiation becomes a story of "rehabilitation" in that Tlali is at pains to emphasize the sense of tradition and community within which the child's values are shaped; this is achieved by code-switching between English and Sotho, with proverbial expressions being used to describe African kinship relations. Far from being an outsider, as seen in the stories by Nyatsumba and Williams, here the narrator experiences a sense of "belonging" in the extended family. However, the story does not romanticize the complex—and for women often oppressive—relationships in the extended family structure, for we learn that the grandmother's suspicion of her son results from her experience of living in a "sea of males": "She grew up to understand and feel the pain of being taken for granted, of being expected to bear burdens and suffer in silence, and to be at the service of others who very rarely appreciated it" (133). This observation gains significance when we are told later that she spent long hours away "working in the homes of whites" (134), and again there is a sense of deflected anger, from "whites" to "males" to her own son.

Deborah McDowell has suggested that one of the characteristic differences in quest stories written by black men and women is that the male's quest frequently takes him "underground," a consequence of his engagement with (white) society on a social and political level, whereas the black woman's quest is primarily a personal one of self-discovery, not one of conflict with hegemonic culture (166). It is possible that the different ways in which the young male and female protagonists respond to their parents here are related to their culturally and gender-determined position in South African society. It is important to note that while in Tlali's story the narrator is recalling the way traditional African family structures operate, Nyatsumba's story is set in the present and deals with the dissolution of some of these values with the emergence of a new class of educated and upwardly mobile black South Africans.

Another aspect of the generational relationship is explored in Riana Scheepers's story "Garden-Gate Green, Privy-Pink, Back-Door Blue," originally written in Afrikaans, dealing with a white working-class family. Here the child narrator, perhaps unconsciously, reveals how her grief at the father's death in a mining accident is channeled into anger directed at her mother's suitors, whom she deliberately drives away. When the mother finally adapts to the absence of the father, not by replacing him with another man, but by appropriating some of the tasks he used to perform, the story suggests an entry into a new adulthood, no longer dominated by the absent father/husband. In fact, the shift to a new order is symbolized by the way the father's paint is used to "transform" and re-color the pantry and privy in unexpected shades. "'Right,' said my mother as we admired our new pantry, both of us tired and spattered with paint. 'Now we can get on with our lives again'" (150).

It would be interesting to trace how descriptions of generational conflict in South African literature will become indicative of broader social processes in the future. Will there be a change from the primarily hostile relationship between children and parents to the kind of "sisterhood" and rehabilitation suggested by Scheepers and Tlali? Gloria Blatt suggests that the negative and often stereotypical portrayal of parents in youth literature fulfills young adults' psychological need for independence as they prepare to break away from home (77). While Blatt is, of course, referring to the Western-style nuclear family, this lends an interesting perspective to Nyatsumba's story. When turning one's attention from narrative strategies to the theme of entry into adulthood through cross-cultural relationships, it becomes clear that the stories in *Crossing Over* represent some of the recent trends in the politics of race and identity.

EXPLORATIONS OF YOUTHFUL CROSS-CULTURAL RELATIONSHIPS

Rudine Sims Bishop identifies four different types of text dealing with interracial relations: first, those that are consciously interracial, intended for a multicultural audience; second, those that represent people of different cultures as interchangeable, thus universalizing these differences; third, those that represent distinct groups, where integration is not the focus; and fourth, those that focus on the effects of racism and discrimination (24). It is important to distinguish between these different representations as applied to centers such as the United Kingdom or the United States, where the first two models would be seen as symptomatic of a melting-pot ideology and would be read in terms of debates on multiculturalism. However, in South Africa an economically and politically powerful minority has been dominant over the majority of South Africans, and an emphasis on ethnic and cultural difference has been viewed with some suspicion as a legacy of apartheid ideology. In the anthology the first two models outlined by Sims Bishop often overlap, while the second and third models (generally harmonizing cultural and ethnic differences in specific communities) are more common for illustrated children's literature being produced at present. This does not privilege one model over another; rather, it provides a dialogue within which to read these representations of cross-cultural relationships. Though the subject is dealt with predominantly by white writers, who dominate the field at present, one can safely assume that different perspectives will be offered in new writing by other South African authors in the future.

Three stories by well-known writers for children and young adults—Dianne Hofmeyr's "The Magic Man," Jenny Hobbs's "Two Fishermen," and Barrie Hough's "The Journey"—represent relationships that include a stillborn child, a thwarted potential relationship, and one that is about to begin. The dialogue that is established when reading the stories in relation to each other suggests a complex negotiation between present, past, and future, as well as between stories of passage and stories of crossing referred to earlier. Significantly, the familiar and usually tragic trope of miscegenation common to serious South African literature is replaced by an emphasis on cross-cultural love stories aimed at a teenage market. As Phillippa Garson puts it, "The times are surely a-changing when the pervasive theme in the latest novels to appear on recommended reading lists for South African teenagers is cross-cultural love" ("Cross-Cultural" 6).

In all three stories the cross-cultural relationship involves not only a sexual or potentially sexual relationship, but also focuses on "voice" and speech in interestingly different ways. For instance, in Hofmeyr's story the mute magic man becomes the agent whereby the young woman can finally tell the "truth" to herself (and the readers) about her stillborn baby, when she shows him a photographic record of her past: "her mother standing in her pink OK Bazaars uniform and the flowered doek [headscarf] in front of the farmhouse with the farmer and his wife and the farmer's son" (70). In another blurred photograph, the son is "smiling into the camera as only he could smile" (70), and these pictures provide a subtext that enables the reader to interpret this as yet another tale of miscegenation, but told from a new angle, for until this moment we have not been made aware of her "colored" status. Whereas the other woman is usually silenced or punished, as in Nadine Gordimer's prototypal story "Country Lovers," in Hofmeyr's story she is able to "share her story," and this becomes a liberating experience when she drops the baby clothes out of the window, and then "step[s] back and close[s] the window firmly" (72). There is a suggestion that the past must be faced before new relationships can be entered into. What attracts her to the magic man is not only his tricksterlike ability to create illusions but more especially his muteness, which paradoxically enables her to speak.

In Jenny Hobbs's "Two Fishermen," a schoolgirl experiences a newfound sense of unease within the close-knit family unit during a seaside holiday with her parents. She is attracted to a fisherman, whom she watches from a distance but cannot approach. The implication is that apartheid social taboos force her into a traumatic sexual awakening with the wrong man. One day she is attacked by a son of family friends, and as she runs weeping from her attacker, she encounters the fisherman again. He speaks to her for the first time, resulting in her acute awareness of missed opportunity.

The question of speech also plays a significant role in Barrie Hough's story "The Journey," but here it is the black adolescent girl who teaches the white boy to overcome his speech impediment; in teaching him to speak, she rehabilitates him literally and figuratively. Thembi and Johan meet when they attend the same model C (partially integrated) school. Thembi is the daughter of a doctor in Botswana, and thus an outsider. Significantly, it is Johan's speech impediment that makes him sensitive to Thembi and to the way other children treat her: "Early on in life, Johan had learnt to read this 'quiet' language—from the time he knew his speech was different to that of other children" (64). Here again speech becomes associated, as in other stories, with dominant hegemonies. Unlike Johan, Thembi is articulate. She becomes chairperson of the debating society, and her ability to code-switch between Setswana ("which few pupils at the school understand"), English, and Afrikaans suggests the context in which cross-cultural exchanges can be achieved in a nonhierarchical way and on her own terms. Johan's attraction to her "difference" is not only a recognition of similarity in outsider status but also a physical reaction when, after she tells him that she will kiss him only when he is able to "whisper without stuttering," he recalls the sweet smell as his lips "brushed against the thin beaded braids as she turned her head away from him" (64). When he finally overcomes his speech impediment, "He shouted, she ululated," and a cross-cultural relationship in which they meet on new ground is suggested at the end of the story (66).

This narrative is in keeping with recent trends in youth literature in which cross-cultural relationships are naturalized—as they are on countless South African television programs for children and young adults—as if to represent the nation to itself as harmoniously and easily nonracial. Tötemeyer states that interracial interactions in young adult literature previously occurred primarily in rural settings where children of farmers and workers are thrown together ("Towards" 82), and this is the case in Hofmeyr's "The Magic Man," where the situation of "the farmer's son on the tractor" suggests his power over the daughter of the worker, whose status is suggested by the mother's uniform and doek. Similarly, the class and color differences between the girl and the fisherman in Hobbs's story thwart the potential attraction between them. However, in the wake of the abolition of the Group Areas Act, interaction has been facilitated through integrated suburbs and schools (which is how Thembi and Johan meet).[7] However, such changes are still class-bound; it will take time for the Reconstruction and Development program to have any real effect on the lives of the majority of South Africans.

Unlike several other stories in the anthology that deal with active participation in the April election, Johan and Thembi's response to the political event is mediated (perhaps typically of teenage self-preoccupation) through their interaction with each other while watching the inauguration of the new state president on television. They comment on the outfits worn by the participants as well as the political significance of the occasion; he teases her for showing emotion in spite of her cynicism about politicians, and, in reply, she calls him "Boertjie," not used derogatively here, but reminding him of his Afrikaans background. This mediated response should be read as part of a broader dialogue on the election, as the anthology offers a variety of perspectives on this watershed event in South Africa's political evolution.[8]

In attempting to identify new trends, however, one should place these stories in the context of other recently published texts aimed at a young adult audience. For instance, the 1994/95 catalogue for Gap Books (Heinemann Centaur) describes how this series focuses on issues that are considered relevant to young people in postelection South Africa. Some of the popular themes are the problems encountered in home and school life in a nonracial South Africa, as in Julie Frederickse's *The Diary without a Key;* the role of young people in society, as in Themba Mabusa's *The Village Rescuers;* understanding one's rural heritage, as in Karen Press's *Let It Come Back;* the search for identity, as in Dawn Garish's *Not Another Love Story;* and friendships and love relationships across class, cultural, and color barriers, as in Dennis Bailey's *Ketho.* The issues of living with a disabled person, sexual molestation of young people by their elders, and the young person's first encounter with death are also woven into these narratives. Ecological issues feature strongly and, as Jenkins notes, this reflects the turn from an ethos of hunting to one of conservation (*Children* 1).

Garson notes that although publishers see youth literature as a growing industry and offer lucrative prizes, these books will reach teenagers primarily through schools and libraries as "booksellers are continuing to turn their backs on the teenage literature market" ("More Than Just" 3). This observation should also be seen in terms of cost, availability, and the extremely low literacy rate in South Africa. A University of Cape Town survey recently found that 80 percent of black and 40 percent of white adults were functionally illiterate beyond standard five, about 12 years of age. Sue McMurry, a librarian, claims that the reason local texts are not likely to become bestsellers is that "they are written too much to reflect the way we are. They are 'worthy' books, not light relief . . . [teenagers] prefer more escapist stuff" (quoted in Garson, "More Than Just" 3). However, Jenni Millward, a librarian and specialist in young adult fiction, believes these books appeal more to black than to white teenagers. Being more attuned to social and political issues affecting them, says Millward, "black teenagers are more interested in the experiences of their white counterparts than vice versa" (quoted in Garson, "More Than Just" 3).

While this appears to confirm the common perception that little has changed in the "new South Africa," there needs to be a vision of the future, even a utopian one such as represented in Hough's "The Journey." At the same time, the past and its painful memories must also be dealt with. Those who have been silent or silenced should be given opportunities to speak and be heard, while those who have spoken in the past must learn to speak "differently." Responding to the variety of voices represented in *Crossing Over,* speaking on what Isabelle Holland describes as a "multiplicity of levels," seems appropriate and necessary for a successful crossing. In order to know where one is going, one also needs to know where one has come from.

NOTES

1. This one-day conference hosted by the *Mail & Guardian* (in association with the South Africa Institute for Librarianship Information Science) was held in Cape Town on September 22, 1995.

2. Commenting on Ernst Fischer's reference to the artist as "commissioned by his society," the South African playwright Athol Fugard refers to his "failure of the imagination" when he describes the difficulty he had in visualizing a "free and democratic" South Africa that he believed in, but of which he "had no image" (quoted in Walder 94).

3. Gerwel comments on features that appear to characterize this "new" literature: "The awakening of an awareness of others, a loosening of the paralysing bounds of fear and suspicion, the dawning sense of self, the possibility of remembering and speaking about pain without unleashing destruction, the emancipation of the personal from the overbearing domination of the political" (n.pg.).

4. See Flockemann, "New Voices, Young Voices, or Voices for the Young?"

5. It should be borne in mind, however, that while this racial categorization seems inconsistent with efforts at constructing a nonracial South Africa, there has recently, and perhaps inevitably, been a resurgence of the discourses of race in the runup to the local elections in November 1995. This phenomenon should also be seen in the context of the implementation of affirmative action policies and a redefinition of old binary categories, such as "black" and "white," to include other minorities such as Indian, Malay, and Colored.

6. Ndebele, who has written for children and adults, made this observation during a class discussion with students at the University of the Western Cape in 1993. In his critical essays, Ndebele has been influential in stressing that South African fiction needs to "rediscover the ordinary," to show that people who have suffered political oppression are not just helpless victims.

7. During the apartheid era, South African schools fell under no less than 17 education departments (Newfield 40). However, discussions are still under way concerning the establishment of a unitary education system.

8. These range from Lesley Beake's celebratory account of an inauguration rally in Cape Town, "The New Beginning," to stories that balance the political event against personal interpretations of it for people from different backgrounds, pointing not only to the price paid in the past but also to the fact that apartheid is not yet dead.

WORKS CITED

Alexander, Neville. "AM Live." SAFM. October 5, 1995.

Bailey, Dennis. *Ketho.* Isando, SA: Heinemann Gap, 1994.

Beake, Lesley."The New Beginning." In Rode and Gerwel. 54–57.

Blatt, Gloria. "The Stereotyped Parent." *Adolescents, Literature and Work with Youth.* New York: Haworth, 1985. 71–80.

Case, Dianne. *92 Queen's Road.* Cape Town: Maskew-Miller-Longman, 1991.

Cilliers, Isabel, ed. Towards Understanding Children's Literature for Southern Africa. Cape Town: Maskew-Miller-Longman, 1988.

Engdahl, Sylvia. "Do Teenage Novels Fill a Need?" In Lenz and Mahood. 41–48.

Evans, Emrys, ed. *Reading against Racism.* Buckingham: Open University Press, 1992.

Flockemann, Miki. "New Voices, Young Voices, or Voices for the Young?" *Current Writing* 4.1 (Apr. 1992): 140–42.

Frederickse, Julie. *The Diary without a Key.* Isando, SA: Heinemann Gap, 1994.

Garish, Dawn. *Not Another Love Story.* Isando, SA: Heinemann Gap, 1994.

Garson, Phillippa. "Cross-Cultural Love Stories for Teens." *Supplement: Weekly Mail & Guardian* (June 1995): 6.

———. "More Than Just a Trashy Romance." *Supplement: Weekly Mail & Guardian* (Aug. 1995): 3.

Gerwel, Jakes. Foreword. In Rode and Gerwel.

Hobbs, Jenny. "Two Fishermen." In Rode and Gerwel. 8–16.

Hofmeyr, Dianne. "The Magic Man." In Rode and Gerwel. 68–72.

Holland, Isabelle. "What Is Adolescent Literature?" In Lenz and Mahood. 33–40.

Hough, Barrie. "The Journey." In Rode and Gerwel. 64–67.

Jansen, Beverley. "Children's Literature in a Post-Apartheid South Africa." In Cilliers. 89–92.

Jenkins, Elwyn. *Children of the Sun: Selected Writers and Themes in South African Children's Literature.* Johannesburg: Ravan, 1993.

———. "Letters." *South African Review of Books* 36 (July/Aug. 1995): 17.

Lenz, Millicent, and Ramona M. Mahood. *Young Adult Literature.* Chicago: American Library Association, 1980.

Mabusa, Themba. *The Village Rescuers.* Isando, SA: Heinemann Gap, 1994.

McDowell, Deborah. "New Directions for Black Feminist Criticism." *Feminist Literary Theory: A Reader.* Ed. Mary Eagleton. Oxford: Basil Blackwood, 1986. 163–69.

Mhlophe, Gcina. "Evesdropping." SAFM. August 9, 1995.

Mitchell, Claudia, and Ann Smith. "More Than Just a Love Story: Investigating the Literary and Social Significance of the Southern African Young Adult Novel." Unpublished paper. Association of University English Teachers of Southern Africa conference. Pietermaritzburg. July 1995.

Naidoo, Beverley. "Can You Fully Understand It? Approaching Issues of Racism with White Students in the English Classroom." In Evans. 104–15.

Newfield, Denise. "Reading against Racism in South Africa." In Evans. 39–63.

Nhlanhla, Manana. "The Availability of Indigenous Literature: The Black Child and His Reading Needs." In Cilliers. 162–66.

Nyatsumba, Kaizer M. "Streets of Hillbrow, Here I Come." In Rode and Gerwel. 138–45.

Press, Karen. *Let It Come Back.* Isando, SA: Heinemann Gap, 1994.

Rode, Linda, and Jakes Gerwel, eds. *Crossing Over: Stories for a New South Africa.* Cape Town: Kwela, 1995.

Scheepers, Riana. "Garden-Gate Green, Privy-Pink, Back-Door Blue." In Rode and Gerwel. 146–150.

Sims Bishop, Rudine. "Children's Books in a Multicultural World: A View from the USA." In Evans. 19–38.

Stevenson, Gordon. "On Constructing Useful Realities: The Uses of Popular Culture in the Uncertain World of the Adolescent." In Lenz and Mahood. 107–17.

Tlali, Miriam. "A Second Look." In Rode and Gerwel. 133–37.

Tötemeyer, Andree-Jeanne. "Racism in Children's Fiction: Towards the Creation of Non-Racist Books in South Africa." In Cilliers. 173–80.

———. "Towards Interracial Understanding through South African Children's and Youth Literature." In Cilliers. 80–88.

VanderStaay, Steven. "Young-Adult Literature: A Writer Strikes the Genre." *English Journal* 81.4 (1992): 48–52.

Walder, Dennis. *Athol Fugard.* London: Macmillan, 1984.

Weiner, Pamela J., and Ruth M. Stein, eds. *Adolescents, Literature and Work with Youth.* New York: Haworth, 1985.

Williams, Michael. "Red Sports Car." In Rode and Gerwel. 1–7.

BIBLIOGRAPHY

'Abd Allah, Muhammad Hasan. *Qisas al-atfal: usuluha al-fanniyah—ruwaduha* (Children's literature: its artistic origins and pioneers). Cairo: al-'Arabi lil-Nashr wa-al-Tawzi', [1992].

Achebe, Chinua. *Hopes and Impediments: Selected Essays.* New York: Doubleday, 1989.

———. *Morning Yet on Creation Day.* Garden City, N.Y.: Anchor-Doubleday, 1975.

African Book Publishing Record, no. 1, 1974–, published quarterly. Ed. Hans M. Zell and Cécile Lomer. London: Hans Zell Publishers.

African Youth Literature Today and Tomorrow. Bonn: German Commission for UNESCO/ Munich: International Youth Library, 1988.

APNET Children's Catalogue 1995/96. Harare: African Publishers Network, 1995.

Ashcroft, Bill, Gareth Griffiths, and Helen Tiffin. *The Empire Writes Back: Theory and Practice in Post-Colonial Literatures.* London: Routledge, 1989.

Bgoya, Walter. "Intra-African Trading in Children's Books: Opportunities and Constraints." *Book Fair Magazine. 3rd Pan African Children's Book Fair.* Nairobi: CHISCI Press, 1994. 30–31.

Bookbird: World of Children's Books 36.1 (Spring 1998). Special issue entitled: African Children's Literature. Ed. Meena Khorana.

Castle, Kathryn. *Britannia's Children: Reading Colonialism through Children's Books and Magazines.* Studies in Imperialism. Manchester: Manchester University Press, 1996.

Chimombo, Steve. *Malawian Oral Literature: The Aesthetics of Indigenous Arts.* Zomba: Centre for Social Research and University of Malawi, 1988.

Chinweizu, Onwuchekwa Jemie, and Ihechukwu Madubuike. *Toward the Decolonization of African Literature.* Vol. 1: *African Fiction and Poetry and Their Critics.* Washington, D.C.: Howard University Press, 1983.

"CHISCI Convenes the APNET Standing Committee on Children's Publishing in Africa." *Kalulu News* 6.4 (Aug. 1994): 2.

Cilliers, Isabel, ed. *Towards More Understanding: The Making and Sharing of Children's Literature in Southern Africa.* 1988. Rpt. Cape Town: Juta, 1993.

Davidson, Basil. *The Search for Africa: A History in the Making.* London: Currey, 1994.

Dixon, Bob. *Catching Them Young: Sex, Race and Class in Children's Fiction*. London: Pluto, 1977.

———. *Catching Them Young (2): Political Ideas in Children's Fiction*. London: Pluto, 1977.

Emenyonu, Ernest N., and Charles E. Nnolim, eds. *Current Trends in Literature and Language Studies in West Africa*. Ibadan: Kraft, 1994.

Fanon, Frantz. *Black Skin, White Masks*. New York: Grove, 1967.

———. *The Wretched of the Earth*. New York: Grove, 1963.

Fayose, Philomena Osazee Esigbemi. *A Guide to Children's Literature for African Teachers, Librarians, and Parents*. Ibadan: AENL Educational, 1995.

Giddings, Robert, ed. *Literature and Imperialism*. New York: St. Martin's, 1991.

Hale, Thomas, and Richard Priebe, eds. *The Teaching of African Literature*. Washington, D.C.: Three Continents/African Literature Association, 1989.

Heale, Jay, ed. *From the Bushveld to Biko: The Growth of South African Children's Literature in English from 1907–1992 Traced through 100 Notable Books*. Grabouw: Bookchat, 1996.

———. *SACBIP 94: South African Children's Books in Print 1994*. Grabouw: Bookchat, 1994.

Ikonne, Chidi, Emelia Oko, and Peter Onwudinjo, eds. *Children's Literature in Africa*. Ibadan: Heinemann, 1992.

Irele, Abiola. *The African Experience in Literature and Ideology*. London: Heinemann, 1981.

Jenkins, Elwyn. *Children of the Sun: Selected Writers and Themes in South African Children's Literature*. Johannesburg: Ravan, 1993.

Jones, Eldred D., ed. *Myth, History and the Contemporary African Writer*. London: Heinemann, 1980.

Journal of African Children's and Youth Literature (JACYL), published annually. Ed. Osayim-wense Osa. Itta Bena: Dept. of English and Foreign Languages, Mississippi Valley State University.

Kabira, Wanjiku Mukabi, and Karega wa Mutahi. *Gikuyu Oral Literature*. Nairobi: Heine-mann, 1988.

Khorana, Meena. *Africa in Literature for Children and Young Adults: An Annotated Biblio-graphy of English-Language Books*. Westport, Conn. and London: Greenwood, 1994.

Laurentin, Marie, and Cécile Lebon, eds. *L'Édition africaine en français pour la jeunesse* (African publishing for children in French). Paris: La Joie par les Livres, 1996.

Laurentin, Marie, and Viviana Quiñones, eds. *Les Livres africains pour la jeunesse* (African books for children). Paris: La Joie par les Livres, 1994.

Lawson, William. *The Western Scar: The Theme of the Been-to in West African Fiction*. Athens, Ohio: Ohio University Press, 1982.

MacCann, Donnarae. *The White Supremacy Myth in Juvenile Books about Blacks, 1830–1900*. Ph.D. diss., University of Iowa, 1988.

MacCann, Donnarae, and Gloria Woodard, eds. *The Black American in Books for Children: Readings on Racism*. 2nd ed. Metuchen, N.J.: Scarecrow, 1985.

Maddy, Yulisa Amadu, and Donnarae MacCann. *African Images in Juvenile Literature: Commentaries on Neocolonialist Fiction*. Jefferson, N.C. and London: McFarland, 1996.

Matatu: Journal for African Culture and Society, no. 17–18 (1997). Double issue entitled: Preserving the Landscape of Imagination: Children's Literature in Africa. Ed. Raoul Granqvist and Jürgen Martini. Amsterdam: Rodopi, 1997.

Mbiti, John S. *African Religions and Philosophy*. London, Ibadan, Nairobi: Heinemann, 1969.

Memmi, Albert. *The Colonizer and the Colonized*. 1965. Rpt. Expanded ed. Boston: Beacon, 1991.

Meyers, Jeffrey. *Fiction and the Colonial Experience.* Totowa, N.J.: Rowman & Littlefield, 1968.

Mwanycky, Serah W. *Children's Reading Needs: The Challenges of the Next Century to Parents, Educators, Publishers and Librarians in Africa.* Nairobi: CHISCI, 1993.

Naidoo, Beverley. *Censoring Reality: An Examination of Books on South Africa.* London: ILEA Centre for Anti-Racist Education and the British Defense and Aid Fund for Southern Africa, 1984.

Nayareth, Peter. *The Third World Writer: His Social Responsibility.* Nairobi: Kenya Literature Bureau, 1978.

Ngugi wa Thiong'o. *Decolonising the Mind: The Politics of Language in African Literature.* London: Currey; Nairobi: Heinemann Kenya; Portsmouth, N.H.: Heinemann, 1986.

Odaga, Asenath Bole. *Literature for Children and Young People in Kenya.* Nairobi: Kenya Literature Bureau, 1985.

———. *Yesterday's Today: The Study of Oral Literature.* Kisumu: Lake Publishers & Enterprises, 1984.

Osa, Osayimwense. *African Children's and Youth Literature.* New York: Twayne, 1995.

———. *Foundation: Essays in Children's Literature and Youth Literature.* Benin City: Paramount, 1987.

———. *Nigerian Youth Literature.* Benin City: Paramount, 1987.

p'Bitek, Okot. *Africa's Cultural Revolution.* Nairobi: Macmillan Books for Africa, 1975.

Pieterse, Jan Nederveen. *White on Black: Images of Africa and Blacks in Western Popular Culture.* New Haven: Yale University Press, 1992.

Richards, Jeffrey, ed. *Imperialism and Juvenile Literature.* Manchester and New York: Manchester University Press, 1989.

Rochman, Hazel. *Against Borders: Promoting Books for a Multicultural World.* Chicago: American Library Association, 1993.

Schmidt, Nancy J. *Children's Books on Africa and Their Authors: An Annotated Bibliography.* New York: Africana, 1975.

———. *Children's Fiction about Africa in English.* Owerri/New York: Conch, 1981.

———. *Supplement to Children's Books on Africa and Their Authors: An Annotated Bibliography.* New York: Africana, 1979.

Schmidt, Nancy J., ed. *Children's Literature and Audio-Visual Materials in Africa.* Owerri/New York: Conch, 1977.

Shohat, Ella, and Robert Stam. *Unthinking Eurocentrism: Multiculturalism and the Media.* London and New York: Routledge, 1994.

Small, Stephen. *Racialised Barriers: The Black Experience in the United States and England in the 1980s.* London and New York: Routledge, 1994.

Soyinka, Wole. *Myth, Literature and the African World.* London and New York: CUP, 1976.

Street, Brian V. *The Savage in Literature.* Boston: Routledge and Kegan Paul, 1975.

Tiffin, Chris, and Alan Lawson. *De-scribing Empire: Post-colonialism and Textuality.* London and New York: Routledge, 1994.

Van Zyl, H. E., and M. M. Botes, eds. *South African Children's Book Illustrators.* Pretoria: South African School Media Association, 1994.

Westra, Pieter E., ed. *Freedom to Read: The Future of Publications Control and the Free Flow of Information in South Africa.* Cape Town: South African Library, 1994.

Zell, Hans M., and Cécile Lomer. *Publishing and Book Development in Sub-Saharan Africa: An Annotated Bibliography.* London: Hans Zell Publishers (in association with African Publisher's Network, Harare, Zimbabwe), 1996.

INDEX

ABOUT THE EDITOR
AND CONTRIBUTORS

MIKI FLOCKEMANN teaches in the Department of English at the University of the Western Cape. Her research interest is diasporic literatures, focusing on comparative studies of women from South Africa, the Caribbean, and North America. She has also published articles on South African performance arts.

MICHAEL SCOTT JOSEPH is a rare book librarian at Rutgers, The State University of New Jersey. He has published numerous bio-critical articles on English and American children's book illustrators, and historical essays on illustrating. He is the author of "A Pre-Modernist Reading of *The Drum*: Chinua Achebe and the Theme of the Eternal Return," in *ARIEL* (January 1997), and "Pictures and Frames," an analysis of postcolonial African children's book illustration based on linguistic schema, in *Bookbird* (Spring 1997). He is also the co-founder and organizer of the Annual New Jersey Book Arts Symposium.

MEENA KHORANA is a professor of English and children's and adolescent literature at Morgan State University. She has published widely on multicultural and international children's literature. She is the author of *The Indian Subcontinent in Literature for Children and Young Adults: An Annotated Bibliography of English-Language Books* (Greenwood, 1991) and *Africa in Literature for Children and Young Adults: An Annotated Bibliography of English-Language Books* (Greenwood, 1994) and the editor of the Dictionary of Literary Biography volume *British Children's Writers, 1800–1880* (1996). She is the editor-in-chief of *Bookbird*, the scholarly journal of the International Board on Books for Young People. She was guest co-editor of the postcolonial children's literature issue of *ARIEL* (January 1997).

GRETA D. LITTLE is an associate professor of English at the University of South Carolina, where she teaches adolescent and children's literature. She has published several articles on children's literature as well as an edition of Christopher Pearse Cranch's fiction for children. Her interest in Arabs and their portrayal in children's books grew out of her experience as a Fulbright lecturer in Morocco in 1993. Research assistance for this essay was provided by the University of South Carolina.

CLAIRE-LISE MALARTE-FELDMAN is an associate professor of French at the University of New Hampshire. She has published extensively on literary fairy tales, contemporary French tales for children, and Charles Perrault. Most recently she edited a special issue of *The Lion and the Unicorn* devoted to French children's literature.

MBARE NGOM is an associate professor of Spanish and French and chairperson of the Department of Foreign Languages at Morgan State University. His particular areas of scholarly research and teaching are French and Francophone literature, Hispanic African literature, and Latin American literature. He has published several articles on Hispanic African literature and is the author of *Diálogos con Guinea* (1996). He is currently compiling an anthology of Hispanic African literature.

ASENATH BOLE ODAGA is a Kenyan author who writes fiction and nonfiction for adults and children. She has written more than forty books—including *Jande's Ambition* and *The Secret of the Monkey Rock*—some of which are being used in educational institutions. She lives in Kisumu, where her family runs Lake Publishers & Enterprises, Ltd.

OSAYIMWENSE OSA is a professor of English and chairperson of the Department of English and Foreign Languages at Mississippi Valley State University. He is the founder and current editor of the *Journal of African Children's and Youth Literature* and the founding editor of *Ekpoma Journal of Languages and Literary Studies*. He is the author of *African Children's and Youth Literature* (1995), *Foundation: Essays in Children's Literature and Youth Literature* (1987), and *Nigerian Youth Literature* (1987).

JEAN PERROT, a professor of comparative literature at Paris-Nord University, has published essays on children's literature: *Du jeu, des enfants et des livres* (1987) and *Art baroque, art d'enfance* (1991). He has also edited several volumes on the subject, such as *Culture, texte et jeune lecteur* (1993) and *Ecriture féminine et littérature de jeunesse* (1995), and has organized a series of conferences on international children's literature.

NANCY J. SCHMIDT is a librarian for African Studies and an adjunct professor of anthropology at Indiana University. She has done research on African children's literature for more than thirty years and is the author of numerous articles, reviews, and three books: *Children's Books on Africa and Their Authors: An Annotated Bibliography* (1975), *Supplement to Children's Books on Africa and Their Authors: An Annotated Bibliography* (1979), and *Children's Fiction about Africa in*

English (1981). She has also edited the volume *Children's Literature and Audio-Visual Materials in Africa* (1977).

KAREN PATRICIA SMITH is a professor at the Queens College Graduate School of Library and Information Studies, New York. She is widely published in the area of children's literature and is the author of *The Fabulous Realm: A Literary-Historical Approach to British Fantasy, 1780–1990* (1993) and *African-American Voices in Young Adult Literature: Tradition, Transition, Transformation* (1994), which won the Carey McWilliams Award for 1994. She has been a guest editor of two issues of *Library Trends* in the area of children's literature, in Winter 1993 and Spring 1996.

JUDY ANNE WHITE is an assistant professor at Morgan State University, where she specializes in medieval and Renaissance literatures as well as Jungian approaches to literature. She has published articles on children's literature, Beowulf, and film.

JACK YEAGER is a professor of French and women's studies at the University of New Hampshire. He is the author of *The Vietnamese Novel in French: A Literary Response to Colonialism* and articles in *L'Esprit Créateur, Présence Francophone,* and *Quebec Studies.* Most recently he coedited *Postcolonial Subjects: Francophone Women Writers.*

ISBN 0-313-29864-5

90000>

EAN

9 780313 298646

HARDCOVER BAR CODE